Managerial
Psychology

Harold J. Leavitt

Managerial Psychology

An introduction to
individuals, pairs, and groups
in organizations

Third Edition

The University of Chicago Press
Chicago & London

The University of Chicago Press, Chicago 60637
The University of Chicago Press, Ltd., London
© 1972 by The University of Chicago
All rights reserved. Published 1972
Printed in the United States of America
ISBN: 0-226-46982-4 (clothbound)
Library of Congress Catalog Card Number: 73-184905

Contents

Contents

Preface to the third edition

Things have changed a lot since the 1964 edition of this book. Relevant knowledge has changed. And times have changed.

I have tried to reflect both changes in this new edition. I've included new findings and ideas which, filtered through my eyes, appeared particularly relevant to management. I've also, on occasion, deleted a few ideas that have not held up in validity or utility.

But I have also tried to include new material for its relevance to the more current state of the world—even if the ideas are not new, or even, in a couple of cases, if hard evidence is scarce. My justification for those inclusions is simply that students of management need to attend to certain large behavioral problems, even if our understanding of them is sparse.

For the reader familiar with the earlier editions, here is a summary of the changes in this one:

In part 1, on the individual, I have left the section on motivation, perception, etc., pretty much intact, except for adding an emphasis on growth motivation to counterbalance the earlier emphasis on deficiency motivation. But the big changes in part 1 come in the realm of cognition. I have added two new chapters, one on cognitive styles as an important dimension of individual differences, and another on attitudes and values, in response both to the good work that has been done in that area and to its growing relevance for organizational decisions. Finally in part 1, the chapter on assessment now includes a chunk on assessment centers, certainly one major new application that has evolved since 1964.

In part 2, on interpersonal influence, the biggest change is the addition of a chapter on power tactics—responsive more to the times than to new knowledge. The earlier absence of a discussion of the coercive uses of power must have been, to say the least, an optimistic oversight. Otherwise, bits and pieces have been added and subtracted in part 2, with the largest net addition in the last chapter on money incentives.

Part 3, on groups, gives increased, but still limited, space to sensitivity training groups and adds a new subunit on leadership. There are other modifications throughout, but no other major additions.

In part 4, on the large organization, I have added one entirely new chapter—in response to the times and to my own interests—on the relationship between the organization and its environment, perhaps the major managerial problem of the 70s. All other chapters have been updated but left essentially intact.

My colleagues at Stanford's Graduate School of Business have been extremely helpful with suggestions for additions and modifications.

Help has come in from many other quarters as well. Colleagues in industry and at other universities, and industrial and governmental executives, both in the United States and abroad, have provided examples and suggestions for change.

And then there are the students! They gave help, too, albeit sometimes in devious, ingenious, and obscure ways.

My special thanks to Mrs. Kathy Bostick who never lost her cool, no matter how heavy the load.

Once again my wife (same wife, even in California) has carried the load of putting the manuscript into shape, on time, under pressure. But the greatest influence on both of us at this point in our lives—and it is reflected in the emphases of this edition—has been our son, Mr. Chocolate Mess.

1

**People one at a time
The units
of Management**

Introductory note

In these next several chapters the reader will find a presentation of the concepts of human behavior that seem most relevant to managerial problems. Such consideration of people and their behavior seems a prerequisite to any conscious attempt to learn how better to "manage" people. "Conscious" is a key word, because many persons (including many businessmen), are extremely skillful managers even though they go about their activities more or less intuitively. Those of us who are not so gifted need to think out loud about human relations and about ourselves as mechanisms for solving business problems.

Although the book as a whole purports to deal with problems of management, this first section focuses almost entirely on the individual human being. The reasons for this "impractical" digression are several: First, the characteristics of people in general are a good base from which to build up to the characteristics of people in industry. Second, managers, unlike parents, must work with used, not new, human beings—human beings whom other people have gotten to first. Third, the manager is his own best management mechanism. An examination of his own makeup should therefore be useful to him.

Part 1 is designed as follows: It starts with some fundamental assumptions about what is "true" of all people everywhere. It moves then to a more detailed examination of the ways people differ from one another and some of the sources of those differences. Next, personality differences and their influence on the ways people see and deal with other things and other people are considered. Two chapters deal with the problem of *pressure*—the effects of frustration and conflict on behavior. Two chapters are concerned with conscious problem-solving, the everyday life of the manager. One chapter is devoted to values and attitudes, the points where thought and feeling meet. Finally one long chapter is given over to the practical problem of assessing people for particular assignments.

The goal of this section is both to simplify and complicate the reader's picture of people—to simplify by systematizing and interrelating some basic ideas (most of which are not new) and to complicate by pointing out the infinite shades of gray and the multitude of interacting variables that can occur in the behaving human organism.

People are alike
Some basic ideas

Businessmen's decisions, like other people's, are usually based on some combination of fact and theory. They are choices made by interpreting things observed in the light of things believed. And in most of their decisions businessmen are reasonably aware of the particular beliefs they are using in interpreting the facts they observe. They take supply-and-demand ideas into account in making marketing decisions, for example. And they often use high-level technical theory in attacking engineering and production problems.

Businessmen also use theory in dealing with human problems. But in the human area theorizing seems to be much more implicit or even unconscious. The theories of human behavior that businessmen hold seem also to be much more diverse than their economic and engineering theories, perhaps because they are much more the private property of individual executives. Here, for instance, are some pairs of theoretical assertions that have been made by business executives. Each of them necessarily reflects some basic assumptions about the nature of man:

People are basically lazy; or, People just want a chance to show what they can do.

Always be careful of an executive who loses his temper; or, Watch out for the man who never loses his temper.

A good salesman sells himself before his product; or, A good product sells itself.

If you give people a finger they'll take the whole arm; or, Kindness begets kindness.

Men need to know exactly what their jobs are; or, Men will work best when they can make their own jobs.

Each of these statements (and the list is not at all exhaustive) is either an assumption about the nature of people or a derivation from such an assumption. Each is a flat, unequivocal generalization, much like the statement, "Air is lighter than water."

The fact that many of these generalizations contradict one another suggests that they cannot all be right and therefore raises difficult questions of proof and consistency. This section of the book does not aim to prove that some are true and some are false. What it does aim to do is to provide a set of internally *consistent* generalizations; generalizations that should be *useful* in predicting human behavior, whether they are fundamentally true or not.

All of us seem to make some kind of generalizations about people, and this is important in deciding what is "practical" and what is "only theoretical." Managers have a reputation for practicality and hardheadedness, a reputation fledgling managers may mistakenly equate with entirely concrete and nongeneral thinking. Yet statements like those above are extremely general, extremely theoretical. They may express poor theory, but they point up the need for theoretical generalizations to serve as a foundation for practicality. Some kind of psychological theory is just as necessary for the manager dealing with human problems as is electrical and mechanical theory for the engineer dealing with machine problems. Without theory the engineer has no way of diagnosing what might be wrong when the engine stops, no way of pre-estimating the effects of a proposed change in design. Without some kind of psychological theory, the manager cannot attach meaning to the red flags of human disturbance; nor can he predict the likely effects of changes in organization or personnel policy.

The particular theoretical position outlined in these early chapters will not be new to most readers. Most of us already accept it but often do not use it. If it is good theory it should lead to useful predictions. Incidentally, if it is good theory it may not necessarily be true theory. No one knows whether some of the things said here are true or false. The reader can decide for himself whether or not they are useful.

Three basic assumptions about people

Suppose we asked this question of many kinds of people: "What are the fundamental, unexceptionable truths of human behavior?" Suppose one asked it of college students, union members, top- and middle-level managers, foremen, salesmen, nurses, and housewives. The answers would include generalizations like these:

People are products of their environment.
People want security.
All people want is bread and butter.

People are fundamentally lazy.
People are fundamentally selfish.
People only do what they have to do.
People are creatures of habit.
People are products of their heredity.

Some of these answers, like the generalizations we talked about earlier, seem to contradict others, but at another level the contradictions disappear. If one organizes them, one comes out with essentially the same generalizations that many modern psychologists would offer. For three major ideas are implicit in that list:

The first is the idea of *causality*, the idea that human behavior is caused, just as the behavior of physical objects is caused by forces that act on those physical objects. Causality is implicit in the beliefs that environment and heredity affect behavior and that what is outside influences what is inside.

Second, there is the idea of *directedness,* the idea that human behavior is not only caused but is also pointed toward something, that behavior is goal-directed, that people want things.

Third, the list includes the concept of *motivation,* that underlying behavior one finds a "push" or a "motive" or a "want" or a "need" or a "drive."

These three ideas can provide the beginning of a system for conceptualizing human behavior. With the help of these ideas, human behavior can be viewed as part of a double play from cause to motive to behavior-toward-a-goal. And it is also helpful to think of the three as generally forming a closed circuit. Arrival at a goal eliminates the cause, which eliminates the motive, which eliminates the behavior. Thus, for instance, a man's stomach is empty; the emptiness stimulates impulses interpreted as "feeling hungry"; the feeling of hunger stimulates action in the direction of food; he gets food. The food fills his stomach, causing cessation of the "feeling hungry" impulses, which in turn eliminates the behavior in search of food.

This closed-circuit conception includes one major danger. Many "psychological," as distinct from "physical," goals are not finite and specific. One can consume a specific quantity of food and thereby temporarily stop feeling hungry for more. It is doubtful, however, that one can consume a specific quantity of prestige, for instance, and feel sated. Prestige and other "psychological" goals seem to be ephemeral and boundless; enough may never be obtained to inactivate the causes and hence the motive.

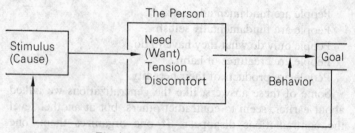

Fig. 1. A basic model of behavior

These assumptions of causality, motivation, and direction are nevertheless useful assumptions if they are accepted as universal. Causality, motivation, and direction can be thought of as applying equally to all people, of all ages, in all cultures, at all times. When one makes such assumptions they should lead one, upon observing human behavior, always to seek motive and, behind motive, cause.

There are many different perspectives on these assumptions, but the basic assumptions remain intact. For example, one can say that behavior is an attempt to get rid of tension. Tension then equals motivation; and the objective of behavior is to eliminate the necessity for behaving. Words like "motives" or "needs" or "drives" are rough synonyms for each other as well as for words like "tensions" or "discomforts" or "disequilibriums." Behavior is thus seen as an effort to eliminate tensions by seeking goals that neutralize the causes of tensions.

Thinking about motivation in terms of tension and discomfort inside the person is useful in another way. It puts the emphasis on the *push* from inside the person rather than on the *pull* from outside. Managers, for instance, often encounter problems with subordinates who "don't know what they want." They feel restless and disturbed but can't seem to say what it is they are after. Most of us behave this way a good deal of the time, feeling the push of tension from inside but not being able to identify the precise goal that would eliminate the tension. We search vaguely, trying one job or another, one boss or another, one idea or another, until—if we are lucky—we hit on something that does the trick. Only then may we be able to tie up that particular feeling of tension with some specific goal, so that next time we can head directly for where we want to go. The baby, after all, doesn't start out saying, "I want a bottle." He starts out saying, "I feel discomfort somewhere inside." He then goes on to try all the different behaviors he can muster until he discovers that the bottle eliminates that particular discomfort. Only then can he identify this goal and narrow down his behavior so that he can get to his goal without exhausting himself.

But no matter how one views these concepts, they suggest that the ultimate condition of man can be thought of as an equilibrium condition in which he need not behave. This ultimate will be unattainable so long as one fly after another goes on landing on man's rump to stir up some new need and to force him to go on swishing his tail.

Of course the same landscape can be drawn from a brighter perspective. The tendency not to behave unless one has to can also account for man's capacity to learn. It can account for the baby's ability to become an increasingly efficient food finder. The diffuse kicking, squalling, and rolling give way over a few years to the simpler and more efficient behavior of learning to find and open the cookie jar. If people were not thus naturally stingy in their expenditures of energy, if they did not abhor unnecessary effort, if they were not lazy, then their factories would probably be no more efficient today than they were fifty years ago, if the factories existed at all.

Until now we have treated human needs as tensions that arise, sometimes distantly, out of *deficiencies,* out of want or lack. In recent years a strong case has been made for what has been called "growth motivation," a self-generating view of at least some major human needs. It is in the nature of man, this argument runs, to reach out for something more no matter what his state of satisfaction. Men do not sit on their duffs even if they are very well fed and very comfortable.

This position is important because it leads one toward a more optimistic posture in approaching the question of motivating people. If one views motivation as arising exclusively out of deficiency, then one begins to think about ways of creating deficiencies for others in order to motivate them. "Let's make him unsatisfied by making him hungry, then he'll work." The growth-motivational view points out that it is when men are satisfied in their more basic needs that the "higher" needs are likely to flower. It is when man is freed from the simple deficiencies that he can really begin to work as a complete man.

This picture allows little room for the idea of "habit," if habit means uncaused or undirected repetitive behavior. If the word "habit" is to fit here, it will have to mean something like "characteristic ways of trying to satisfy certain needs." The disorderly file clerk is not, then, just disorderly because he has disorderly habits. He is disorderly because he has learned to try to satisfy his needs by what we consider disorderly means. Nor is the inmate of the booby hatch just a different kind of human being from those on the outside. He is in there because his best methods for satisfying his needs have landed him there.

So these three assumptions (cause, motivation, direction) become theoretical starting points. Perhaps they are worth careful thought. For the reader should consider the implications of these ideas for such concepts as "free will," "habit," and "insane behavior." Accepting these assumptions will probably require some revision of the usual meaning of these ideas.

In summary

This chapter has made three interrelated assumptions about human behavior:
1. Behavior is caused.
2. Behavior is motivated.
3. Behavior is goal directed.

In the process some alternative assumptions have been implicitly discarded. We have discarded the idea that behavior is "random," i.e., that it is going nowhere, for no reason. But we have left room for other ideas, such as the idea of growth motivation, which is not directly generated out of deficiency.

Moreover, the three assumptions are assumed to be interrelated in a circular sequence: from cause to motivation to goal direction. Arrival at the goal inactivates the cause, and hence eliminates the motive, and hence eliminates the goal-directed behavior; although some goals may not be finite.

Many different words can be used to deal with these three ideas. Words like "drive," "tension," "need," and "disequilibrium," for example, are all approximate synonyms for the word "motive."

2

**People are different
The growth of
individuality**

While people are alike, they are also different. They are alike
in that their behavior is caused, motivated, and goal-directed
and their physical equipment is roughly similar. They are different to the extent that they are subject to different kinds of
stimulation, that they vary in kinds and degrees of motivation, that they behave in many different ways to achieve
many different goals, and that they have different sizes and
powers in their physical equipment. The purpose of this
chapter is to try to account (only at the broadest level) for the
range and kinds of differences that every manager has observed among those around him.

The range of motives

Consider the variety of motives which seem to occur in
human behavior. Consider, for example, the class of behavior
called "work." What are the motives for work; what are the
tensions or discomforts that people try to eliminate through
work? Why should people sacrifice so much of the good life
to walk into the plant morning after morning, year after year?
Clearly, different individuals will give different answers to
such questions, and each answer may be perfectly true for
each person. Clearly, too, any single individual may come up
with a variety of motives to fit his particular case. Direct
questioning of a random portion of the American population
would certainly include such answers as these:

I work for money and the food, shelter, and goods money
buys.

I work for status and recognition.

I work to belong, to be part of a group.

I work to get to the top.

I work because it's only right that people should work.

I work for knowledge and understanding.

I work for security.

I work for the feeling of accomplishment I get from a job
well done.

This list is not exhaustive. Some of the statements are concrete and specific; others are vague and shadowy. Some seem to overlap one another in meaning. Perhaps the reader will, nevertheless, go along with the generalization that most people work for some variety of reasons like these and that most people would also be willing to do some work for almost any one of the reasons listed, even if the others did not exist. But perhaps before he will go along, the reader may want to add at least one qualification: these motives may be real only for *most people in America this year*. Although some of them may be universal, others may be specific to our culture or to certain subgroups within our culture. This would be a valid qualification.

The classes of needs

Looking back over the list of motives, one can classify them into at least two major groups. Some arise from needs that are essentially physical and "basic": needs for food, for water, for warmth. One could add others: needs to urinate, to defecate, to sleep, and so on. These are clear-cut, unambiguous needs; they are physiological; they are universal; they are present in infants as well as adults; they are even present in most other classes of animals. They seem unquestionably to be part of the person's original inborn equipment.

The second large class of needs, however, is less easily definable. Needs for achievement, status, and "belongingness" are much more "psychological," more clearly limited to human beings, and for the most part not immediately observable in the newborn. They also seem highly individualistic—much more so than the basic physical needs. They seem to be present to an extreme degree in some people and almost nonexistent in others. We do not ordinarily characterize one another as "food seekers," but we do often characterize a person as a "power seeker" or a "prestige seeker." In fact, our judgment of the intensities of psychological needs in other people makes up a large part of our judgment of their personalities. Application blanks for industrial jobs seldom include questions about how much water a man drinks or how many sandwiches he eats for lunch. But they do include questions about his ambitions and his social interests.

It is in these so-called psychological needs that the bulk of industrially-significant personality differences lies; we must try to account for the differential development of these needs in different individuals. This problem could lead us quickly into the question of the importance of heredity and environment, but that would be an unprofitable venture. If the reader prefers to believe that the psychological needs are acquired out of our environment, such a belief will not affect the position taken here. If he prefers to believe that the seeds of psychological needs lie in the genes and that environment only fertilizes and nurtures them, that position is also tenable.

Dependency and the development of personality

The most important issue seems to be this one: Can we, with as few assumptions as possible, account for the development of individually different adult personalities? For the back-slapping sales manager and the quiet, methodical comptroller?

A theory, it has been said, is as good as its ratio of predictions to assumptions. To economize on assumptions, we may assume here that only the basic physical needs are inherited and then go on from there. It is then possible to account broadly for the elaborate complex of needs that exists in a twenty-year-old while assuming that all he had to begin with were (1) his basic physical needs and (2) his body. In his "body" we must include his sense organs, plus his memory—a mechanism for retaining information picked up by the sense organs—plus a decision-making mechanism, plus a tendency to be stingy in the expenditure of energy, plus a muscular system that allows the person to move and act upon his environment. If that is the person's original basic equipment, it is almost enough to account for the accessories he will have added by the time he is ten or twenty or forty. But he still needs one more characteristic, a characteristic that is not so much a part of the person as of the relationship between the person and the world. This additional characteristic is *dependency*—the dependency of the newborn infant on parents for the satisfaction of his needs; the dependency of the growing child on parents, teachers, and friends; of husband on wife; and of people in industry on their bosses; and vice versa.

If the human infant came into the world with almost complete physical development, like some other animal young, then we might have to devise quite a different theory to account for the adult personality. In fact, if the infant could fend for himself from the start, the adult personality would be noticeably different from what it is.

But any infant who survives to adulthood has necessarily

passed through a period in which he was almost entirely dependent upon other people for the satisfaction of his basic physical needs. And this dependency, coupled with the presence of physical needs and a good but incomplete physical plant, may give us the leverage to account for the development of a great many secondary and tertiary mental needs. To see how this dependency lever might work, consider this entirely hypothetical illustration:

Suppose that you suffer from a magical ailment. The major symptom of the ailment is paralysis—complete paralysis. But though you are paralyzed, your head is perfectly clear and your senses are perfectly keen. You can hear, you can see, you can feel, you can think—but you can't move.

You have a brother who possesses a magical gift. Whenever his hand is on your shoulder you are cured; you can move as well as anyone else. But when he takes his hand away the paralysis immediately returns.

Assume that your brother is a nice guy; he spends a good deal of his time with his hand on your shoulder, and he goes through considerable inconvenience to do this. Through his help you can lead something approximating a normal life. You have not had this disease very long, but by now you have gotten over the shock that it entailed, and you are trying to settle down to the best life you can work out.

This morning you awake, but of course you cannot move. You lie in bed until your brother comes in to put his hand on your shoulder. Whereupon you rise, dress, and wash. You have breakfast, chat, and read the morning paper. You do everything that you may have done before you had the disease.

Over breakfast your brother announces that he forgot to tell you he has a dentist's appointment this morning. He will have to leave the house about ten. He probably will not be back until noon. This is a matter of no great concern to you, since it's just a two-hour absence.

With his hand on your shoulder you arrange a comfortable place in which you can sit while your brother is gone. You set an easy chair by the window, put your feet on an ottoman, and tune in a radio to a program you particularly like. You open the window to let the warm air and sun in and to see what's going on outside. You settle down for the two-hour absence.

Your brother leaves.

For half an hour or so, as you expected, things are fine. You are perfectly comfortable; there's enough activity outdoors to keep you interested; and the radio program is good.

At ten-thirty the program changes to the thing you hate most—hillbilly music—but that's of no major concern. A fly manages to get through a hole in the screen and begins to buzz around your nose—but this is just one of those inconveniences you have now learned to bear.

By eleven o'clock there's a little itch from a rough place in the chair, but that's bearable, too. The fly is still around. The hillbilly music goes on. At eleven-thirty the sky clouds over. The air gets cold and windy. At a quarter to twelve it's raining hard. You're getting wet and cold. If you could shiver, you would. The itches increase. Your bladder begins to get a little too full for comfort.

But you reassure yourself: fifteen minutes more.

At noon you're waiting hopefully for your brother's step, but you don't hear it. He doesn't show at twelve-fifteen. The cold and the wet and the itches and the bladder and the fly and the radio become almost unbearable. By twelve-forty-five you're on the verge of explosion. One o'clock and no brother, but more rain, more discomfort.

At just about one-thirty you hear footfalls. Brother walks in, puts his hand on your shoulder, and says: "I was caught in a traffic jam. I'm sorry I'm late."

Now let the reader seriously ask himself these questions:

1. Just how would you *feel* about your brother at this moment?

2. What do you think you would *do* to your brother at this moment?

Your answers probably fall into one of these major categories: (1) I would feel angry and resentful. (2) I would feel extremely relieved; extremely grateful that he had finally arrived. (3) I would feel mixed up: angry and resentful, on the one hand, and relieved and grateful, on the other.

To the action question, answers range from: (1) I would sock him on the nose to (2) I would throw my arms around him and kiss him.

Each of these answers is appropriate and understandable.

Together they represent the necessary conflict of feelings that derive from the complete dependency of one individual on another. The person who says he would feel angry and hostile will probably be ready to admit that those would be predominant but not exclusive feelings. While he feels angry, he may at the same time feel affectionate and grateful. The man who says he will feel grateful and relieved will probably admit that he is also angry and irritated. Some admixture of these almost polar feelings will probably be present in everyone. This is the peculiar phenomenon of *ambivalence,* of the simultaneous existence of opposite feelings in the same place at the same time.

Similarly, at the action level, the man who says, "I would sock my brother on the nose," might be willing to add, "But I might feel awfully sorry afterward." And the man who says, "I would throw my arms around him," might add that his embrace would include a touch of a bear hug.

Suppose further that this sort of incident happened often, for month after month. Might you then develop an increasing wish for independence from your brother? Might you also seek ways of controlling your brother, of "getting something on him," so that you would not have to count impotently on his good will? And suppose he was a particularly bad brother who didn't care much for you? Wouldn't that intensify your wishes for independence from him or power over him?

Extreme dependency thus serves as a lever for initiating other kinds of needs. To the extent that dependency yields ready satisfaction of existing needs that one cannot satisfy independently—to that extent one's feelings are likely to be positive, friendly, affectionate, protective, grateful, and one is likely to develop strong *social* needs. To the extent that dependency does not satisfy, but rather frustrates—to that extent one is likely to develop feelings of anger and hostility and to wish more strongly for independence and autonomy, to develop strong *egoistic* needs.

The infant suffers from this kind of magical paralysis. He is entirely dependent on adults for the satisfaction of his inborn physical needs. But because no parent can be entirely satisfying (or entirely frustrating), each child must necessarily develop some mixture of plus and minus feelings, first toward the parents and then, since the parents very often are the world, toward the world.

No parents can entirely satisfy or entirely frustrate an infant for these reasons: Infants who encounter only frustration in their very early attempts to satisfy their needs simply do not survive. Children who don't get fed die. At the other end of the scale, however, no infant can hope for perfect satisfaction. No parent has the prescience to foresee all the infant's wants before they arise or the patience to satisfy every want he does foresee. So no adult in the world grew up through complete frustration in infancy or through complete satisfaction.

The working range is the range between the extremes on the satisfaction-frustration scale. Parents can consciously or inadvertently work predominantly near one end of the scale or the other. And the extent to which the predominance actually is at one end or the other, together with the physiological givens, probably accounts for the *general* pattern of early personality development in any particular child. Teachers, bosses, and other people can perform in the same range later to finish off personality development.

To be more accurate, one can put it this way: Some infants face a world that is mostly non-satisfying, non-predictable, and non-controllable from the beginning. Some infants face a world that is more satisfying, more predictable, and more controllable. Children faced with an unpredictable and un-controllable world are more likely to grow fearful and hostile early. They are more likely to wish strongly for independence. And they are more likely to be concerned with *egoistic* needs, with mechanisms by which independence may be gained, i.e., with power, ingratiation, acquisition of goods, and so on.

On the other hand, children whose early years are mostly satisfying are more likely to be secure and dependent. They are more likely to develop predominantly *social* needs, with only secondary concern (unless they learn it later) about autonomy and independence.

These acquired sets of feelings can now be thought of as two new classes of learned needs. One set is of essentially social needs, for dependency, for affiliation with people (because people satisfy needs), for affection, and the like. The other set is egoistic, i.e., concerned with the self in relation to other people rather than with other people per se. In this class belong the emerging needs for independence, for power (over other people), for prestige (as one kind of power over other people), for knowledge (another kind of power), and the like.

The extent of parental control

Theoretically, the relative development of one of these sets of needs or the other in a child is partially controllable by an outsider, the parent. He can encourage social needs by satisfying physical needs, and he can encourage egoistic needs by frustrating physical needs. In practice, the problem is not quite so simple. For one thing, frustration of physical needs in infancy is likely to be accompanied by two by-products—hostility and fearfulness—as well as by a wish for independence. Moreover, if one were really to frustrate continuously, he would soon have to frustrate not only physical needs but the egoistic needs that begin to emerge from the early frustrations. So now the frustrating parent, having developed in his child a wish for independence, must withhold the right to independence. The next step then is the child who wants independence but cannot successfully get it. Nothing he does for himself is right or successful. Where then? Perhaps a retreat from the world, a kind of internal or fantasy independence. When he grows up a little this behavior may earn him a complicated psychiatric label.

There is another key factor in this picture. When a child, or an adult for that matter, is prevented from getting what he wants, he is apt to become angry and to attack the thing that blocks him. The child strikes out blindly at Mama, the adolescent uses his fists, the adult often attacks with words. Suppose our hypothetical parent frustrates the child so that he wants to attack the parent. He kicks and he bites and he howls. Does the parent now decide to satisfy or to frustrate this new behavior? Does he let himself be attacked successfully, or does he frustrate the attack by using his superior force to retaliate? If he does the first, what becomes of his dignity? If he does the second, what does he teach the child? Probably he teaches the child that he must suppress or repress his hostility. But the *suppression* of hostility is not the same as the *absence* of hostility. The child who is not allowed to kick still feels like kicking. Extend this behavior over time, day after day, incident after incident, and the pattern becomes one of internalized, unexpressed, "sat upon" hatred and anger, sometimes with a cover of equanimity and calm.

This is not to say that the child is forever what he becomes in, say, his first year of life. On the contrary, the child is always something more than his history. And present needs plus dependency can account for the development of new needs in adults as well as in children. But the outgrowth of very early experiences (experiences in trying to satisfy one's physical needs through a wholly dependent relationship) is a foundation for the broad outlines of later personality. The

first years have a good deal to do with determining whether
or not the child feels essentially secure or insecure about his
place in the world and essentially optimistic or pessimistic
about other people.

Dependency in industry

The things people learn in this first and most important
dependency relationship probably also have a good deal to
do with the way they face and deal with the less extreme
dependency relationships of later life—like the relationship
one has with his superiors in industrial organizations.

In fact, if we want to put this story in managerial terms,
we need only to go over the last few pages and change a few
labels. We can read "manager" for "parent," and "employee"
for "child." And then we go on to tone down all the
consequences a few notches. The employee, a "used" model
of a child, enters a less extreme dependency relationship when
he goes to work, and he enters with already existent social
and egoistic as well as physical needs. If people in the company are "good brothers," the probability that the employee
will learn to feel trustful and affiliative is pretty good—if he is
already reasonably trustful of people with power. If people in
the company are "bad brothers," his predominant local feelings (superimposed in a complicated way on the general feelings he brought in) are more likely to be hostile and competitive.

It is important to point out here that this view about early
dependency may conflict with some widespread beliefs about
training both children and employees. For example, this position suggests that strong discipline for the infant will probably lead to hostility and fear and to active power and
independence seeking. It suggests further that a history of
frustration probably makes later frustrations *more* difficult to
take rather than easier. And, in a situation in which great
psychological pressure is to be put on a man, holders of this
position would place their money on the man who had *not*
gone through an infantile school of hard psychological
knocks. They would pick the man whose parental relationships and preferably his later ones had been comfortable
and relatively free from psychological want. (Incidentally, the
evidence from studies of successful executives is consonant
with this view. Successful executives tend to come from har-
monious, higher-income homes and to have liked their families and teachers.) For the first year or two, the best way to
"spoil" a child would therefore seem to be to deny him what

he wants. The best way not to "spoil" him is to help him get everything he wants. And, if one considers the new employee instead of the new baby, the same conclusions might hold. But more of this in later chapters.

The hierarchy of needs

One outstanding exponent of growth motivation has pointed out that certain needs take operational precedence over others if both are unsatisfied at the same time. The ambitious man who is lost in the desert pays attention to his thirst, not his ambition. In general, the ordering of needs seems to be from the physical needs, which take first place when unsatisfied, to the social needs, to the egoistic needs, and perhaps beyond what we have called the egoistic group, to needs for self-actualization—that is, to needs for fulfilling one's self in one's own way.

Suppose that such a hierarchy does operate; suppose we begin to get interested in social relationships after our bellies are filled, and in achievement after our social relationships are secure, and in doing our thing when we have filled all our other needs. What implications does the hierarchy have for management? One implication is that when management tries to reward or punish, it had better reward or punish the needs that are operational and not those above or below that operational level. If I feel psychologically safe about my physical needs, threats or rewards will have effects different from those produced by the same threats or rewards in someone who is operating primarily at the level of physical safety. Conversely, if my next meal is the problem that is real to me, don't expect me to be diverted with offers of promotion or threats to my status.

It has been suggested, in fact, that the general level of operational needs in a society changes as the society develops and that managers often lag behind that development in their methods of management. They may thus use incentives or threats that would have worked in the less developed America of a hundred years ago, but are as meaningless in our present affluent society as a penny is to today's teenagers. Our society, in other words, is probably at a stage in which social or egoistic needs are more operational for most of us than physical or safety needs.

In summary

People are born with physical needs. They later either acquire or blossom out with a host of other social and egoistic needs.

These new psychological needs can be thought of as out-growths of (1) physical needs, (2) the nervous system of the physical body, plus (3) dependency on other people.

The child is dependent on adults. Adults can make that dependency predominantly satisfying or predominantly frustrating. Satisfaction builds security and social needs; frustration builds insecurity, hostility, and egoistic needs.

The dependency conditions of infancy recur in later life in industry and elsewhere. The same infantile learning formula may prevail at the adult level.

But the operational needs of adults may be different. For the needs we respond to tend to form a hierarchy, with physical needs taking precedence *if they are severely threatened*. But if we are physically secure, social, followed by egoistic, followed by self-actualizing, needs become the ones we work to satisfy.

Perception
From the inside
looking out

The two preceding chapters were about the world's influence on the development of the person; in this one the issue is the person's influence on the world. The major questions are these: How and why do people see things differently? How objective can people be? Do people see only what they want to see? Or don't want to see? What part do people's personal views of the world play in the supervisory process?

The perceptual world

Most of us recognize that the world-as-we-see-it is not necessarily the same as the world-as-it-"really"-is. Our answer depends on what we heard, not on what was really said. The housewife buys what she likes best, not what is best. Whether we feel hot or cold depends on us, not on the thermometer. The same job may look like a good job to one of us and a sloppy job to another.

Fig. 2. Wife or mother-in-law?

To specify the problem, consider the line drawing in figure 2. This is a picture of a woman. Here are some questions about it: (1) How old is the woman at the time of the picture? (2) Does she have any outstanding physical characteristics? (3) Is she "reasonably attractive" or "downright ugly"?

Show the picture to ten other people. Do they all see the same thing? If some think she looks between twenty and thirty, does anyone think she's over fifty? If some think she's over fifty, does anyone think she's between twenty and thirty? How does one account for the conflicts? Are the differences simply differences in taste? Or in standards of beauty? Or is each person distorting the "real" world in a different way?

This old psychology-textbook picture is intentionally ambiguous. It can be seen either as an ugly old hag with a long and crooked nose and toothless mouth or as a reasonably attractive young girl with head turned away so that one can barely see one eyelash and part of a nose. More importantly, the picture will be based on the "facts" as they are seen by the viewer, which may be different from the "facts" seen by another viewer.

Incidentally, if the reader still sees only one of the two figures, he is getting a good feeling of what a "need" is. The tension or discomfort that one feels when he thinks he is missing some things others can see or when he feels he hasn't quite closed a gap in his knowledge—that is a need. And it will probably be difficult to concentrate on reading further until he satisfies that unsatisfied need by finding the second face in the picture.

The influence of our needs
on our perceptions

The hag picture is another demonstration of a commonplace observation, i.e., that people see things differently, that the world is what we make it, that everyone wears his own rose-colored glasses. But consider some additional questions: Whence the rose-colored glasses? Are the glasses always rose-colored? That is, does one always see what he wants to see, or does he see what he is afraid he will see, or both?

These questions are important because the primary issue of "human relations" is to consider ways in which individuals can affect the behavior of other individuals. If it is true that people behave on the basis of the perceived world, then changing behavior in a predetermined direction can be made easier by understanding the individual's present perception of the world. For if there is any common human-relations mistake made by industrial superiors in their relations with subordinates, it is the mistake of assuming that the "real" world is all that counts, that everyone works for the same goals, that the facts speak for themselves.

But if people do act on their perceptions, different people perceive things differently. How, then, is the manager, for example, to know what to expect? What determines how particular people will perceive particular things?

The answer has already been given in the preceding chapters. People's perceptions are determined by their needs. Like the mirrors at amusement parks, we distort the world in relation to our own tensions. Children from poorer homes, when asked to draw a quarter, draw a bigger than actual one. Industrial employees, when asked to describe the people they work with, talk more about their bosses (the people more important to their needs) than about their peers or subordinates, and so on.

But the problem is more complicated than that. People may perceive what is important to their needs, but does this mean people see what they want to see, or what they are afraid to see? Both wishes and fears are important to one's needs. The answer seems to be that we perceive both, but according to certain rules. We magnify a compliment from higher up in the organization but we also magnify a word of disapproval. We dream of blondes, but we also have nightmares. And sometimes we just don't pay attention at all to things that are quite relevant. We forget dentist's appointments; we oversleep when we have examinations coming up; we manage to forget to clean the basement or to call on this particular customer.

Selective perception

What, then, are the rules of selective perception? The best answer we can give is this one: If one reexamines his memories of the past, he may find that his recall of positive, satisfying things is better than his recall of negative, unpleasant things. He may find it easier to wake early to go fishing than to get to a dentist's appointment. He may look forward, in fact, to doing pleasant, satisfying jobs but may evade mildly disturbing and unpleasant jobs. A senior executive once commented to the author that the biggest problem he encounters with young management people is their tendency to avoid the little unpleasant decisions—like disciplining people or digging through boring and repetitive records or writing unpleasant letters. This executive felt that his younger men would be far more effective if they could learn to deal as promptly with these uncomfortable little decisions as they did with the big ones.

But we can see some sense in this selective remembering if we look for it. There are some advantages to a person in being blind to unpleasantness, even if such blindness cuts down his working effectiveness. Ignoring the unpleasant may represent more than "laziness." It may be a sensible defensive device, psychologically speaking. Thus, most people are able to ignore soft background conversation while working. In effect they are psychologically deaf to a potentially distracting part of the real world. And this defense helps them to concentrate on their work. Similarly, most people manage to ignore the threat of the hydrogen bomb and to go on eating and sleeping as though this dangerous part of the real world were not here. It can even be shown experimentally that words with unpleasant connotations tend to be recognized more slowly when exposed for very brief intervals than words with pleasant connotations.

The strange part of this defensive process, however, is that in order *not* to hear the distracting music or *not* to see the unpleasant words one must first hear and see them. One has to see the word, recognize that it is unpleasant, and reject it almost simultaneously, so that one can say, "No. I didn't see what that word was." Hence the label "defense" attached to this phenomenon—defense against the entry of preselected things mildly disturbing to one's equilibrium. So two of our rules of selective perception become: (1) see what promises to help satisfy needs, and (2) ignore mildly disturbing things.

Suppose, though, that while one is successfully ignoring background talk someone back there starts to shout; or, while one is successfully ignoring the H-bomb, an H-bomb falls on London. At those points, when the unpleasantness becomes intense and dangerous, people stop defending and begin attacking. They stop ignoring the irritation and start directing all their attention to it. This reversal seems to happen suddenly, at some specific threshold. The distant irritation increases to a point at which it becomes so real, so imminent, and so threatening that we reverse our course, discard the blindfold, and preoccupy ourselves completely with the thing previously ignored.

This is the third rule: Pay attention to things that are really dangerous. The whole picture now begins to look like this: *People perceive what they think will help satisfy needs; ignore what is disturbing; and again perceive disturbances that persist and increase.*

There is yet a fourth step in this process. What can happen

when perceived threats become even more intense and imminent? When the soldier in combat watches his buddies die around him? That one we shall consider later, in the chapter on conflict.

This process may not seem entirely logical to an outside observer, but it is quite reasonable psychologically. For this kind of self-imposed psychological blindness helps the person to maintain his equilibrium while moving toward his objectives. An organism lacking this ability to fend off minor threats might well find itself torn apart in its attempt to deal simultaneously with all of them. Or, at least, an individual unable to ignore unpleasant realities might spend so much of his energy dealing with them that he would make little progress toward his major goals. For once a person has learned to perceive a multitude of threats and dangers in his world he needs a system of defense against them. One should add, however, that some individuals may see relatively few things as dangerous and therefore have little need for defense, while for others the world holds dangers at every turn.

In the preceding chapter we suggested that a person who has encountered a relatively helpful world is likely to perceive more of his environment as potentially helpful. If, however, the world has been mostly frustrating, then more of it, and especially new things in it, will be seen as potentially dangerous. Being dangerous, they must be fended off. But, paradoxically, to be fended off they must first be seen. So to protect himself from more insecurity, the insecure person must first see the things that will provoke insecurity and then manage to deny to himself that he has seen them.

Projections of the perceived world

The basic point of this chapter, the point that the world as it is perceived is the world that is behaviorally important, underlies the development of the now generally familiar projective tests. Originally projectives were designed for the diagnosis of aberrations in personality, but the chapter on assessment will show how they are being used industrially. The same idea also underlies what market researchers now call "motivation research" into consumer attitudes, techniques for discovering people's personal views of the "facts" of advertising and product design. Consumer research in general can be thought of as an attempt to make a diagnosis of the relevant parts of the consumer's view of the world so that products can be designed to be seen as aids rather than obstacles.

For managerial purposes, the importance of the perceptual world is clear. If one's concern as a supervisor or counselor or committee member is to try to effect some change in the behavior of other people, and if in turn people's present behavior is determined largely by their perceptions of their environments, then it is critical that one seek to understand their perceptions if one is to understand the circumstances under which their behavior might change.

For example, managers assume almost universally that subordinates want promotions. And yet more than one subordinate has been driven into panic and disappointment because he felt psychologically forced to accept a promotion that no one (sometimes even himself) bothered to find out he did not want.

Often assumptions about the perceptions of others are wrong because they are incomplete. One may assume correctly that employees want more money, but he may fail to understand that more money is acceptable only within a certain framework of independence. This is the paternalism problem.

Sometimes the problem is simple lack of sensitivity for other people. Thus a foreman once complained to the writer about how odd people seemed. He said one of his employees had gotten terribly upset "for no reason at all." The foreman had said, "Hey, boy, go over there and pick that up!" The employee got angry. He had said, "Don't call me 'boy'; I have a name!" The foreman couldn't understand why the employee, a Negro, should get angry about a "perfectly reasonable" request like that.

Or again many parents argue for the importance of heredity over environment because their own children seem to be so different from one another. "Our second child," they will say, "was just a completely different person from the first, though we treated them both *exactly* alike." Parents may be truthful in feeling that they treated two children alike, but it is unwise to assume that the children were therefore treated alike. The first child's world did not include the second child; but the second's did include the first. Indeed the evidence is now quite good that certain personality variables are related to the birth order of children in families. First-born children tend to be more affiliative and more dependent than later-born, for example, and generally more susceptible to social pressure. Moreover, for the infant whose slate is relatively blank, the minor marks made by parents may be major marks for the child. Thus many parents pass lightly over the differences between feeding an infant now or ten minutes from now. But the child is not likely to pass over the same thing nearly so lightly. The manager is likely to pay little attention to his criticism of a subordinate's work. But for the subordinate it is a week's food for worry.

One more example. Sales managers often complain of the difficulties they encounter in getting salesmen to make cold calls. The salesman says he was too busy, or there were better prospects, or he had to catch up on some reports. Is he lazy? Or just defending himself—perhaps unconsciously—against a perceived threat? If it is a defensive process, there are two general ways in which the manager can try to shake the salesman loose. He can teach him to feel comfortable about cold calls, or he can change the mild threat to a major one so that it can no longer safely be ignored. But if he chooses the latter course he had better consider the by-products.

Perceiving oneself

So far we have talked about perceptions of things and other people. But one of the people each of us perceives is himself, as he is, and also as he would like other people to see him. Each of us struts his own act before the world, as it were, in an effort to have other people see us as the kind of person we value.

Quite early in life, we begin to learn what kinds of groups we want to join, what kinds of social classes to aspire to, what kinds of status to achieve. Two of us may have equally intense needs for status and prestige, but if we have grown up in different environments, one of us may seek that status by acting masculine and powerful, or by affecting long hair and a beard. Another may seek to fulfill the same needs by costuming himself in high-style fashions or by donning the pinstriped uniform of the executive.

Teenagers are often painfully awkward as they strive to perfect their own private acts. They seem to feel it terribly important to appear to be what they doubt they really are. Later they become more skilful, either because their acts are better or because their acts are not very far from what the actors really are.

Note that our acts are functional for us. They are performed by both teenagers and adults for good reasons. An act is a way of filling a role. It is also a way of protecting the vulnerable parts of ourselves from real or fancied attack. But our act is effective in performing its functions only if other people accept it. And other people usually accept acts when the gap between our acting selves and their estimate of our "real" selves is small. Other people tend to be reasonably accurate judges, too. So acting problems arise as the distance between act and reality increases.

It is also true that acts are often uncomfortable for the actor. The girl friend happily abandons the courting dance as soon as the wedding is over. But until she has the man tied down and delivered, she must play her version of the coquette, no matter how much worry and fret it requires. Similarly the company executive must act decisively, though privately he may yearn for a chance to weep on someone's shoulder.

But though our acts are functional, they contribute to a social world full of distorted signals. You are trying to tell me that you are strong, worldly, and decisive (and you may be—or you may not), and I am just as busily trying to communicate to you that I am the sagacious, understanding, intellectually stimulating character I would like to be (and may actually be—or may not). We have both been practicing our acts for a long time. So we have both developed clever ways of being convincing, ways that the poor inept adolescent has not even dreamed of. But we have also developed clever ways of spotting the other guy's act.

Our relationship becomes even further confounded by the fact that we read one another's cover stories through our own need-distorted glasses. While you stand there trying to radiate strength and decisiveness, I see you as brash and immature. And you, wanting action and recognition, see my efforts at quiet, pipe-smoking wisdom as dullness and lack of imagination. Looked at this way the wonder is not that we find it so difficult to understand one another, but that we are able to understand one another at all.

The first big problem then is the problem of accuracy, of somehow gaining more accurate information about other people—estimating the discrepancy between the actor and the "real" person. The second problem is to estimate how well our act is working. For surely we are in considerable trouble if the self we want to present to the world is presented so badly, so weakly, so transparently that everyone else is discounting it. We are in a bad way if the people around us are saying: "There is a man who is trying to act decisive and sure of himself, while in fact it is as plain as the nose on your face that he is really unsure of himself, indecisive, anxious."

To the best of this writer's knowledge there is only one general mechanism by which such distortions in relationships can be reduced, and that is the mechanism of *feedback*. If somehow we can develop better ways by which we can learn from other people how our act is getting across, then we can either modify it so that it gets across more fully or we can try to reduce the discrepancy between the act and ourselves, so that it is an easier act to play convincingly. The first course leads to a world of intrigue and gamesmanship; the second, to a simpler, less distorted world.

By this reasoning, other people, if we can get them to provide us with appropriate feedback, can do us considerable service in helping us to bring what we wish to be closer to what we are, and to reduce our uncertainty and anxiety in the process.

We shall talk more about feedback in part 2, when we consider problems of influence and persuasion.

In summary

People see things differently. Even "facts" may be seen quite differently by different people. Relevance to one's needs is the most important determinant of one's personal view of the world. Things that seem to be aids to satisfying one's needs are seen quickly. But things that look like obstacles, if they are not critically threatening, may also be seen quickly, only then to be denied so that they appear not to have been seen at all. By denying obstacles, people "protect" themselves temporarily from them. If they really become dangerous, however, people drop the blinders and face the obstacles.

One of the things we perceive is ourselves and other people. To protect and enhance ourselves, we try to manipulate the picture other people have of us by putting up a front that will make them think we are what we want to be. The problem of our act, and getting it across successfully, depends mostly on our ability to pick up audience reactions accurately. And accurate audience reactions are hard to come by because the audience is acting too.

To ignore differences in perception is to ignore a major determinant of behavior. Yet it is easy to assume unwarrantedly that everyone views the world from the same perspective as the viewer. Time spent trying to reach a common view is not wasted time.

4

Frustration
The roadblock

The hypothetical manager we have been talking about is now struggling continually to reach unattainable goals by a variety of means: first, by behaving in an attempt to satisfy his unsatisfied needs; second, by distorting his perceptions of the real world, i.e., by denying a multitude of minor obstacles in his environment that would push him into greater and greater disequilibrium and by spotlighting things that could be aids to the satisfaction of his needs; and, finally, by periodically stopping on his path toward some goals to deal with obstacles so significant he can no longer ignore them.

Another step is left in the development of this picture. It is the step of actually dealing with these serious obstacles between the person and his goals. The major questions are these: How do people behave under one special kind of pressure—the pressure created by a serious block between the person and what he wants? What kinds of people behave in what ways in the face of such blocks? Why do some people seem to run into more roadblocks than others? Why do some managers blow up so easily? Why don't some people seem to recognize what's good for them?

The obstacle course

Here is a hypothetical case that may illustrate some aspects of the problem:

> Let's go back, if we can, to the days when we were eighteen or so. We have met a girl and taken her out once, and we like her. Now the junior prom is coming up and we decide to invite her. We extend our invitation, and Mary accepts.
>
> This prom is important. It's the big event of the year. It will cost some money, and we don't have much, so we start saving our pennies. We take on extra odd jobs, washing cars, delivering groceries. We manage to borrow a car. We even work it so that a close friend and

his girl will come with us and share the cost of the gas. We manage to scrounge up enough money so that by prom night we've rented a tux, gassed the car, and bought a corsage. Primped and combed and polished, we drive over to pick up our friend, and from there to Mary's house. We park at the gate and go up the walk with our corsage clutched in our little hot fist.

We've never met Mary's parents. When we ring the doorbell and a man appears, we correctly assume it is Mary's father.

We: "Is Mary home?"

Mary's Dad, gruffly, newspaper in one hand, pipe in the other: "Why no, Mary's gone out for the evening."

End of scene. Two questions for the reader: (1) How would you feel? (2) How would you act?

People's reactions to this situation may be grouped into three major classes:

First, there are those whose predominant reaction is *anger* —at Mary.

Second, many people do not feel nearly so angry as they feel *ashamed* and *disappointed* in themselves.

Third—and very rarely—essentially rational rather than emotional feelings occur, i.e., "I wonder which one of us forgot the right date?"

The actions that may follow these feelings can, of course, be direct expressions of the feelings. The man who feels angry may express himself in action—in door slamming, cussing, or in seeking out Mary for verbal or physical attack. But there is another possibility. He may suppress his feelings and act as though he feels calm. Similarly, the man who feels ashamed and inadequate may act accordingly—with weeping and wailing. On the other hand he may act in many other ways. He may, for example, *act* angry as a face-saving device —though he doesn't feel angry.

The rare third man may feel neither angry nor ashamed. He may simply view the situation as a not-very-important problem to be solved. He thus has an infinite variety of actions open to him—to double check, or find another date, or go alone, or spend his money elsewhere—all without major emotional upset.

*Two kinds of aggression and who
shows them*

The third man is a rarity. Most people would feel like one of the other two. These two have one thing in common: intense emotional feelings of aggression. In one case the aggression is directed toward some outside object—toward Mary or toward her parents or toward women in general. In the other case it is directed toward one's self, one's lack of ability in these realms, one's unattractiveness for women, one's stupidity in getting involved with a girl like Mary.

Probably there is some admixture of these feelings in almost everyone, much as in the dependency relationship of infancy. But the sets of feelings that would predominate can be guessed at fairly accurately if we know just a little about the person in the situation.

For example, suppose man A is the Beau Brummel of the high school. Every girl in town would love to go out with him. He is perfectly self-confident about his ability to handle women. This is his area of major success, though in many other areas he is less sure of himself. Now he gets stood up by Mary.

Contrast him with B, the low man on the high-school totem pole. This boy has acne. He knows he is not very successful in his social relationships. The girls tease him but pay little serious attention to him. He didn't want to go to the prom in the first place, but you, one of his friends, urged him to. You almost had to force him ("for his own good") to call Mary.

What differences would one expect in the way that these two personalities would handle this situation?

Secure, self-confident A, moving toward an important goal and encountering an entirely unexpected and apparently insurmountable obstacle will probably want to attack the obstacle directly. He will be angry. He will want to fight.

B, who is pessimistic about his abilities but who nevertheless would like very much to be successful, might behave quite differently. When he encounters the sudden, insurmountable obstacle, his anger and hostility will probably be directed toward himself—at this further proof of his own inadequacy, at his stupidity in even venturing into this danger area. He will be just that much harder to entice into boy-girl relations in the future.

Frustration is a feeling

This area begins to look like this: When people meet serious obstacles between themselves and their important goals, they get aggressive. If they are optimistic about their ability to reach their goal, they get aggressive outwardly—they attack the obstacle. If they are pessimistic about their own ability, they get aggressive inwardly—they attack themselves.

Clearly a *series* of frustrations can begin to turn the secure optimist into an insecure pessimist. The Beau Brummel may lose his confidence if, having been stood up once, he bounces back only to find himself stood up again—and again and again and again. A point may be reached in the process at which he can no longer feel certain that the world has gone wrong. At this point he will begin unhappily to worry about himself. Similarly, a series of successes may turn the shy boy into a Beau Brummel.

The rare third man is still worth thinking about. He is the one who feels no emotional upset—no anger at Mary or at himself. He treats the incident the way most of us might treat running out of ink in the middle of a letter—troublesome, but not worth getting into a stew about.

An explanation of the third man requires us to go back to the chapter on perception. Different people perceive the world in different ways. What kind of world can the third man be perceiving that permits him to toss off this obstacle so lightly? His world probably includes, for one thing, a wide range of alternative behaviors to fall back on when he meets a roadblock, so that no single roadblock seems insurmountable. His is a bigger world. It is probably also a world in which most of his other egoistic needs have been successfully satisfied, so that being stood up is not so important.

But what distinguishes an important goal from an unimportant one? The word "important" here means something like personal, or where-the-hair-is-short, or dear-to-one's-self-esteem-or-survival. For what is the goal that is blocked for our frustrated subject? He is not upset because he cannot get to the dance. He is upset because his personal egoistic needs for status and self-esteem are challenged. Most of us will agree that being stood up on an important date might have been a major frustration when we were adolescents. But as older adults whose social relationships have jelled, whose range of interests has expanded, we are likely in this situation to be more like the third man. Just the experience of a few years may make the problem look much less important or even emotionally minor. Adult security and self-assurance usually hang on firmer threads, not so readily ruptured by a single social setback.

Incidentally, we usually save the word "frustration" for incidents that cause emotional reactions. For the third man, and for most "minor" obstacles, we talk about "deprivation."

The explosive businessman

Some odd implications evolve out of these generalizations about who reacts to frustration in one way and who reacts in another. The position taken here, in effect, is that the confident, secure person will be less likely to encounter serious (for him) obstacles, but that he will be more likely to blow up at such obstacles when he does encounter them.

Yet, although it is generally true that industry prefers secure, solid, optimistic people to shy, withdrawn, insecure people, it is also true that industry is likely to look askance at executives who have emotional outbursts. Emotional blowoff is seen as unbusinesslike behavior that earns the young executive only black marks on his boss's evaluation sheet. Hence we are likely to find in industry many cases of internal emotion and the external appearance of calm.

Thus it is possible for the secure optimist to avoid part of this problem—he can *feel* like blowing up but then stifle his corresponding actions so that what the boss sees is a controlled and rational facade. In fact, many executives in industry probably do just that, thereby perhaps contributing to the psychosomatic illnesses industrial executives are said to develop. For chronic failure to express intense emotion and through that expression to utilize the physiological products of emotion can lead to chronic physiological disturbance. Moreover, encountering an obstacle, then wanting to attack it, and then finding the avenue of attack is cut off by the disapproval of organizational superiors—such a series itself constitutes a secondary kind of frustration.

The occasional blowoff, therefore, ought to be viewed as an appropriate reaction by an imperfect but hard-working, highly-motivated individual when he encounters, as he must at times, a difficult, unexpected, and apparently insurmountable obstacle.

It may be true that an executive would be an even better executive if he did not get frustrated to begin with; that is, if obstacles that were important for other people seemed minor to him, so that he did not even feel an emotional reaction. Most of us would consider it ideal if our model executive could be the rare third man, who would simply shrug his shoulders (both at himself and at the world) and start thinking about where to go from there. An ideal executive might then be one whose tolerance for things frustrating to other people would be so great, whose areas of personal security would be so broad, whose breadth of perception would be so wide, that only very, very few incidents in his lifetime would include insurmountable obstacles (because he would always have ways around them) or really important self-esteem needs (because his self-esteem would be so solid that few things could threaten it). His egoistic needs instead would be needs for accomplishment of organizational goals.

The problem is one of people's expectations about their ability to satisfy their needs; and expectations are, in turn, largely determined by past successes and failures. If through life one has come to expect failure, to feel unsure of his ability to satisfy his personal egoistic needs, then these needs loom larger in his perceptions than they do for the next man. The martini that is not dry enough stops being just a deprivation, i.e., just a martini that is not dry enough. It becomes instead a sign of disrespect from the bartender—a threat to one's self-esteem.

It follows that people whose self-esteem is easily threatened are less likely to be rational about their efforts to satisfy their needs. It follows, too, that if one can build up people's feelings of self-confidence, so that their expectations are optimistic, they will be able to deal with problems more rationally and objectively.

Frustration and standards of success

Perhaps the most important key to whether we encounter frequent frustration or not is our own individual standard of success. Two men may both want to make money, but "to make money" for one may mean $10,000 a year while for the other "to make money" means $100,000. If two such men are of about equal ability and have about equal opportunity, and if both actually achieve $25,000 a year, then one will be satisfied and the other frustrated. Both have achieved the same external level of success, but one may perceive himself a failure.

This problem has many facets: It is a question of the relationship between our aspirations and our ability to achieve our aspirations. If the two are close together, frustration is relatively unlikely. If our ability exceeds our level of aspiration—if we are much *better* than we need to be—then society probably suffers because we do not contribute as much as we can. If aspiration and ability are out of line in the other direction—if we want what we do not have the capacity to obtain—then we have a potential source of serious frustration.

It is useful to examine the ways in which people develop their individual ideas of how good is good and how high is high. Many of them seem to develop early in life. Even when quite young, some children seem always to need to win any game they play while others seem to want only to be "better than average." And occasionally we see still others who apparently can be perfectly happy as low man on the totem pole. Similarly, in industry some people seem consistently ready to accept the level at which they are working or only want to move ahead in small (but perhaps steady) steps. Others feel they are at the bottom unless they are at the top.

An illustration may show how such differences develop: Suppose someone puts a target on a wall and then leaves you alone with a set of darts and the target. Suppose you have never thrown darts before and have shown no particular interest in dart throwing. Do you set yourself a score to shoot for before you throw the darts for the first time? Probably not. But suppose you throw the five darts and score 75 out of a possible 250? Now what do you do? Before you throw the next dart do you set yourself a standard? Is the standard 250? Or is it anything better than 75? For most of us it would be the latter. In situations in which we are perfectly free to set our own standards, we are most likely to keep setting our goals just slightly ahead of our present abilities. Thereby, through learning and training and exercise, we can feel that we are continually moving ahead successfully.

Let us suppose, however, that instead of being alone in the room with the target and the darts, someone else is present—another man who has been a constant competitor of yours. The other man throws first and hits 100. Now what is your goal? And now how do you feel when you hit only 75?

Once other people enter into the goal-setting process the more or less "natural" tendency to set goals a little ahead of past achievement begins to give way. Goals may then, in fact, be set without any regard to ability. Thus one occasionally encounters a person who *must* become a great industrialist because his parents have hammered that notion into him since childhood. Failing to become a great industrialist constitutes failing to satisfy the people he wants most to satisfy and, hence, means frustration.

Take the case of a young engineer who was unhappy on his job. He had never wanted to be an engineer; he had always wanted to be a coach. But his father had been an engineer. His father, on his deathbed, had extracted a promise from the student that he would become an engineer, and a good one. So the fellow was stuck first with a goal that had been imposed on him and, second, with abilities and interests that were not likely to allow him to reach that goal. He had no good solution to the problem except to continue through life jumping for the ring he would probably never reach—unless he could somehow change his attitude toward his now unreachable father.

It is a commonplace in industrial work situations to feel that one must set high standards for employees to "motivate" them. But may not standards beyond an individual's reach lead him into one of two other behaviors? They may lead him into a hopeless struggle to reach a goal that his abilities will not allow him to reach, and hence into a series of failures, and hence again into panic and insecurity. Or else overly high standards may lead a better-adjusted individual simply to remove himself physically or psychologically from the situation, to refuse to accept the standards that are set for him.

Perhaps one can argue that a person who is in a position to set standards for other people has a responsibility to set those standards neither so low as to provide inadequate opportunity for full expression nor so high as to guarantee feelings of failure.

In summary

Frustration is a "feeling" rather than a "fact." It is a feeling that arises when one encounters certain kinds of blocks on paths to certain kinds of goals. These feelings arise when the block seems insurmountable and when failure to surmount it threatens one's personal well-being—when the goal involves the self.

When people encounter such obstacles, they react with aggression; aggression mostly toward the obstacle when the person is sure of his own ability and aggression mostly toward oneself when the person is pessimistic about his ability, i.e., when he has had a history of failure.

Many obstacle situations are depriving rather than frustrating because the obstacles do not seem insurmountable or the goals are not central to the self. Some people may therefore meet fewer frustrations than others because they have more ways around more obstacles or because they are self-confident enough so that their self-esteem does not have to be proved again by every new problem they encounter.

Moreover, if a person's goals are in line with his abilities, then he may avoid another major source of frustration. If his objectives extend far beyond his abilities, he may consider himself a chronic failure because he cannot see that the carrot is really tied to his own nose.

Other people—parents, peers, managers—have a good deal to do with the development of self-confidence and hence with the ways people deal with obstacles. For self-confidence is tied to success, and success is in large part what other people may decide it is.

Psychological conflict Roadblocks on the inside

Conflict may be thought of as a class of frustration, the class characterized by a pulling in two directions at the same time. The obstacles one meets are not brick walls but drags that pull back as one goes forward. Conflict situations are frying-pan-and-fire situations, or donkey-between-the-bales-of-hay situations. They are choice situations, decision-making situations. And this class of psychological situations underlies both major emotional upset and irrationality in everyday problem solving.

Conflicts occur at all levels of personality and in all degrees of importance to the person. Some are minor. Few persons are likely to be psychologically crippled by trying to decide between two movies, though the presence of conflict is often visible in a tendency to vacillate before the choice is made. Nor is the donkey nearly so likely to be paralyzed between the bales of hay as the old story makes out. On the contrary, most of us encounter numberless conflicts in the course of everyday life, conflicts we manage to resolve in short order and without permanent scars.

Some of the same generalizations that apply to frustration also apply to conflict. Some conflict situations involve important central needs that appear to be inescapably opposed. Others involve relatively unimportant needs or offer so many substitute possibilities that we hardly recognize their existence. As with frustration, serious trouble arises from conflicts between intense central needs involving long-term critical goals, where no satisfactory alternatives are visible. Such conflicts can be a real threat to the personality.

In this chapter some extreme illustrations of more serious personality conflicts will be presented, in search both of better understanding of the process itself and of some ways in which the industrial environment can irritate or even create such conflicts. Then, after looking at some samples, alternative ways of handling and resolving them will be considered.

40

An extreme illustration

Here is a nightmarish illustration:

Suppose I build a large cage and put you in it. Suppose you live in it for a long time and get used to it. This is home. Life is dull but not unbearable. You have a good bed and the food is good. But there is a peculiarity about the food. On the table in one corner of the cage is a box. The box has a cover. When you get hungry you lift the cover and inside you find an attractive meal. So whenever you get hungry, you just open the box, take a few things you like, and let the cover close again. You eat and then you go over to your bed and take a nap.

One day something happens. When you get hungry, you go to the box as usual. You reach out to lift the lid, but when your fingers hit it you get a strong electric shock.

You draw back and rub your hand. You think about it for a while. You decide it must have been static electricity and reach out again. This time you get another shock, one that seems more intense than the first. This upsets you somewhat, so you begin to look around to see if there is something wrong. You look for a plug or a wire you can pull out. You look for some rubber gloves. But you can't find anything that will do the job. Of course, you're not very hungry—yet.

An hour later, you are hungrier, so you go over again. You say: "What the devil; so I'll get a little shock, so what?" You touch the cover, but the shock has now grown quite intense. It really hurts. You drop the lid in a hurry. You again sit down on your cot and think for a while. After twelve hours of this, with no food, you begin to get a little frantic. You begin to poke around the place, looking for the answer to the electrified box. You call for help. Nothing seems to work. You start looking seriously for a way out of the cage, something you haven't done since the first few days you were in it. You try to pull the bars apart, to break the lock, to crawl out. Nothing works.

You can smell the food in the box and your hunger begins to get desperate. You decide to risk it. You pull open the lid, get knocked back, but you still manage to reach in and grab a bit before you let the lid drop. You eat your morsel and go back to your cot to think the thing over again.

The situation goes on. As you get hungrier, the shock seems to get stronger. As you approach the box, driven by your hunger, you can almost feel the pain of the shock you'll get when you touch it. You manage to get enough food to stay alive, but instead of adapting to the shock you seem to get more sensitive to it.

What do you do?

The sanity in insanity

The conflict here is an extreme one involving two basic, critical, physical needs: the need for food, and the need for the avoidance of pain. There is no physical escape, and the needs increase in intensity with time.

What, then, would happen?

Probably you would "go crazy." After some days of this, you would probably be huddled in a corner in a dazed and stuporous state. If we opened the cage and took you out, you would probably stay dazed and stuporous for a long time. If we tried to feed you, you probably wouldn't eat. If we tried to wake you, you probably wouldn't wake up. You're gone— even though you're alive and there's no specific physical defect.

If we sent you down to Florida and put you out to bask in the sun, if we held your hand and talked with you and reassured you, and if we used some of the methods that have been developed in psychiatry, we might be able to get back into contact with you. We might tease you into accepting food and into discovering thereby that things have changed and the world is no longer what it had been during those terrible days in the cage. We might, in other words, be able to cure you of the effects of this intense conflict. The cure might be complete, but most probably, no matter how many years passed, you would still get upset when you met up with cages or electric shocks.

Now suppose that we step inside your mind while you're in this stuporous state. What will we be likely to find? You may be off in some fantasy world. You may be the gourmet of gourmets, eating your way continuously through quantities of delicacies while in one fist you hold the only key to the master electric switch. You would be dealing with the conflict by escaping upward into unreality and fantasy. You cannot escape physically; you cannot handle the stresses as they exist; so you escape psychologically, through a neurosis or psychosis.

Such behavior thus becomes, in a sense, reasonable behavior. It fits with the view that the organism defends itself from intolerable attack and seeks to keep itself together. Cutting off one's communication with the real world in favor of a world of fantasy is a desperation measure for meeting intolerable conflict. It is not necessarily a healthy way of meeting it, but to a person at a particular time it may be the best available way.

This illustration is extreme, of course. And it can only work because a cage exists. If we had not enclosed you in the cage, then you would have dealt with the conflict simply by walking away from it and looking for food elsewhere. In fact, one might say that the presence or absence of the cage makes the difference between conflicts that lead to extreme emotional reaction, especially withdrawal reaction, and conflicts that are handled more easily. But the cages one encounters in real life are usually built of social and cultural bars rather than steel ones.

Consider just one more illustration of major conflict before taking up the question of conflict in industrial situations. Consider two husbands, A and B, each married to an impossible shrew. Both have been married for a long time, both have children. A has a political job. He is in the public eye. He has no religious values of any significance. He is not interested in his children. He has no scruples about divorce. B loves his children, is intensely religious, and feels that divorce is sinful. Assume that the wives of A and B continue to make their lives miserable, and suppose further that the intensity of this misery increases continually. Suppose that A and B reach the same point at about the same time. Each decides he can stand it no longer and runs away.

Which one will be more successful in his attempt to escape? Which one will be able to settle down to life and work in a new community? The answer clearly is that A may be quite successful, and B quite unsuccessful.

The conflict for A is between his career and his desire to escape. Though much intensified in degree, this choice is not essentially different from the choice one must make in deciding between two radio programs broadcast at the same time. A's choice involves little guilt, little threat to his idealized picture of himself. The stimuli are largely external to his person. All he can lose is his career. But for B, leaving the field is no escape at all. His conflict resides entirely within himself. It involves his conscience, his self-esteem. No matter how far he may be from the physical location of the conflict tomorrow morning, his feelings of guilt and his loss of self-respect will be with him, for he has no easy way of cutting out communication within himself.

The troublesome conflicts, then, are those that involve needs "central" or "internal" to the personality. Usually these turn out to be conflicts between needs at different *levels* of the personality—between more or less basically impulsive needs and "conscience" needs.

Conflict in people in industry

Much supervision is an attempt to control others through the use of conflict. For example, the threat of discipline to prevent some unwanted behavior is an attempt to introduce a conflict into another person's (B's) perceptual world. Where B had only one need, to get what he wanted, now he has a second and conflicting one, to avoid the punishment that getting what he wants now entails.

Such control, through conflict, cannot be classed glibly either as good or as bad. For the most part such measures do not introduce dangerous conflicts because they do not set up situations that involve feelings of guilt or threaten people's feelings of self-esteem. They are largely external to the personality. But insofar as some people may see rules as a challenge to their basic autonomy, the reaction may be intense.

Other uses of conflict as devices for controlling behavior can get more serious. Suppose, instead of the threat of discipline, we choose to try to develop "positive" feelings of loyalty and duty to the company—suppose we try to build a "company conscience" into our employees as we do into our children. If we succeed, we are setting up *internal* conflicts this time. Now it is not the boss that the employee must worry about, but his own feelings of guilt. People who thus begin to feel honor-bound can get themselves into a tense emotional tizzy. And the probabilities of an irrational emotional blowoff are consequently greater. Paternalism is that kind of problem. One simply showers employees with gifts or benefits and then makes it clear that they are expected to show their gratitude by submission. For those with strong needs for independence, the resulting conflict is essentially internal, and it includes the possibility of violent reaction.

There are many other places in industry where one may find serious long-term emotional conflicts. Many of these center in the same fundamental desires for independence and autonomy, on the one hand, versus one's desires for dependence and support, on the other. The whole pattern of industrial organization encourages this sort of conflict.

Subordinates are by definition dependent on their superiors. Subordinates are therefore bound to feel ambivalent to some degree, i.e., to feel uncomfortably bound and yet pleasantly protected.

Sometimes one finds individuals who have managed to strike a balance between their needs for autonomy and for dependency, perhaps by finding a particular job at a particular level that satisfied both needs—like a job as assistant to a powerful superior. Or an executive may find himself a middle-level spot at which he feels both competent to do the jobs assigned to him and satisfied with his prestige and status. Often, however, higher management, blind to the subordinate's perception of the world, decides to "reward" him by promoting him. Promotion for one who has thus struck a satisfactory compromise between conflicting needs may result only in reinstating the old enervating conflict with greater intensity than ever. Now perhaps our subject begins to feel panicky about his ability to do this bigger job. It frightens him. However, he wants the status and the money it will bring, and he wants to conform to the social necessity of accepting a promotion. ("You'd be crazy to refuse an offer like that!") Shortly following such a promotion, one often sees beginning signs of active conflict: anxiety; "unpredictable" lashing out against subordinates; "inexplicable" refusal to delegate authority; self-isolation from peers and subordinates and, if possible, from superiors; and so on. In fact, many such cases end up in physical illness or alcoholic escapes or some other industrially unacceptable solution. Top management then usually decides it has misjudged the man—he wasn't as good as he looked.

This is not to suggest that fear of promotion should keep people from accepting promotion. Fears can be overcome by success in meeting them. But awareness of the existence of needs that drag against the rewards of promotion can help a promoter to plan the promotional process more wisely.

Sometimes a job demands of a man some activities that do not mesh with his conception of what is right or his conception of what is dignified or proper for him as a member of society. Salesmen seem to suffer from this conflict more than some other occupational groups. Sales managers beat the drums and wave the flag to get them to go out to sell Ajax iceboxes to Eskimos. But some Eskimos seem not to need iceboxes; or some other iceboxes look more useful than Ajax; or the salesman feels uneasy and uncomfortable about putting his foot in people's doors when he hasn't been invited.

Some sales managers try to resolve this job vs. moral-

social conflict by "proving" to the salesman the social importance of selling. They point up the white man's burden of
carrying the good life to the ignorant consumer. They try to
resolve the conflict by building up the pressure on one side to
such an extent that it overrides the other. The difficulties here
are two: First comes the problem of the morning after. His
enthusiasm drummed up by "inspirational" sales meetings,
the salesman goes out and sells—temporarily satisfying his
job needs and reducing them to zero. He then finds himself
feeling depressed and guilty because the still unsatisfied
moral-social needs are now naked and exposed. The second
difficulty with this inspirational method is that it requires
continual recharging. The sales manager must maintain the
initiative by injecting periodic shots of enthusiasm, lest the
salesman wake up one morning deciding his product and his
job are really no damn good.

Finally, one can mention the role of conflict in consumer
decisions. All the recent activity in motivational research
centers in a conception of the human personality as a multi-
storied structure. The occupants on each floor are at war with
the others. Thus some people may deny that they buy a product for its snob value, because their self-respect requires such
denial; but they may be able to buy the product for its snob
value nevertheless, if the snobbery-self-respect conflict can
be rationalized in terms of "good value," or "quality," or
"utility."

Conscience

The conflict problem seems to be one of disorder in nature itself. If the development of human personality were entirely
orderly, perhaps the need system of an individual would be
so designed that there would never be two opposing simultaneous needs. But people do not grow up with any such well-
integrated system of needs. On the contrary, they seem from
the very beginning to develop more or less opposing needs
which frequently demand simultaneous satisfaction. People
get hungry and sleepy at the same time; they want to fight
and to run at the same time; to love and to hate; to overpow-
er and to submit.

Although the mere presence of opposing needs accounts
for the existence of conflicts, it does not account for the intensity or the variety of reactions to conflict. What is required
to account for these interpersonal differences in reactions to
conflict is an additional dimension in the picture of the structure of human personality. We need to introduce the concept

of conscience, of internal control by the person of his own behavior.

The development of conscience seems to pass through several phases, and you often can actually see them going on in a child. First, the child begins to avoid some things he wants to do because he fears reprisals from his parents or because he wants to please them by showing his self-restraint. When he finds he gets punished for throwing his milk at Mama, he may begin to think twice about throwing it. The next time the same impulse shows up, he may try to do it when Mama's not looking. But as he gets more socialized, as he begins to realize he can't outguess Mama, he begins to internalize and accept as his own the restrictions that originally came from Mama. At that point he begins to act, for himself, *like his parents.* He may throw his milk to satisfy the impulse, but then he will slap his own wrist to punish himself for what he has done. The final stage in this process is the child's refusal to throw the milk because *he* now feels it is a wrong act.

This is conscience. It is the difference between the person who is aware of the law but is afraid only of getting caught and the person who himself feels that the law is right and proper and that to break it is morally wrong. So learned conscience needs can be satisfied only by denying the satisfaction of other needs.

The conflicts that cause difficulty are long-term conflicts between increasingly strong action needs and severe conscience needs. Thus, in the military situation, one troublesome conflict may center in the soldier's duty and loyalty needs at the conscience level and his desire to avoid danger at a more basic level. In a husband-wife case, the conflict may be between the conscience notions of morality and propriety and the desires to escape physical and psychological harassment at the hands of a shrew. In industry the conflict may be between desires for psychological safety and the conscience wish to be what people expect one to be.

If, in early life, we develop an oversized conscience—if many things come to be seen as sinful or improper or dangerous—then we may encounter many serious conflicts. If one learns early that aggressiveness or sensuality or hostility are wrong and to be feared, and yet, in the course of living, one encounters situations that call for aggression or stir up sensual impulses or engender hostility, then one may be caught up in conflict much more than the next man. And if one's perceptual breadth is too limited to find ways around such problems, then the conflicts will be severe.

On the other hand, if a man develops an undersized conscience, if he can lie, or steal, or manipulate people without guilt, then he may suffer very little, although society may suffer a whole lot. Such people are usually labeled "psychopaths." They sit in a special psychiatric filing category because they are not exactly sick, except socially. They may make other people sick, but they themselves feel fine.

Unconsciousness

At this point we must add one more concept to the whole picture: the concept of unconsciousness. It has been pointed out that one extreme way to handle conscience-impulse conflicts is to deny the existence of one or both of the needs. Amnesiacs do this. This process of denying from memory something the conscience disapproves of is the process that is now called *repression*. It is another defense mechanism, another way of holding a personality together in the face of otherwise unsolvable problems. If there is no acceptable solution in reality, then the solution must somehow be found in unreality, and repression is a way of denying reality by literally forgetting about it. The conflict then no longer exists. Thus the soldier with combat fatigue is in a completely stuporous state and remembers nothing of what has happened. Except, of course, that he actually does remember. In fact, one might say he remembers too well, since his memories may be so threatening and so dangerous that he must deny them to himself. So unconsciousness is the burial ground for dangerous or guilt-provoking needs and experiences. Day dreaming and night dreaming are cues to such unconscious activity. Temporary, voluntary escape into unconsciousness through alcohol or hobbies or movies are other less extreme ways of temporarily holding oneself together by forgetting the conflict. Psychosomatic (psychologically caused but physically manifested) illnesses are often unconscious ways of channeling off some of the tension that deep-seated conflicts may engender.

Handling conflict

Obviously none of these many unconscious or semiconscious methods of handling conflict is particularly satisfactory from the point of view of mental health. Each of them is a last-ditch holding maneuver which itself requires a great deal of energy. So much energy, in fact, may be devoted to repressing what is feared that not much is left for the behavior required to satisfy the multitudes of other more mundane needs that most of us must satisfy in order to survive.

So we are left with this question: How can one *really* resolve emotional conflicts? Conflicts, like other psychological phenomena, are conflicts only because they are perceived as such. They are not part of the real, but of the perceived, world. A conflict exists for a person because to him certain needs seem mutually exclusive. His conflict would be resolved if (1) he could find some new, previously unknown means to satisfy both needs fully, (2) he could change his mind about one of the needs so that he was no longer interested in it, or (3) he could reorganize, in one of a number of other ways, his view of the world so as to set the conflict in a new and less significant perspective.

For example, consider a husband caught between an impossible wife and his social duty. Several alternative resolutions are *theoretically* available. First, he may come to feel differently about his notions of duty. If he decides it is, say, socially, religiously, and morally appropriate to leave his wife, then perhaps he can do so without trouble. Or he may somehow come to see his wife in a new light, so that instead of an ogress she becomes an unhappy human being in need of help. Still again, a man may be able to change his expectations about life, to reorient his standards and philosophy so that the sufferings he endures are not so much sufferings as the-things-one-must-expect-from-life.

This is not to say that one can resolve conflicts simply by asserting, "I feel differently about this." The problem is really to feel differently. The counselor and the psychiatrist offer to help people reorganize their perceptions of problems so that they can perhaps find new solutions.

One way to illustrate the idea of "reorganizing perceptions" is to ask the reader to compare himself today with himself as an adolescent. Consider what a skin rash might have meant in adolescence and what it would mean when he is thirty-five and settled down. The problem is simply not the same problem. As our worlds have grown, as new knowledge and new experience have been added, we have changed our perspectives, reorganized our perceptions.

Sometimes an adult conflict exists only because a person cuts off his channels of information from the world. The combat-fatigue victim, for example, may withdraw completely into himself, apparently seeking to avoid emotional repetition of arduous experiences. Unless he eventually opens his channels, he will never get an opportunity to learn that the world has changed and that he is surrounded by sunlight instead of explosions. Similarly, the process of repressing old conflicts so preoccupies many of us that we cannot observe our changing environments. We do not learn that elaborate defenses are unnecessary because now nothing needs defending. Thus, the poorly educated executive, after a series of perceived failures in coping with technical innovations, may go on avoiding technological change, never realizing that now he is—if he can bring himself to try it—perfectly capable of handling the situations that he is expected to handle. This tendency to narrow one's incoming communication channels in order to avoid psychological dangers is one major social cost of conflict. People avoid much of the world because they fear much of themselves. They "take leave of their senses," literally.

But though many reactions to emotional conflict are psychologically unhealthy and inefficient, they remain psychologically lawful reactions. They, like other behavior, can be thought of as attempts by the organism to bring itself into equilibrium.

Conflicts, beliefs, and decisions: The great balancing act

These processes for dealing with emotional conflict—efforts to reorganize or to reduce incoming communication—have their parallels in the less emotional but equally important processes of making decisions and solving problems. In the next chapter, we will concentrate on the thinking part of man, so at the end of this one it is useful to build a bridge between the emotional side that we have discussed so far and that other everyday problem-solving side. The processes that we use to deal with conflict provide such a bridge; for conflicts occur not only in the guts but also in the brains of men. Decisions, the essence of managerial life, are, after all, resolutions of conflicts.

Some of the dilemmas that need explaining are things like the apparent irrationality of many decisions, even hardheaded business decisions; the frequent failure of businessmen to abandon a course of action even after it seems obviously to be the wrong one; and the tendency to believe in our plans more after we have decided to carry them out than we ever did before.

All of these can be thought of as a part of a great balancing act taking place in the emotions of most of us as well as in our heads. We search for consonance, for consistency, for balance, in business decisions and in the choices of everyday life. When we have invested a large amount in a course of action—like a new line of products— we find it hard to accept reports showing that the products aren't selling. To

maintain an internal balance, to reduce psychological dissonance, we may do "irrational" things—like blaming the sales
force or investing *more* in promotion and advertising, on the
grounds that we haven't given our ideas a fair test.

When the scientist puts a year's work into a problem and
his hypotheses don't check out, he is in a state of dissonance,
too. He can either give up the hypotheses—to which he has
given much of himself—or he can seek a larger grant to develop finer instruments to give his ideas a "really" fair test.

And so on. A well-known study of an offbeat group that
predicted the end of the world is a good example. They
predicted the end would occur at a special hour on a special
date. They disposed of their worldly goods, informed the
newspapers, and gathered at an appointed place to await the
end. When the hour passed and nothing happened, did they
quit and go home? Not at all. Too much inbalance, too much
dissonance. Instead they "received" a late message from
outer space telling them that this had been a test run to check
their readiness and their faith. A new hour was then duly set,
and it passed. And now how could the imbalance be
handled? It was handled ingeniously. A new message arrived.
It announced that because of the faithfulness of this little
group the earth would be spared for a few centuries more.

The salesman changes companies and begins to sell for
competitor B after firmly believing in product A for twenty
years. How can he sell B if he thinks A is better? Dissonance
again. So he looks into B "more carefully," and he "discovers" that it is a far better product than he had thought. Quality control is much better, etc. Now he can get back in
balance.

The lame duck executive is likely to have the same
problem. If he has been obviously shunted aside by the company he has been loyal to and is on the way out, he is in
imbalance. How to resolve it? Either by admitting that he is
less good than he thought—which is difficult indeed and
ought to create greater dissonance—or by beginning to look
on the company differently; to mobilize his list of the company's weaknesses and stupidities; to prove that they don't
deserve him. That's the more likely course. He makes himself
ready to leave by searching more than ever for the negative
side of what he is leaving. By so doing, of course, he speeds
up the process, irritating his colleagues even further; in their
turn, they can assuage their guilt and uncertainty by using his
present negative behavior as evidence that they were right in
unloading him.

Of course, the company that decides to try a third or

fourth test market may be right, or the salesman, or the departing executive. So we must be careful here, as elsewhere, about "psychologizing" too easily to explain things our way. The problem is to distinguish "real" logic from the selective logic generated to deal with psychological dissonance.

So the feelings and the facts get intertwined and almost inseparable (though we often think of them separately) in many of our problems. It is the whole man who makes the choices, not just the logical part of him.

In summary

The development of personality allows for the coexistence of opposing needs. Conflict situations are those requiring decisions between such coexistent opposing needs.

When conflicts involve critical needs and seem to offer no ways out, reactions may be severe. Fantasy, delusions, and amnesia are such extreme ways out of conflicts.

Conflicts that require extreme solutions usually involve "conscience" needs, centering in morality and social propriety. Extreme solutions often require the person to push one of the needs into unconsciousness and thereby—by forgetting —to deny the conflict.

But such repressive defenses cost energy. Less enervating solutions call for reorganization of perceptions, finding new ways out of apparently dead-end situations.

Serious chronic conflicts may develop in the industrial organization. Conflicts between needs for dependence and for independence are especially prevalent because the industrial environment emphasizes dependency but values independence.

Less deep but equally important conflicts occur in everyday decision-making situations. There emotional and logical mechanisms get mixed into one another. It often then becomes hard to tell how much of our commitment to a course of action is objective and logical and how much of it is an effort to maintain our psychological balance. For human beings seem to want to maintain balance, to avoid dissonance between mutually contradictory beliefs and ideas. Hence, when we make a difficult decision, we tend to build up our support for our solution and to find more and more reasons for feeling we were right in rejecting the alternative.

6

Learning, thinking, problem-solving Some reasoning parts of people

A first purpose of this chapter is to counterbalance the general impression of human irrationality and emotionality we have built up thus far. In preceding chapters we emphasized emotional, unconscious, "illogical" aspects of human action. But even a cursory look at people's behavior will show that much of it is quite reasonable. It represents conscious effort to satisfy conscious needs. Students learn to type and to solve arithmetic problems; workingmen search for ways to add to their incomes and their job security; architects try to improve the beauty and functionality of their plans; managers try to choose the most effective ways of budgeting their capital and of designing and marketing their products.

Not long ago, however, a chapter about these matters probably would not have been included in this book. Psychologists and social scientists were so deeply concerned with the emotional life of man that they ignored his conscious thinking life altogether.

This emotional emphasis was partly a reaction against still earlier, entirely rational approaches. Forty or fifty years ago, for instance, we assumed that workers worked only to earn money and that managers, in turn, sought only to maximize their profits. We built theories of economic behavior and industrial organization around these assumptions. Early industrial engineering grew up as a logical, "scientific" process, treating irrational human quirks like hostility and resistance as outside the realm of science. Later, with the emergence of such odd bedfellows as Freud and the Western Electric studies, attitudes turned in the opposite direction. Foggy conceptions of social and egoistic needs took precedence. Workers sought to satisfy ephemeral needs for "belongingness"; managers were not managing, they were unconsciously competing with childhood images of their fathers.

Only very recently have social scientists from many fields set about to integrate and modify these views; to deal with

the undeniable whole man—the manager who may be unconsciously competitive but who also spends a fair share of his
time trying to decide what materials to buy and what marketing strategies to follow. This chapter, then, is about those
conscious efforts to learn, to think, and to solve problems—
efforts that most managers work at for many hours each day.

What does it take to learn?

Earlier chapters have already said a good deal about
learning. In effect they have said that people learn continuously; they learn their personalities; they learn many of their
social and egoistic needs, their attitudes, and their habitual
ways of behaving. At the same time they learn to speak, to
walk, to read, to build model airplanes, and to make managerial decisions. They are learning whenever their behavior at
time 2 is modified as a consequence of experience at time 1.

The question now before us is this: What does it take for
someone to be able to learn? If we set about to build a
"thing" capable of learning, what would we have to build
into it? And just how would the thing work?

This thing we are trying to build must demonstrate that it
is a learning thing by behaving more effectively—perhaps
more quickly and with fewer mistakes—the second or third
time it tries to solve a problem than it did the first time.
What characteristics do we have to build into it to permit it
to pass such a test?

Our thing will really need two kinds of mechanisms in
order to learn. It will need some hardware, some gadgets,
some devices that will "allow" it to do certain kinds of things.
But it will also need some "rules"—it will need a program
that will permit it to decide which of the several alternatives
to select.

On the hardware side, our thing will first require some
input channels so that it can have "experiences" to learn
from. It will need some means of getting information into
itself from outside itself, something like human eyes or ears
(some photoelectric cells will do).

Second, it will need some *output devices,* some ways of
acting and searching. It will have to be capable of moving
through the world or of sending signals out into the world. It
will need some equivalents to human muscles or the human
voice, like wheels or a typewriter. For how can it modify its
behavior if it cannot behave? How can it search for easier
paths if it cannot explore?

We are not through yet. If this machine is to improve performance with experience, it needs to remember its experience. It needs a *memory device* for storing up its experiences as well as a way of using this stored-up information when faced with new problems. Lacking such a storehouse, or lacking access to it, each experience will be a first experience.

Besides these external mechanisms it will need several inside gadgets. It will need some *associative device* to connect inputs with outputs. The device may be a simple one that makes only one choice—to connect or not to connect a given input with a given output. But without such a device the thing won't be able to close the circuit between what comes in and what goes out and hence will be unable to profit behaviorally from its experience.

Besides all this hardware, which allows the thing to receive, process, and put out information, the gadget will need a program, a set of rules so that it doesn't just input and output completely at random.

One of these rules ought to be a *stinginess rule*. If the selective device has a choice among outputs, it can be built either to select the most "efficient" of all outputs—the simplest and shortest one—or to select the first output it comes across that will work (which may be easier in the long run) or to use some other specified decision rule.

It will also need a *response rule*. It cannot be allowed to sit still and ignore all inputs. It has to be built so that it is *on* when inputs are coming in and so that it stays on until it gets an answer. It will have to have, in other words, something vaguely like human needs—some motivation to work.

One final requirement: the thing will need some way of getting *inputs about its own outputs*. It has to know whether its own actions were right or wrong. If the archer could not see that he had missed the target, he could never know how to modify his aim. If the manager could never learn about the effects of his past changes in plant layout, he could not know by himself how to improve his layout. But this means that the input mechanisms have to be somehow related to the output mechanisms. If the only input device in our gadget is a photoelectric cell that is sensitive to light, and our only output gadget is a buzzer that signals with sound, then our thing might have a tough time learning. So there has to be some kind of correspondence between the nature of the input and the nature of the output. If it inputs and outputs in the same language, it can learn about itself.

Given all these characteristics, our learning thing begins to look like figure 3.

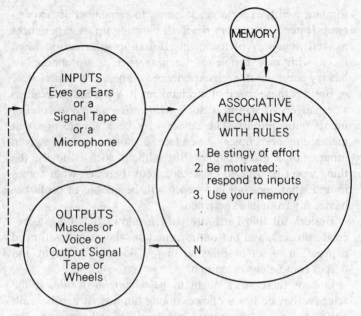

Fig. 3. A learning mechanism

Notice that the thing is full of closed loops, with the arrows completing full circles. It is also a relatively elaborate system; it is not a cellulose sponge. Notice, too, that it looks a little like the design of a control system that one might find in many engineering situations.

Theoretically, then, if we could build a thing like this, it could learn. If any of these characteristics were missing, it could not learn; nor, theoretically, could people. If we knock out all a person's input senses—his sight, hearing, touch, taste, smell—he can't improve his performance over time because he can't find out how he did the first time. If we knock out his memory, he can't learn because each new try is his first try. If we knock out his outputs—his voice and his muscles—he can't try at all. If he has no brain to make choices, he can't improve because he can't change; he can only repeat his behavior. If we knock out the stinginess principle or his needs, he won't improve because he doesn't give a damn—the hard way is as good for him as the easy way, and no behavior at all is as good as anything else. And if he can't see or feel his own hand—that is, if he can't determine the effects of his own outputs—he has no way of deciding how to change his outputs.

If we put all these requirements together, we come out

with an essentially mechanical but nevertheless dynamic view of learning—learning as a process of doing things, finding out and evaluating what has happened, storing the experience, and trying again—using past experience as a jumping-off place. Psychologically speaking, one can say that (1) we act, (2) we perceive the effects of our actions, (3) we reorganize and remember our perceptions, and (4) we act again on the basis of our reorganized perceptions.

Feedback and machines that learn

Engineers have been able to design machine equivalents for each of these requirements for learning in order to build machines that can learn. Using such machines—highspeed computers are the best example—psychologists, mathematicians, and others are able to program them not only to solve problems but to learn to solve similar problems faster after experience. Computers can be programmed to learn to solve problems in symbolic logic or chess or to work out answers to riddles in ways that are surprisingly human. In fact, as of this writing, computers have been programmed to make a variety of rather complex decisions. One program, for example, can simulate an investment officer at a bank so that it will make almost the same selection of stocks that he would make, when the two—man and machine—are given the same data to work with.

Sometimes the computer programs behave very differently from human beings, working in a routine mechanical way and checking out every possible choice no matter how patently foolish it is. But other programs are quite human. Such *heuristic* programs (as distinct from *algorithmic* ones) are designed to behave like people. They are built by observing how people solve problems and then programming the computer to do likewise. And heuristically programmed computers therefore make mistakes much like the mistakes made by people when they are learning new games or solving new problems.

Some of us remember, for instance, the way our geometry textbooks used to trap us back in high school, by giving us a series of similar problems and then springing a new one on us. We would generate a rule about how to solve the first lot, and then try to use the rule on the new problem that looked like the old one. After hitting dead ends half a dozen times, we would finally realize that the rule simply didn't apply to this problem, and we would finally go off in a new, perhaps simpler direction.

Heuristically programmed computers behave in much the same way. They do not behave as machines "normally" do. They do not just try everything whether it looks sensible or not, nor do they forever keep banging their heads against walls. Instead they are specifically programmed to behave in a human way. They use strategies or heuristics of the sort that people use—for example, "If the problem is complex, try to reduce it to a simpler form first" or, "If this problem looks like a problem you can remember that you have already solved, first try the method you used to solve that other problem."

While these machine programs simulate human learning and problem-solving methods they do not at all simulate the human brain. The simulation is not of neurons and synapses; but of information-processing methods.

Several questions about these man-machine comparisons have stirred up considerable emotional heat. It seems clear that by usual definitions of learning, machines really can learn to solve difficult, nonroutine problems. They can do much more than arithmetic. It is not clear that machines are necessarily going to end up smarter or dumber or more important than people, though many observers, including this one, are convinced that many present-day management jobs will ultimately be filled by programmed problem-solving machines—after an intervening period of programmed problem-solving people.

But perhaps the most important issue that needs to be stressed here is not whether or not machines can learn, but the critical importance of the closed loop, of the feedback system in both human and machine learning. *It is only by obtaining accurate information about the effects of our own behavior that we can correct and modify our own behavior.* It is only by knowing what and how we have done that we can learn to do differently.

Feedback—the flow of return information about our own outputs—is important not only in learning to solve intellectual problems; it is also critical in learning to solve social problems. To learn to be skilful in our relationships with other people, we must rely upon the feedback we get from other people about our impact on them. And therein lies the problem we shall be discussing at much further length in later sections of this book. The problem is this: It is relatively easy to get feedback about the effects of our actions on *things.* We can see whether or not the ball has gone down the fairway or off into the rough. And we can then make efforts to correct our stroke on our next drive. We can put a part into a jigsaw puzzle and see whether or not it fits. We can play a note and hear whether or not it is off pitch. But when we say something to someone else, we do not necessarily or automatically get immediate feedback to tell us whether or not he heard what we intended. For now we are working through the perceptual filters of another person. And his outputs in response to our inputs are subject to great distortion.

While we *know* that the golf ball sank into the water hazard, we do not always know whether or not the bright idea we just gave to our boss sank into his brain.

Teaching Machines

It is probably worth pointing out to the reader that teaching machines and other programmed-learning techniques are applications of the feedback principle to human learning. The essence of the teaching machine idea is to provide the student with factual and immediate feedback about the effects of his own performance. The student fills in the blank and immediately learns whether or not he was right. But in much regular nonprogrammed teaching there are long intervals between learning and feedback—between lecture and examination, for example. And in many areas no evaluative feedback is ever forthcoming.

Some complicating factors in human learning and problem-solving

People's decision rules about what is relevant to a problem are usually broader and more diffuse than those programmable into a machine. Our rules reflect the complexity of memories and needs that exist within us at any one moment. As a result, we are likely to learn more from an experience than we intend to learn. The new management trainee not only learns about the company's finances; he also learns that the financial vice-president likes to push people around. He learns not only geometry but the geometry teacher and attitudes toward geometry. He perceives all these as parts of the problem-to-be-solved because his need satisfactions are tied up with all of them. Learning to solve the geometry problem is only one of several potential satisfactions to be gained by the student. Learning to please the teacher is another; learning that geometry is something to stay near, or to escape from, is another.

Certainly one difficult task of a teacher who sets out to

teach geometry (or management, for that matter) is to be sure that it is geometry and not himself that the students see as the major problem-to-be-solved. In fact, one of the major advantages of the movement toward impersonal teaching machines may turn out to lie precisely in this area. By eliminating many activities now done by the human teacher we also eliminate many special and often irrelevant learning problems that the human teacher creates for the student. With the machine almost all the student needs to learn is the subject matter. In the classroom he needs to learn both subject matter and people in an inextricably interrelated way.

Another complexity stems from people's limited storage capacity. We cannot hold many raw bits of information in our memories unless we classify and categorize them. It is as though we had only a limited number of file folders to work with but could label them any way we chose. If we insist on putting just one piece of information in one folder we soon run out of space. But if we can find useful ways of grouping information, the same set of folders can hold an almost limitless quantity of information.

The problem of finding appropriate categories thus becomes a key issue in developing our ability to learn. The manager who insists on separately classifying each bit of information about his operation will soon be overwhelmed by detail, as some managers are. But if he can set up an efficient system of categories, he can handle all he needs to remember.

Unfortunately, categorizing systems, once set up, are difficult to break down. The clerk has difficulty giving up his clerical categories even though he is now in a managerial job. He goes on "thinking like a clerk." As a later chapter on management development will point out, one weakness in up-through-the-ranks and job rotational training is that it demands frequent and difficult recategorization at each step on the ladder. Why, one may ask, teach a man to think like a clerk if we later want him to act like a manager?

A third source of complexity in human learning lies in the fact that mistakes in problem-solving are both costly and valuable. We often (being stingy) want to learn only the "right" way of doing things. But learning only what is right means that all the other possibilities are unknown, uncharted, and unstored; and, hence, they cannot be categorized for dealing with similar but not identical problems in the future.

Suppose, for instance, that you are in a hotel in a strange city. You want to drive to plant X. The hotel clerk gives you directions, and you follow and memorize them. What have you learned?

Suppose, instead, that you just got into your car and started out, stopping to ask for help, noticing landmarks, and finally, after many mistakes, getting to X. Then you try again the next day, and the next, until you end up on the same route the clerk would have given you anyhow. Now what have you learned?

By the first method you learned one efficient path through an otherwise unknown jungle. By the second you learned a lot about the jungle and alternative ways of getting through it. You have a list of alternatives against which to apply your decision rules—but at the cost of time and energy.

Now suppose the clerk's route gets dug up for road repairs one day; so you must detour. The advantage of earlier explorations becomes obvious: you have a mental map to work from. You can "feel" your way through the city; the list of mistakes you have stored up will help you solve this new problem.

Insofar, then, as the world of the manager is a world of new problems, one must worry about balancing what the fledgling manager learns by costly experiment and exploration against the high cost of those explorations. If management were a series of repeatable routines, the choice would be easy. But if every problem in management is a new problem, why teach routines?

Problem-solving as a two-stage process

Learning and problem-solving are inseparable processes. When we solve problems we learn about them. But for convenience let's shift our attention now to the problem-solving part of the learning-problem-solving process.

One of the first issues that arises, is this: Just what, after all, constitutes a "solution" to a problem? What is *the* best solution to the problem of college for the children? Or *the* solution to the problem of allocating our capital budget?

We used to assume, especially in economic theory, that *the* solution existed, and that people would look for it; that people would rationally select the one very best alternative from an array of all possible alternatives laid out before them.

There are two things wrong with this assumption. The first is that we do not usually have anything like a complete array of alternatives laid out before us. The manager does not know all the machines on the market or all possible market-

ing strategies, and *it would cost him a great deal to find out*.
The second thing wrong is the idea that only the best actually
satisfies most people most of the time. In practice, people
often save themselves a great deal of time and effort by
searching only until they find something that works well
enough to meet their own private standards of satisfaction. In
fact (as the chapter on frustration pointed out), it is precisely
when people feel impelled to find the very best method, when
their levels of aspiration are set (usually by others) far above
their abilities, that they are likely to be inefficient problem-
solvers, unable to decide and act because every available
decision and action looks less than satisfactory.

Notice that we have been talking about problem-solving as
a two-stage process. Usually when we think of solving a
problem we are apt to think only in terms of finding the right
answer from among the possibilities. But we have tried to
define problem-solving here in a little broader sense, so that
it includes not only the selection or decision process, but also
the *search* process that must precede it. For it is very seldom
indeed that the world supplies us with free road maps fully
describing all possible routes, all possible choices. Before we
can solve a problem we must search for paths, routes, ideas,
tools. This search involves the expenditure of time and
energy, and often the expenditure of money or other
resources. So part of the problem of deciding which car to
buy is the search problem of deciding which cars to look at
and how much to shop around. In the new car market, at
least in big cities, the search process costs relatively little.
Most of the makes are likely to be lined up in a single street.

But suppose we enter the private used-car market. How
many classified ads shall we respond to? How many newspapers shall we study? How many individually owned cars do
we go out to see before we decide to buy? How far will we go
to see them? Will we ever reach the point where all the potentially satisfactory used cars are simultaneously known to
us, in full detail, so that we can make a choice among them?
This is quite unlikely, because the market is dynamic; while
we are searching for the last car, the first ones have already
been sold. And it is also unlikely because few of us are
willing to pay the price of such a thorough search. Instead we
search until we have some idea of the comparative advantages of different kinds of cars and then on until we find a
satisfactory one. From there on, with any luck at all, our balancing processes go to work to help us support the decision
we have already made. But we all know perfectly well that

there may still have been a better buy that we never found. So the search process and the costs associated with it become a large part of the problem-solving process.

Another large part of the problem-solving process is, of course, the decision itself. Having gathered as much information as we can afford; having arrayed as many alternatives as we are willing to, what then? Then apparently we combine some of our emotional balancing processes with our brains, and either select some standard guaranteed tools for making the choice or we use *heuristics*.

Heuristics are rules of thumb, strategies for making complex decisions. Sometimes our heuristics are not very good. Sometimes they aren't bad. We kick the tire on the used car. We start the engine and look at the exhaust to see if it is burning oil. We try to figure out whether or not the car has been repainted. And on the basis of some of these less than perfect tests (plus our emotional reactions) we make a decision. Some of us have longer check lists than others. Some of us find a mechanic we can trust and bring him along with us to help make the decision.

Man as a "satisficer"

But notice that in most cases, whether selecting a wife or a used car, deciding which of several package designs to adopt, or trying to choose among several applicants for a job, we follow what some authors have recently called a *satisficing* model. We usually indulge in a limited amount of search, until we reach a *satisfactory* rather than an optimal alternative.

This model of man as a satisficing problem-solver—as an individual using both his head and his guts with a limited degree of rationality and with large elements of strategic guesswork—this is quite a different model from others that have existed in the past. Some earlier conceptions of problem-solving laid almost exclusive emphasis on the impulsive and emotional aspects of behavior. That kind of model is still finding lively application in such areas as motivational research in marketing.

But these emotional ideas are not negated by the satisficing model; they are simply placed in a different setting. When one talks about the "cost" of search, one must take into account the *psychological* cost. And the locus of search —the segment of the market in which the buyer searches— may be very much a function of his unconscious (or conscious) need for status and prestige. Some buyers may look only at used Lincolns and Cadillacs; others, only at used sports cars. And their selection of these areas to search is quite likely to be related to their personalities.

The satisficing model is also very different from still a third model that many of us carry around with us. The third is a rational model of problem-solving behavior.

The rational model began as a description of how people *ought* to solve problems rather than how they do solve them. Somewhere along the line this distinction became blurred; researchers and even industrial problem-solvers now sometimes treat the rational model as though it were a description of the way people actually behave in problem situations. The rational model, of course, assumes that people will behave rationally—that is, in terms of our two phases of problem-solving, that they will first perform a complete and rational search and that they will then select the optimal alternative from among the alternatives evoked by the search.

To borrow an apt analogy, the distinction between the rational and the satisficing models is made clear when one thinks of a man looking for a needle in a haystack. The "rational" man searches all through the haystack collecting all the needles he can find there. He then measures the sharpness of each needle and selects that one needle which is the sharpest. The satisficing man searches through the haystack until he finds a needle; then he tries it and if it is sharp enough to sew with he gets on with his sewing; and that's the end of it. If not, he searches some more until he finds one that is satisfactory.

It seems quite clear that most of us do behave more like the second man than the first, whether we ought to or not.

Can some people satisfice better than others?

There is another big issue in the problem-solving process that we have only touched upon, and that is the whole question of the way we *analyze* problems; the way we analyze the search part and the way we analyze alternatives in the decision part. If we are really satisficers, and if we often use heuristic rules for solving problems, then we are rather closely bound by our earlier experiences. Faced with a new problem, we try heuristic rules that we have found to work well on earlier problems that look similar. It is as though most of us carried around a rule saying, "If it worked before, do it again; if it doesn't work, try another." This is a kind of *local* problem-solving process. In the television industry someone tries a program about doctors or cowboys, and if it works, other people pick it up and try it the next year. When the ratings begin to drop off, the producers begin to search for new themes. If we have had pretty good luck using engineering students from a particular college, we are apt to go on recruiting from that school. We keep our ears and eyes open to see whether or not this year's students from that school are doing all right, and only if they aren't do we begin to search in other schools.

But of course it is possible that somewhere in the world there are potential employees who will do this job a good deal better than the ones we are now getting. Or that there are better television themes. But as long as present results are *satisfactory,* our search for new solutions is likely to stay minimal. If there are better solutions, we won't know it until someone else gets them first. Or so it will be *unless we have better analytic tools than the next man*—unless we can use an X-ray on the haystack, or can take finer measurements of sharpness.

Consider this example:

Suppose I have a big box in which I tell you truthfully there are a thousand marbles: 750 black and 250 white ones. I tell you I am going to select 25 marbles, one at a time, and I want you to predict what color the next marble will be.

I am now ready to reach into the box and pull out the first marble. What color do you think it will be? Black or white? Write the answer down before I pull the marble out.

In fact that first marble was *black.*

Now predict the second marble.

In fact the second was *black.*

Now predict the third.

In fact the third was *white.*

Now predict the fourth.

In fact the fourth was *black.*

Now predict the fifth.

In fact the fifth was *black.*

Now predict the sixth.

How did you go about working on this problem?

If you are like most undergraduate students, you begin to develop *local* hypotheses. You notice that there were two blacks followed by a white and then two blacks, so you begin perhaps to generate a hypothesis like this: "There should be more blacks than whites because there are more blacks than whites in the box; and there were two blacks and then a white and then two blacks, so it looks as though there may be a pattern of two blacks and a white. So I will guess that the next one will be white." And you would go on developing new hypotheses as your experience increased. If the next one was in fact white, then you might feel more sure of your theory about two blacks and a white. But if that pattern broke, you would search for a new theory. If five whites came up in a row, you would probably even bet that white was less likely to come up on the sixth, and therefore bet on black.

But a statistician, a trained analyst of these kinds of problems, would not use this approach at all. He would say something like this: Three-quarters of the marbles in the box are black; one-quarter is white. So on any try the probability is 3 out of 4 that a black will come up. I shall, therefore, *always* predict black. And the trained analyst would beat you most of the time, *because he had a better analytic tool than you did*.

The point is that there may be methods in the world for solving problems which are unknown to some of us. And which in fact seem almost contrary to "common sense." Some of us learn some of these tools and apply them quite natural-ly. Some readers, I am sure, were not for a moment trapped by the marbles problem, because they were armed with a tool that they were not likely to have developed for them-selves out of common sense. Someone else developed it, and they were taught it, probably in a classroom in college.

In the history of man, great numbers of tools have been developed and have passed eventually into the realm of common sense. None of us has to figure out any more how to add two and two. Other people have long since worked out rules, and we learned them in the second grade. But in more complex problem areas, where very few tools have existed, new ones are being developed. And especially in manage-ment, the competitive advantage may often lie with that man-ager who is expert with such tools, or who is expert enough to realize that other people are expert with such tools. Man-agers do not always take easily to the notion that other methods better than their own are being developed. They resist the staff analyst's, or the operations researcher's, complex formulations for solving simple problems. But in many cases (not all cases) their own local methods simply do not work as well.

We shall have much more to say about individual styles of thinking in the next chapter, not only in support of analysts, but in support of other types as well.

Active and passive learning and problem-solving

Learning and problem-solving, as we have been looking at them, are *active* rather than *passive* processes. People don't absorb things, they *work* at learning. They search for information, they make decisions, they act upon their decisions, they remember, and they modify their decisions after observing the effects of their actions. People do learn from exposure to experience, but, in this context, experience means doing things to the world as well as letting the world do things to you.

This distinction between active and passive learning is important in management. If we take the passive view, it follows that the trainee should be pumped full of knowledge and experience. So we probably invest heavily in classrooms, lectures, and job-rotation schemes. If we take the active view, we invest in projects, problems, coaching staffs, and the like.

If we take the passive view, we go on to count heavily on the wisdom and experience of superiors—that wisdom and experience to be communicated to the youngsters through advice, written and verbal. We encourage juniors to learn from authoritative seniors. If we take the active view, the wisdom and experience of seniors is relegated to a supportive, behind-the-lines category, available when juniors need it. We encourage juniors to learn first from the problems they are trying to solve, and only secondarily from seniors.

If we take the passive view, we assume that learning should precede action—that we should first learn potentially useful things and *then* try to apply them. If we take the active view, we, in effect, encourage the learner to get himself stymied and then to search for useful ways out.

Moreover, if we generalize a little, the passive view would probably support the sequence of school first and job practice afterward. It would suggest that the business school ought to come before the business job. The active view would support a back-and-forth sequence; one that started with the job, then went *back* to school, and so on—back and forth as, and if, required by the problems encountered on the job.

In defense of schools of business, however, even the most assiduous activist must face up to one dilemma. If we start with active problem-solving, how does the problem-solver know *where* to search for solutions? How can he know what better tools may be available?

One answer might be that the motivated business problem-solver is probably highly accessible to new tools and ideas, because he has competitors and because his level of aspiration doesn't ever quite settle down. But to get to those new tools, he, or their inventors, had better open up channels of communication. This is to say that industry, with its host of opportunities for trying to solve problems, is an ideal active learning ground for management—a better one, in many ways, than any university can hope to be—*if* it can maintain close and solid communication with universities and other tool-developing groups.

Learning and motivation

Active learning occurs, we said earlier, when people are motivated; and people are motivated, we also said earlier, when they are *not* satisfied. So we come up against another curiosity. On the one hand, psychologists, this one included, have been arguing that stability, security, objectivity, and many other fine things emerge when needs are satisfied. But now we discover that effective problem-solving, which is what business is all about, emerges when needs are *not* satisfied. What's the escape from that paradox?

One answer is that there need be no escape. If the purpose of business is to get things done at a profit, and if things get done by discontented people, then let's keep people discontented, whether they are stable and secure or not.

But even if we argue that people's stability and security are not the business of the businessman, objectivity is. We would like problems to be solved "reasonably," "rationally," "sensibly," and unstable people may not be objective ones. So we are still in a box.

Another way out can be derived from the distinction made, in the chapter on frustration, between the words "frustration" and "deprivation," or from the earlier idea of growth motivation and the need hierarchy. People can be dissatisfied, it was pointed out, without being frustrated. They can want to solve problems without being in an emotional uproar, if they feel reasonably confident that they can satisfy their lower-level emotional needs. So the trick (if that's a fair word) would be to let people develop their own dissatisfactions about job problems—about making the sale or designing the package—while staying comfortable about more basic needs, about being competent, appreciated salesmen or package designers. Then they can concentrate their energies on the job to be done and do it with some degree of objectivity.

Note that if we learn actively through motivation, experience itself need have little to do with learning. Repeated experience, without appropriate motivation or feedback may teach us almost nothing. Pulling dollar bills out of our pockets for years has not taught most of us much about dollar bills as such. We have learned a good deal about their use, but whose picture is on them? How many signatures? Whose? How many times does the number 1 appear? Where?

Repetition of an act may help people to perform the act more skilfully, not *because* of the repetition but because the repetition gives a chance to try out different methods long enough to find a good one. So let's not assume that frequent exposure to selling situations has *necessarily* taught the veteran to be a better salesman than the novice. It has only given him the *opportunity* to learn. Whether he took the opportunity, and what he learned—these are quite separate questions.

In summary

People are not perfectly rational, but neither are they incapable of thinking and learning reasonably and consciously. They are endowed with all the equipment they need: input senses, output muscles, memory apparatus, motivation, and a decision or choice mechanism. Only recently have we come even close to equipping machines with like endowments so that they can perform a few intellectual acts as well as competent people can.

On the other hand, people seem to use their endowments with considerable inefficiency. Partly because their equipment is too good, they can and do "learn too much." They learn feelings and attitudes that often interfere with other learning.

People's capacities for learning are in one sense limited; in another, almost unlimited. By devising categories—systems by which they can classify and remember things that are appropriate to the levels of problems they are dealing with—they can store and use huge amounts of information.

If capable people are not lured by the rest of the world into seeking "perfect" solutions for their problems but limit their searches instead to finding satisfactory solutions, they can operate with considerable savings in effort. For to find a *good* product design usually costs far less, in both money and psychic energy, than to find *the best* product design.

But this is not to say that some tools for searching and deciding are not better than others. On the contrary, new analytic tools are being invented every day; and they are likely to be very different from the common sense methods of today—though our children may use them as we now use addition and subtraction.

It is useful to consider thinking and learning as active processes that begin with motivation. All the activities of searching the world and the memory, of making choices, of trying out new behaviors—all get actively underway when people want something.

7

**Thinking and problem-solving II
My style and yours**

We said in earlier chapters that people are all alike and yet people are all different. We were referring then to the emotional sides of people—to their needs, their conflicts, their feelings. But people are alike and different in another important dimension, too—in their thinking styles. We all think, but we think differently. Some kids grow up with a "natural" skill at numbers, for instance, but others are "intuitive" or "good with words." Women, some men like to say, tend to think "illogically." Women prefer to call it "intuition." We may say of one person, "He has a logical, orderly mind. He reasons things out"; and of another, "He's tremendously imaginative. He thinks up ideas that would never occur to me."

Such differences in the ways people think and solve problems are both real and important. To some extent these differences may be inborn, and to some extent they are related to general intelligence. But it is also quite clear by now that the whole process of formal and informal education strongly influences the particular "style" of our later thinking, if not its quality. At the extremes, that effect of education isn't hard to see. The engineer's professional education teaches him not only facts but manners of thought, analytic manners of approaching problems. An arts education teaches thinking manners, too, but probably quite different ones; and those manners are likely to carry over into other parts of life. Moreover, such differences in style may lead to interesting and significant organizational problems. For instance, individuals in an organization who think in one "language" may have trouble communicating with individuals who think in other languages. The sales manager complains that he can't understand those whiz kids in systems analysis. The account exec in the advertising agency handles his creative people with kid gloves, because they think in peculiar ways which the rest of us simple folk cannot comprehend.

In this chapter we shall consider some categories of thinking styles, and then talk about the normative question of whether some styles are "better" than others for solving organizational problems. Finally we shall consider some of the implications of these differences for getting coordinated action in big organizations where many people with many different styles have to solve problems together.

Some different kinds of styles

I ask you to throw six dice. They come up like this:

I now tell you that in the set you have just thrown there are three windblown roses and six petals. You ask, "What the hell is a 'windblown rose'?" I reply, "That's the game. Your job is to tell me what a windblown rose is and what petals are. So now throw your dice again and tell me how many roses and how many petals you come up with this time."

So you throw again and this time the dice fall like this:

Now how many roses are there? How many petals? The right answer this time is that there are two windblown roses and four petals.

Have you caught on yet? Have you developed a rule? Do you know what a windblown rose and a petal are? If you think you do, or if you think you don't, here are three more samples:

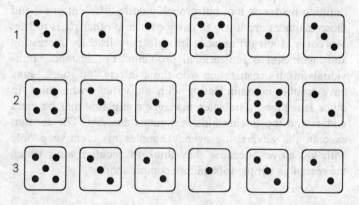

Now have you got it?

Here's the answer, or more properly, here is an answer. The only relevant dice are the odd-numbered ones. Every odd-numbered die has one rose, because the rose is the dot in the middle. The number of petals is the number of dots other than the center one on odd-numbered dice. So the die with the face showing one is a rose with no petals. A three is a rose with two petals; a five is a rose with four petals.

But that's only one way to express the answer or to think about the problem. And indeed it's a very difficult problem to solve if you do think about it that way; that is, if you think about it as a numbers problem. If you don't think of it that way, if you forget about numbers, and if you think about the phrase "windblown rose" and imagine the picture of a rose, the problem is much easier to solve. What does a windblown rose look like? A real windblown rose? It's a rose blown by the wind with just a few petals left on it. Now the face of each die is not a number but a picture, a kind of skeletonized picture. The dot in the center is the center of the rose; the dots around it are petals.

The windblown-roses problem is apt to be solved more quickly by people who think in pictures than by people who think more symbolically. Children do pretty well at it; so do artists; so do women. Accountants and many engineers have a lot of trouble with it.

Let's elaborate on that idea of pictorial (or iconic) thinking versus symbolic thinking.

In recent years developmental psychologists have tried to observe the ways that children go about finding meaning in things. The development of such understanding in children seems to move through three gross stages. Very young children tend to find meaning in things *enactively*. Enactive here means acting upon the thing, touching it, feeling it, handling it. An apple is what it feels like.

Later, around the age of five or so, children begin, by some unclear maturing process, to think in images. They begin to understand things *iconically*. If you ask them now about an apple, they tend to generate an internal mental picture of an apple, an almost one-for-one representation of the real object.

Later still, children go to another stage in their thinking process. Now an apple can be understood *symbolically* by using abstract symbols to think with. It becomes an edible fruit of about such-and-such a size with such-and-such attributes. It is understood with word symbols or perhaps with numbers. Reasonably enough, the rate and extent of symbolic thinking is closely related to education, since most of the symbols we think with are man-made and taught to us by other humans. Thus some children and some societies develop symbolic vocabularies more quickly or over a wider range than others.

This whole developmental idea provides one way of thinking about thinking styles. It may be, for example, that particular kinds of occupations or educations encourage more elaborate and skillful thinking in enactive terms; others in iconic terms; still others in symbolic terms. A mathematician or an accountant couldn't get very far unless he could manipulate abstract symbols pretty darn well. But perhaps a painter or a photographer or (if we allow for sound images) certain musicians might develop high degrees of skill in the iconic realm. And perhaps a ballerina or a good mechanic might develop a large enactive "vocabulary," developing an ability to sense very small differences that the rest of us might miss entirely.

But there seems to be at least one other quite separate dimension to the problem. Not only are some people more skillful than others at manipulating images or tactual sensations or symbols, but some people think much more *analytically* than others, and some think much more *imaginatively* than others. The words *analytic* and *imaginative* are rather difficult to pin down in fine detail; but grossly, the reader can quickly sense their flavor. An analytic thinker is one who can take a complex problem apart, break it down into its logically interconnected pieces, and then put it together again. An imaginative thinker is one who might be quick in generating ideas and multiple solutions to problems or who will move through a problem in a "local," trial-and-error way, taking step one and then seeing where he is, and then trying for step two and seeing where he is, and so on. Contrast him with a more analytic type who lays the whole problem-map out in front of him and then finds the best route. Psychologists have tried to measure analytic ability with logic tests and arithmetic reasoning tests. The sloppier concept of imaginativeness has been tested by giving people problems like this: In the next three minutes think up all the uses you can for a brick.

And again, as the reader might guess, certain occupational groups—engineers, most scientists, accountants—tend to score higher on analytic than on imaginative tests, while art students and salesmen tend to score higher on imaginative tests. In fact, in one study which compared freshman engineering students with senior engineering students and freshman fine arts students with senior fine arts students, the following results emerged: The senior engineers were much more analytic than their freshman counterparts, but significantly less skillful on imaginative tests. The seniors in fine arts on the other hand, got higher scores on imaginative tests, while they fared worse than their freshman counterparts on analytic tests. The four years of professional education had succeeded, it seemed, in spreading the two groups apart, increasing the engineer's analytic skill, apparently at the expense of his imaginative powers, and increasing the fine arts student's imaginative powers at the expense of his analytic skill.

That finding might be important. If one unexpected outcome of professional education in those two fields is to spread the thinking styles of the two groups apart, another effect may be increased difficulty of communication between the two professions.

Which style is best?

We come now to the normative issue: Is imaginative thinking "better" or "worse" than analytic thinking? Is symbolic thinking "better" or "worse" than iconic or enactive thinking?

Clearly the thrust of most education in the Western world has been toward developing symbolic and analytic skills. We have put much less effort, in our formal educational processes, into developing imaginativeness or iconic skill. What, for example, is your model of a good thinker? Isn't it the scientist, skillful with symbolic tools, analytic in process? Or the philosopher? And don't we tend to pooh-pooh those people who are "irrationally" intuitive? Or to believe that it is a little simpleminded and childish for people to think in pictures?

And clearly, too, the progress of man, as we usually define it, has been very heavily dependent on his skillful use of symbolic languages and analytic methods. For it is by those means that knowledge has been passed along and institutionalized, and the complex made simple. If, for example, we said to a senior scientist, "Here's an interesting finding: science and engineering students after four years of education score better on analytic tests than freshmen do," he might well reply that the finding didn't seem interesting at all. For what, after all, was scientific education all about if not to teach the analytic methodology of science? If, on the other hand, we said to him, "But after four years of education, science and engineering students seem to be less capable of solving intuitive-imaginative problems than were freshmen," that might upset him. For most scientists and engineers this author knows are not anti-imagination, they are just pro-analysis. They are pro-analysis for two reasons: first, it has worked; second, the buildup of functional analysis is the foundation from which the next generation of the profession will advance to new knowledge. We need transferable languages and transferable analytic procedures.

If we turn to the artist, on the other hand, we may find that he thinks quite differently about all this. He may be much less interested in transferability or uniformity, and much more interested in uniqueness. The education of the artist reflects that difference. Certainly one key variable in his education is his *individuality,* with the hoped-for consequence that every work he produces will be a unique reflection of himself. Can you imagine an engineer whose training aims for uniqueness, whose professor criticizes the way he has solved a problem because, "That isn't *you*! That isn't unique!"? But such criticism is common for the artist.

Another aspect of the normative problem: The analytic-symbolic approach to the world not only places a positive value on "objective" thinking, but in some ways it places a negative value on "emotional" thinking. Some observers have argued that an important effect of this imbalance in favor of symbolic-analytic thinking is an impoverished emotional development in our society. We have not educated our people to attend to, to understand, and to express feelings and other perceptions which are not easily symbolized or analyzed. By this argument educational emphasis on the symbolic-analytic has yielded a significant unforeseen cost to the humanness of human beings, although some of the deficit is being made up by the recent wave of interest in sensitivity training and encounter groups.

One more normative issue: Just from the point of view of the quality of problem-solving itself, is it true that the symbolic-analytic kind of approach is better? In many realms it clearly is. The application of symbolic-analytic style has led to the solution of many complex problems that people unequipped with those tools have simply been unable either to discover or to solve.

But curiously enough, people less competent in analytic-symbolic realms, but more competent in imaginative-iconic styles, sometimes discover solutions which the analysts miss, because the analysts may limit their search to those segments of the world predefined by their languages. We refer our reader back to the windblown roses game, but we can find many other examples of "better" solutions by nonanalysts, even when "better" is defined by analytic criteria. One can legitimately ask whether a world of highly analytic but not very imaginative thinkers will necessarily turn out better, by any standards, than one peopled by more imaginative but less analytic types.

How can people talk to one another if they think differently?

We need, don't we, both analysis and imagination. We need symbols; we need pictures; and we need to feel. We need many kinds of people with many kinds of education and training and many kinds of thinking propensities. But beyond that, we need some way to bring them together into that beautiful blend that will yield the best of all possible worlds.

But that bringing together is rather difficult. As the languages and thought-modes of specialists move further and further apart, the problem of reuniting the specialists becomes harder. Thus the arts and engineering students we talked about earlier move away from, rather than toward, one another over the four years of college. Male freshman engineers might date fine arts freshman girls, but by their senior years the engineers are living in one world and the art students in another. Their differences show in their dress, in where they choose to live, in their haircuts.

One British author has pointed to a variant on this problem on a much larger scale. He has argued that the entire cultures of science and the humanities have grown quite apart in western societies. Scientists deal with critical problems in ways that are simply not comprehended by less scientific types, and yet it is the less scientific politicians who govern the world that scientists are so rapidly and independently changing.

Certainly within the organization the dangers are real, though on a smaller scale. The notoriously frequent failures of technical people to implement their analytic solutions are a case in point. So too is all the laughing talk by general managers about "longhaired" computer nuts and "weird" operations researchers and "unrealistic" systems analysts. In our view, integrating the many thought-styles of many occupational specialties into some kind of organizational whole is becoming a major problem in modern, differentiated organizations.

Although we can offer no easy solutions, we do know some things that *don't* work. It is not enough, for instance, to "bring people together." The engineers and art students we talked about earlier occupy buildings that are within fifty yards of one another, but the two groups have nevertheless moved apart. A better solution may be to develop a new breed of interpreters, generalists with feet in all camps, who can translate one thought-language into another. In some ways the modern M.B.A. has tended to perform that function. Another suggestion (offered, of course, by an analytic type) is to devise computer programs which will serve as interpreters, converting symbolic data into iconic form or vice versa.

The present fact of the matter, however, is that we don't know very much about how to *un*educate people who have been so educated into one style that they cannot think in others. Perhaps we shall have to learn a good deal more about uneducation in the next decade or two. Meanwhile, encouraging people to speak to one another in mutually foreign languages will not in itself breed understanding.

In summary

People differ in their languages and process of thought just as they differ in other aspects of personality. Education, particularly professional and vocational education, tends to emphasize particular thought-languages, symbolic languages, iconic (pictorial) languages, and enactive (touch and feel) languages. One can conceive of processes differing, too, along a scale from analytic to imaginative.

It is not perfectly obvious that any particular combination of these languages or processes is "better" than another. But it is obvious that people trained in and connected to one style may find it difficult to communicate with those committed to another. Hence we might expect greater emphasis within organizations, as they build in more and more specialists, on bridging this communication gap by introducing "thought interpreters" or other means of increasing understanding.

Attitudes and values
Motherhood, Old Glory, and off the pigs

People not only develop needs and styles of problem-solving, they also develop beliefs and opinions and attitudes and values. Those people believe in God; and these are atheists. Those over there think women's place is in the kitchen, and these are parading for women's lib. Those others believe that if you work hard, you'll get ahead; but these think work is a form of slavery set up by the establishment, and who wants to get ahead in a materialistic society anyway?

This collection of "stuff " in people properly belongs neither in the realm of emotionality nor in the realm of cognitive problem-solving. This realm of beliefs and values seems rather to constitute some mixture of the reasoning and the nonreasoning parts of people.

Moreover, the mixture appears to be changing in some very important ways. People don't seem really to believe what they used to believe. Their thinking processes haven't changed much, nor have their emotional processes; but surely values, beliefs, and opinions are changing fast. Viewing from one side, one can argue that Americans seem to be losing their pride and interest in work, and that they seem to be losing their traditional standards about sex and morality. Viewing from another side, one might say that people are becoming freer and less hypocritical, and that they are fulfilling themselves!

The purpose of this chapter is to consider attitudes and values from a psychological perspective. We shall put forward several questions: Conceptually, what are attitudes and values? Where do they come from? How do they change? What do changing attitudes and values mean for the processes of management?

What are attitudes and values?

Junior has just come home from college on his Christmas vacation. He and papa are chatting after dinner.

"What did you take this quarter, son?"

79

"Well, let's see. I took a course in Chinese art and a seminar on religions of the East. Then I had a course on the history of revolutions. Oh, and then I had a great course in ancient Welsh mythology."

Pause.

Papa says, "Well, that's nice, son. Did you take any math?"

"Oh, Dad, you know I'm not interested in math."

"Did you take any science?"

"No, Dad, science is for the birds. I'll have to take one science course to graduate, but I think I can get credit for that astrology course I took last year."

Pause.

"Tell me, son, what do you plan to do when you graduate?"

"Well, Dad, I thought the first year after I'm out I might kick around Europe. There's this girl I've gotten friendly with. And she and I decided that we might bum around together for a year or so."

Longer pause.

"And what will you do after that?"

"Well, I'm not sure, Dad, but I've always been interested in leatherworking. I think I might make belts. Or sandals."

Another long pause, then papa says, "I think you ought to get more math and science and things like that into your program."

"Why?"

"Because those are the things that will be useful to you, that will help you get ahead in the long run."

"But I don't want to get ahead in the long run."

"You'll change your mind about that, son. Wait 'til you have a wife and kids to feed."

"I'm not sure I ever want a wife, and as for kids, there are too many of them in the world already. Why, Dad, do you know how many people there will be in the world by 2000?"

With some emotion: "Oh, you can spout crap like that now, son, but you'll change your mind. You know, I'm not always going to support you."

"So if you don't support me, I'll support myself, Dad. That's not a problem; it's trivial. You have this funny, old-fashioned idea that somehow I'm supposed to go to college and then go to work and get married and live in the suburbs and retire at age sixty-five and go and live in Florida until I die. That's not my picture of life at all."

And so on.

Papa is trying hard to keep his blood pressure down, to understand, to maintain communication. This kid doesn't seem to want to go to work the way papa did. He doesn't see college as vocational preparation. He doesn't value math and science as instrumentalities to success; indeed, he doesn't seem to value success itself. He doesn't seem to worry about traveling around Europe with a girl to whom he isn't married. And he doesn't seem to be very much concerned with planning ahead. His attitudes and papa's are different. His values and papa's are different. If junior ever does take a "normal" job (which, incidentally, he probably will), he will probably take it not as an instrumentality to papa's kind of success, but as a means of getting enough bread so that he can go skin diving. Or so that he can take another trip to Europe.

Attitudes and values, viewed this way, are orientations toward things in the world. Generally, values are considered to be more basic, more fundamental. Attitudes are a little more direct: propensities to look at more or less specific things in particular ways. What's your attitude toward the Catholic church? Toward big business? An attitude is a readiness to respond, an overall framework within which to cast particular beliefs or opinions. Attitudes are usually pretty conscious. People can express them, although in many cases they may choose not to. We tend to call the same kind of things values when they are a little broader, a little more deep-seated, and include more unconscious elements. We usually treat as values people's deeper orientations toward issues like getting ahead, or justice, or virginity, or family.

Two quite contradictory points about people's attitudes and values are particularly worth noting.

On the one hand, there is a kind of patterning of attitudes and values, so that if we know some of a person's attitudes or values, we can make better than chance guesses about many others. If we know an American's attitude toward communism, we might make some pretty good guesses about his attitudes toward women's liberation, religion, management, and so on. There is a certain amount of consistency in people's patterns of attitudes and values.

On the other hand, and contrariwise, patterns of beliefs and attitudes often seem highly illogical. Junior tries to pin dad by saying, "If you say you're against war, how can you be for winning a victory in Vietnam?" Papa retorts, "If you're a conscientious objector, how can you justify violence on the campus?" Junior adds, "You're against pot, but you smoke and drink." Papa retorts, "You're all for punishing the car manufacturers for ecological problems, but you want a fast sports car!" So we need to worry about a paradox: consistent patterns of attitudes and values along with inconsistencies.

Changing attitudes:
Again the great cognitive balancing act

Back in the chapter on conflict, we talked about cognitive balance. Much of this paradox can be dealt with by calling once more upon this concept.

The balance idea is simply that human beings try to maintain *internal* consistency and balance among their attitudes, values, and decisions. Hence, any of us is apt to stay stubbornly with a position long after it is seen by others as either rationally wrong or inconsistent with other positions we have held.

If we return to papa and junior, perhaps we can account for their apparently irrational inconsistencies in attitudes and values in the same way. Junior, for example, thinking of himself as a pacifist, even registers as a conscientious objector. Some of his other attitudes and values certainly appear consistent with pacifism. He doesn't believe in hunting; he begins to think football is too violent. But then he gets picked up one night for helping to smash windows in the applied physics lab. If we now confront him with the inconsistency between his violent acts and his nonviolent ideology, will he acknowledge the conflict? Not likely. The window smashing is a road toward peace, he may argue, because by stopping war research he is stopping violence, and so on.

Maybe it is because we often sense just this propensity in ourselves and our organizations that we seek help from uncommitted outsiders. Because they are uncommitted, they can examine some areas about which our involvement has created psychological blind spots. On the other hand, though outsiders may be more objective in their judgments, they may have a tough time communicating these judgments to us. For if the effect of truth, as outside judges report it, is to aggravate the imbalance, we will have a strong inclination to reject it. The consultant who tells us that our decision was wrong is just another dissonant force with which we need to cope. And one easy way to cope is to find reasons for believing that we hired the wrong consultant, unless, of course, this is a very expensive consultant—in which case firing him may create more dissonance than sticking with him.

This balancing mechanism thus provides the individual

with a way, sometimes tortuous and unsuccessful, of trying to pull things together psychologically so that he can feel emotionally comfortable; in effect, he tries to do it by modifying the psycho-logic of his position, and then bending the logic to it. It is, after all, the whole man who makes choices, not just the reasoning part of him. So if we want to predict or to change patterns of attitudes and beliefs, we must use our knowledge of the whole man. If we try to predict only by considering logical, rational connections among attitudes, our predictions may be rather poor.

My father, for example, was both an active atheist and an active Republican—and a right-wing Republican, at that. I, and others, used to chide him about the logical inconsistency of being both. Good Republicans, we argued, were God-fearing men. It was the left-wingers who were atheists. But the discrepancy didn't bother him at all. He could argue for hours about how the two positions were perfectly consistent with one another. No one, I am convinced, could have argued him out of his position on *logical* grounds.

The psychological consistency of his pattern emerged because he was an immigrant to the United States. He wanted very much to make it on the American scene—to be a real American. That meant giving up the traditional, old-country ways and really joining up with America. So he went into business and became, naturally enough, a republican businessman. But if he had also remained an orthodox, old-country Jew, how could he have become a real American? Hence, atheism. I don't think the same problem would have arisen if he had been a Scottish Presbyterian. That could have been consistent with business and Republicanism. But traditional European Judaism seemed to him old-fashioned, unprogressive, and irrelevant to this new world of his. For the whole man, his pattern made sense. Viewed by external logic, it was an inconsistent set of positions. But he had no trouble walking the tightrope.

Values

We've used the word *values* as well as the word *attitudes*. Values are the more primitive, basic, all-encompassing of these two concepts. A useful way to think about values is to consider them as a pervasive, underlying set of attitudes, not always conscious. A pervasive belief in individual initiative is a value. So is a belief in the inviolacy of the family. So is a deep faith in science.

Such values may remain only quasi-conscious until something comes along to spotlight them. Since, in a given community, many values are widely shared, we may not even realize we hold them until we enter another community. While I was working with a group in France about ten years ago, one of my unconscious values was made obvious and apparent. The group had been arguing for a long time, and I had been taking an increasingly strong position in favor of getting everybody together into a cooperative team to solve some problems. One of the Frenchmen turned on me at this point. "Ever since you've been here," he said, "you've been making a pitch about all of us cooperating to solve problems. What makes you so sure that cooperation is such a wonderful thing?" I was stunned by this reaction, because the questioner had pointed out something I hadn't consciously realized: my strong, underlying value about cooperation as a basic way of approaching social problems. I had never questioned, indeed never even thought about it. How many Americans have?

Not only are values apt to be semiconscious, they tend also to take shape early in life and to last long. Not that they can't be changed, but the process is slow. Peer groups, for example, can be extremely influential in modifying one's values. Thus one study shows that, as undergraduates, college girls tend gradually to take on the values of the college group. But that part is no surprise. Most of us know that we take on much of the coloration of our local peer-group culture, especially if we are exposed to it intensively in a cultural island like a girls' college. But the values thus picked up by girls tend still to be there fifteen or twenty years later when they have become suburban, executives' wives. If they had become political liberals during those college years, they were still showing strong liberal leanings twenty years out. Which means, of course, that if we expect those radical college kids to "come to their senses" as soon as they have to earn a living in the real, harsh world, we're probably wrong. There may be modifications, but turnabout is unlikely. Besides, don't we also try to match our jobs and careers to our values? So won't emancipated kids look for career patterns that will support their emancipated life style?

More on changing attitudes and values

Most of what we shall have to say about changing attitudes and values will be said in the next section of this book, when we discuss influence and persuasion. But one or two ideas are more appropriate here.

Consider the relationships between people's attitudes and their behavior. Note that changed attitudes are not always reflected in changed behavior. We may change (or have changed for us) our attitude toward cigarettes, but we may also go on smoking. However, there is a gross connection, isn't there? We tend to bring our behavior into line with our attitudes over the long pull. That's what advertising is for. To a considerable extent, that's what education is for.

So one way to change behavior is to change attitudes. And the ways we try to change attitudes are legion: peer-group pressures, propaganda, simple reward for expressing the attitudes we want—and introducing dissonance may help, forcing the person to reassess his existing attitudes. If a man who is strongly anti-Semitic falls in love, for example, and then discovers his girl is Jewish, he may begin to reassess his attitudes—or his girl.

But it is also true that one can change the attitude by changing behavior *first*. Not only does behavior gradually line up with attitudes, attitudes line up with behavior!

For example, if I can get you to debate in favor of X, even though you don't like X, you will probably hold a more positive attitude toward X after the debate than before. If I can get you to sing my commercials, you will probably feel more favorable toward the product. If I can get you to throw a rock at the draft-board window, your attitudes toward the draft will become more negative. If I can get you, the union steward, to argue with your men in the company's behalf, you will feel more positive toward the company.

Values develop or change more slowly than attitudes, but the principle holds for them, too.

In summary

People not only develop thinking styles and patterns of needs, they also hold patterns of attitudes and values. Attitudes and values have strong cognitive components and are usually publicly supported by elaborate rationales. But there are strong emotional factors supporting them, too, so it is not easy to change them by argument or rational debate.

If one wants to change attitudes or values, it is useful to think of the human being as a "cognitive balancer," who tries to keep his attitudes and values grossly consistent with one another. Hence, we find more or less clear attitude and value patterns in most people. If we know some attitudes, we can usually guess others. But that isn't a perfectly safe bet, because most of us also can do balancing tricks that allow us to feel comfortable with patterns that look inconsistent to outsiders.

The important thing is that people try to reduce internal dissonance, to get things into internal balance. If we look at the internal behavior process, rather than the rational facts, we can often better understand and predict attitudes and, moreover, change them much more effectively than by logical argument.

While we can often change behavior by first changing attitudes, the reverse is also true: to change a man's attitudes, change his relevant behavior.

9

The assessment of people
One application of personality theory

Two equally appropriate subtitles might have been attached to this chapter. One could have been: "How not to be snowed by test salesmen." The other might have been: "How not to be snowed by anti-test salesmen." For management people are under attack from two fronts: from those who offer tests as a solution to selection problems and from those who attack tests as unethical, unscientific, and anti-individualistic.

This last chapter in part 1, then, is devoted to a practical problem: the problem of assessment. Its function is to show how the material in the preceding chapters can be applied to a large and real area of managerial decision-making.

The scope of the assessment problem

People in industry continually need to forecast the behavior not only of the economy, of competition, of prices, but also of one another. "Assessment," "selection," and "evaluation" are all varieties of people-forecasting.

Both professionals and laymen have frequently failed miserably in forecasting how people will behave in specified jobs. One reason is the difficulty of the job. If our earlier chapters were right, what has to be predicted is the result of a complex maze of hard-to-specify interrelated forces. Forecasting the behavior of one individual is much like trying to predict exactly what pattern of cracks will result when a particular thrower throws a particular ball against a particular pane of glass. We can be fairly certain that the glass will crack. But we seldom know enough about the ball, the air currents, the thrower, and the particular pane to be sure about the directions and lengths of the cracks that will result.

Nevertheless, we cannot escape in industry from the problem of having to assess people for tasks. Every job assignment that a manager makes includes the requirement that he assess the people available against the job he has in mind.

Every contact with a customer, with a new member of his own organization, with every individual who is relevant to the manager's work, includes some need for assessment—some evaluation of how this person will behave when faced with this kind of suggestion, or that kind of job, or this other kind of person.

So assessment is not limited to "formal" problems like selecting new employees or rating the qualifications of old ones, nor is it limited to the assessment of personality. It must necessarily involve assessment of knowledge, experience, education, and many other aspects of the person.

For the formal phases, like personnel selection and merit rating, a good deal of research and experience is available. Every executive in industry these days is aware of personality tests, patterned interviews, personnel-rating forms, and the like. Underlying each of these is a large (but not large enough) body of theory and empirical research. Unfortunately no comparable amount of work has been done on the day-to-day problems of assessment to help the business executive make increasingly accurate spot judgments about other people. Even so, some useful things are coming to be known. So, when the boss asks, "well, what did you think of him?" the executive can honestly say something more than, "He's a nice guy" or "I don't like him."

Formal methods of selection and evaluation

One can single out at least three more or less separate formal approaches to the selection and evaluation of personnel for industry. Looked at right now, the separations among the three are indistinct, for they have been growing together. But historically, each has made its way over a different route.

Pencil-and-paper tests and the empirical method. The first approach, one largely American in origin, can be roughly labeled the "pencil-and-paper-test approach." The great bulk of short intelligence tests, aptitude tests, etc., belong under this heading. So too, for the most part, do standard interview forms, most merit-rating scales, fitness reports, and the like. Until recently, they were mostly tests of specific skill or abilities, like numerical ability, finger dexterity, and so on.

These are typically American products in the sense that they derive from American behaviorism, with its emphasis on quantification and measurement and on empirical data gathering and with its corresponding de-emphasis on unquantified, introspective, judgmental data. As a consequence, the pencil-and-paper approach has been characterized by efforts to improve the empirical reliability and validity of the procedures more than by efforts to improve the rationale or depth of the material being sought. It is considerably harder to apply to overall personality than to specific aptitudes or abilities.

The pencil-and-paper position is this: The task of selecting people for jobs is a task of predicting in advance how people will behave. Clearly, then, what is required are some measurable advance predictions and some corresponding measurements, taken at some later time, of how people actually performed. If the task is to select salesmen, these are the appropriate procedural steps:

1. We gather—in a standard way—information about people who come to look for jobs as salesmen. We can do this by setting up standard questions about, for example, education, asking them of job applicants, and coding the answers into several categories. We can do the same with questions about home ownership and applicants' preferences for one kind of occupation or another, and we can measure the time required by applicants to solve certain arithmetic problems, and so on.

2. Ideally, we next lock up the test answers in the nearest safe and allow *all* the applicants to go to work as salesmen.

3. Now we wait a predetermined time, perhaps a year.

4. During that year, or before it, we set up some standards about what constitutes success in selling. What is needed is an unequivocal, quantifiable criterion of success. In selling, a theoretically ideal approach would be to permit all test subjects to work in the same territory or exactly comparable ones, with precisely the same amount of training and precisely the same selling tools. One might then use dollar sales at the end of the year, or number of sales, or percentage of returns, or some combination of them all as the criterion of successful behavior.

5. The tester now has available (*a*) the scores of test-subject Jones on the tests he took a year ago, showing his rank on the test in relation to the other applicants, and (*b*) a measure of his subsequent actual job performance in relation to the other applicants. The next move is statistical: to measure the relationship between predictions and performance, to estimate the reliability of this relationship (i.e., to guess how frequently we could expect the relationship to be about like this in the future), and then to decide if any of the tests are worth keeping.

We may discover that a test of intelligence actually predicted sales performance somewhat better than chance. The tester would then consider his intelligence test useful for selection. And, logically, it would not matter what direction the test-performance relationship might take. That is, it would not matter if more successful salesmen were significantly more intelligent, or significantly less intelligent, than the less successful ones. For the method is rigorous here. The problem is not whether the predictions make sense, but whether they predict. If they predict, they are useful; if they do not predict, they are not useful.

The only connection between this kind of rigorous pencil-and-paper approach and any theory of personality lies in the manner in which particular tests are selected and constructed. For the pencil-and-paper approach is itself a method of measurement rather than a theory of man's behavior. Any theorist of any persuasion may use it. Some test items may be based on a theory of physiognomy, some on Freudian psychodynamics, some on the color of a man's shoes. In actual practice, the current pencil-and-paper personality tests used in business derive largely from a semibehavioristic theory of personality. They have been, until recently, notable for their failure to include "deep" areas of personality.

This pencil-and-paper method has a great many advantages and some practical disadvantages. It has the huge advantage of quantification and empiricism. It also has dollar advantages. Pencil-and-paper tests, once standardized, are easy to manufacture, administer, and score. Professional testers are often needed only in the developmental stages because administration can usually be turned over to trained, but not professional, technicians. Such devices are not very time consuming, so that large numbers of people can be tested, frequently in groups of indefinite size, at reasonable costs.

Perhaps the greatest disadvantage of such procedures is that they are designed for statistical, rather than individual, prediction. That is, they are most useful in making predictions about the behavior of large numbers of people rather than about particular individuals. Thus, a pencil-and-paper tester may be able truthfully to tell management that, if his tests are adopted, "Of every fifty applicants whom my tests pass, you can expect an adequate job performance from forty. Under your present selection methods, you can expect adequate job performance from only twenty-five." The tester could not go on, however, to say whether or not Joe Doaks, subject number 23, who received adequate test scores, would be among the successful forty or the unsuccessful ten. Further, the tester would also have to admit that some rejected applicants would be "false positives"—people who would have been successful but whom the tests nevertheless rejected. He could not predict who those individuals would be.

This tendency of pencil-and-paper methods to predict en masse rather than individually raises two questions. The first is an ethical question and perhaps a specious one. Is it "right" to turn any job applicant away, even if he is only one in a hundred, who would have been perfectly competent if he had been hired? Is it "fair" to the applicant to so depersonalize him that he becomes simply a score among hundreds of scores, his fate inexorably tied to a numerical system? Perhaps these are valid questions, and perhaps it is somehow more fair to tie an applicant's fate to the rose-colored perceptions of a nonquantitative interviewer. It would seem, however, that the ethical issue properly attaches to the whole selection problem itself, not to the issue of selection by tests.

The second question that can be asked is about the utility of pencil-and-paper devices at higher organizational levels, where the number of applicants for particular positions may be small. The usual statistical indexes of validity do not apply to very small samples. So if the task is to select assistant general managers rather than typists, the utility of the method is sharply reduced. It is even more sharply reduced when the task is to decide which of two applicants ought to be selected for a particular key post in, let us say, the research and development division of an electronics corporation. At this level so much depends on the correctness of a specific prediction, and similar testing experience is usually so rare, that the pencil-and-paper method becomes inapplicable.

Projective tests and the clinical method. A second approach to formal selection lays much more emphasis on the dynamics of personality, much less on empirical validity. The approach may be labeled, somewhat unfairly, the projective approach. Projectives are much more "head doctor" techniques than pencil and paper tests. They are European in origin, springing theoretically from Freud and technically from the Swiss psychiatrist Rorschach. They build on the internal, perceptual frame of reference talked about in chapter 3, assuming that one can get a valid picture of a person quickly by assessing the way he projects his personality onto some standard, ambiguous parts of the world. All projectives contain these elements of standardization and ambiguity. The "questions" on the Rorschach test are some standardized ink blots that the subject is asked to describe. The tester then interprets the number, quality, and variety of the subject's responses against the tester's theory of personality and against his and others' experience with the responses of other people to the same blots.

Similarly, in the Thematic Apperception Test, the subject is asked to tell stories about a standard series of pictures. The tester records the stories and the subject's behavior. He then interprets the subject's personality in the light of the themes used in his stories.

The end result of a battery of projective tests, then, is not a numerical score comparing subject X with other subjects. It is a verbal report assessing the subject's dominant needs and ambitions, his tolerance of frustrations, his attitudes toward authority, the major conflicts that seem to be operating in his personality, and so on. Given such a report, a manager clearly must decide for himself whether the tester's judgment deserves heavy weighting in the final decision.

One important industrial advantage of projectives is also their scientific weakness. They are essentially individualistic, and they cannot be easily "proved" right or wrong, even by their proponents. Projectives, therefore, push decision-making back to where it belongs anyway, into the hands of management. The projective tester says to the manager, in effect, "Here is my expert judgment of John Jones. You have your judgment of him to which you can now add mine. I have tried to add information to your fund of relevant information, but I cannot guarantee that my judgment will be right. You make the decision."

When one considers the history of projective tests, it is reasonable that they should be used in this way. Projectives have their origin in clinical psychology, in the atmosphere of psychiatry and pathology, rather than in education or industry. It is only in the last few years that these tests have even appeared on the industrial scene. In the clinic and the hospital, their primary function has been to help the physician seeking to diagnose the meaning of the psychological pains of a new patient. Perhaps, if the physician had known his new patient intimately for five or ten years, he would have no need for the projective tester. But the patient is an individual, and it is his individuality that accounts for his illness; so the physician needs a highly individualized, relatively detailed and speedy picture of this personality. This is what the projective tester tries to give him.

Unlike the pencil-and-paper tests, projectives seldom get to the stage at which they can be scored by technicians, because the interpretation always remains individual. The judgment of the tester is a large factor. When management buys pencil-and-paper tests, it buys a quantitative tool from which most subjective elements of interpretation have been eliminated. Any honest technician counting up the yeses and noes on an interest inventory will come up with the same score as any other honest technician. Not so with honest projective testers. The professional judgment of the test administrator plays a far more important part than the projective tests themselves in determining what comes out. In effect, then, when management buys projective tests, it buys the tester, just as when one buys a chest X ray, one buys the judgment and experience of the interpreting physician rather than the plate itself.

Projectives are expensive. Although efforts are being made to standardize and simplify them for mass administration, they remain largely one-at-a-time tests. A professional tester may spend eight hours or more testing and interpreting a single subject. Consequently, projectives have entered industry at the level at which they are most likely to be both useful and worth the money—at the executive level where pencil-and-paper tests are relatively useless.

Management's only bases for determining whether projectives are worth the investment are, first, its own opinion of the tester it has hired, and, second, *its experience over time in relating the actual behavior of applicants with the predictions that testers have made.*

In the face of these difficulties, one wonders how projectives have made their way into supposedly hardheaded business circles at all. One reason may be that projective reports seem to catch the subtle realities of executive behavior better than most pencil-and-paper tests. The reports are complicated and qualified, full of ifs and buts, somewhat like managerial life itself.

Here is a typical excerpt taken from a test report on an applicant for an executive position:

> Mr. X is of superior intelligence. Problem situations, even those for which he is momentarily unprepared, do not throw him. He usually does not become emotionally involved when he has to work on a problem but adheres

to, as he says, a strict formula which forces him into an intellectual and rational approach. . . . The problem is uppermost and feelings are disregarded. More specifically the feelings of others are disregarded, for when his own personal satisfaction is involved then his approach to problems is somewhat less systematic. For example, he wants others to think that he is a very capable individual and tries hard to maintain this impression because of the satisfaction that this gives him. However, because of this attitude he is apt to become too self-confident, or "cocky," and thus makes errors in very simple situations or problems that he usually would not make under such circumstances. The amount of effort he puts forth on a problem varies with how difficult he thinks the problem is. The more complicated the problem the more interested he becomes—and in turn more systematic, planful and analytical in his approach. In a sense, he feels that he is "on the spot" under the circumstances described above, and he puts forth all his energy to demonstrate to others his capabilities through the solution of the problem. . . .

Mr. X is an overly-controlled individual in the sense that feelings play a minor role in the execution of a job. The job is paramount in his mind and he believes that he and others should subjugate themselves to it. Consequently, he is highly critical of the performance of others who work for him—but he demands as much of them as he demands of himself. Furthermore, because the job is so important to him, he does not take sufficient time out to realize the nature of the personalities working with him. He does not accomplish a job by the "human approach" but by insisting that there is a job to be done and all must do it regardless of their personal needs. The only personal needs he does become aware of are his own. *He* feels the sense of accomplishment and *he* feels that *he* has done well. In this sense he is an egocentric individual. He realizes this attitude full well. It should be pointed out that if he could realize that other people may have the same needs as he and that they, too, may want the satisfactions that he wants and that by giving them these satisfactions they will in no way threaten his position, then he may become more effective on the job than he is now. . . .

Being a competitive individual with a high level of aspiration, Mr. X may be a member of a group with whom he is associated but he will not feel as part of them sharing with them all that he knows, etc. To some extent he feels superior to those with whom he is associated; he feels that he could direct and lead them. But he does not win their confidence since he is too forward in this regard and they may resent his attempts to be in the limelight. When working with his subordinates, his status is well-defined; but with colleagues, when he has to win the status he desires, he is somewhat uncomfortable. This lack of comfort makes him put forth even more effort to demonstrate his brilliance and ability which in turn is definitely resented by the group. He is apt to be impatient with those with whom he is working because they do not see things as quickly as he. Although he tries to control himself under such circumstances, his impatience is obvious. Others would work more effectively with him and he would become more successful if he could pay more attention to and accept more of what others have to say.

Managers sometimes react against these qualifications, wishing for more "practical," black-and-white[1] decisions. Realistically, though, selecting an executive is not a black-and-white problem. It is not usually true that people simply succeed or fail. They succeed or fail "if," or they would have succeeded or failed "but." They might have succeeded if they had worked for another kind of superior, or if management had given them a little looser or a little tighter rein, or if they had been provided with a high-powered assistant, or if the job description had been rewritten so that the new man was given more responsibility in area A and less in area B. For success on a job, especially a decision-making managerial job, is not a function of personality alone but of a personality in an environment. Any testing procedure that tends to describe the complications of a personality, rather than to contract and simplify it, provides extra data for relating the person to the environment. If the person is relatively unmodifiable, perhaps the environment is not.

If a projective tester, therefore, can start management worrying about whether to put a new employee to work for sys-

1. Here is an example of how our perceptions are influenced by our times. When I first wrote this, "black-and-white" popularly meant "clear and definitive." Now it also has racial meaning. So I'll leave it in, since *both* meanings are relevant here.

tematic department-head Smith or for loose, easy-going department-head Jones, that in itself may be a considerable service to the company.

Sociometric methods. Sociometrically, people are not assessed by tests or by testers but by other people: peers or subordinates or superiors. The "buddy rating" system used by the military in the Second World War is a typical sociometric device. A platoon of potential officer candidates, for example, trains together for several weeks. Then each member is asked to nominate the three men he thinks would make the best combat officers and the three he thinks would make the worst combat officers. They might be asked, too, to rate their budies on honesty or intelligence or sense of humor or any of a number of other characteristics. Positive and negative votes received by each man are totaled and a score assigned to that man. The score represents his peers' joint estimate of his aptitude for a particular job.

Sociometric techniques do not require the judge to give a rationale for his judgment. No explanation is demanded. Individuals are simply asked to express their overall feelings about other individuals. The sociometric method thereby shortcuts across an area of great difficulty, since both our language and our communicable knowledge about men are usually inadequate. Moreover, what we do know about personality, however inadequate, suggests that personality is not a thing to be torn apart and dealt with as a set of separable elements but is more susceptible to a kind of all-at-once, whole-man evaluation. For, as the first five chapters of this book tried to show, personality—if it can be thought of as an entity at all—is an elaborately interacting and dynamic kind of entity. When, sociometrically, one simply asks men to make an overall judgment of one another, one is, in a way, automatically taking the wholeness of personality into account.

This coin has another side. When data consist of the general feelings of some people about some other people, the dangers of distortion are many. Such distortions may be partially eliminated by using large numbers of judgments. Although the judgment made by one platoon member may be far off base, the judgments of fifty platoon members are reasonably valid—at least more valid, as World War II experience showed, than many paper-and-pencil tests, rating scales, and even military-school grades.

Sociometric methods have been used in a variety of ways

for a variety of purposes. Sometimes one asks several judges to observe and listen to a group of applicants talking to one another. The judges sit on the periphery and observe the applicants. They then decide which one of the applicants would best perform a particular job. A number of variations of this "leaderless group" method are in current use.

Only in the last few years have sociometric methods picked up speed in industrial use, though their validity has been known for decades. A partial explanation for their lagging development may be the indirect organizational implications of their use. Sociometric methods, especially buddy ratings, are something like the voting process. Voting democracy in industry carries many dangers for traditional managerial "prerogatives" and for the whole power balance within an organization. If operators are allowed to select their own foremen, managers will argue, political plots and fixed "elections" may not be far behind. Selection by "popularity," they add, will replace selection by ability, despite the fact that research to date has shown that such ratings are not popularity contests.

The assessment center

Despite these objections, sociometric methods are taking hold, particularly in executive selection. Several major companies have, in the last few years, established assessment centers for their executives, either as separate entities or as parts of management development centers.

These assessment centers typically lean heavily on sociometric measurements of several kinds. Usually they work like this:

Some small numbers of middle- to high-level executives are brought together at a special site for, say, three days. The assessment staff includes one or two professionals —psychologists usually—and several senior line executives who arrive in advance for a short period of training in assessment procedures. This assessment staff then puts the "subject" executives through a series of tests and exercises. The tests may be conventional ones—pencil and paper or projectives. The exercises have a sociometric flavor. Groups of the subject executives are given, for example, a group task—a company problem—and asked to discuss it and put forth some recommendations. This discussion is observed by the senior executive staff, often with one senior executive particularly observing just one or two subject executives as they debate and discuss the issue. This process is repeated in several forms, several times, with the seniors building up their observations of each man relative to the others.

Usually peer assessments are added. Subject executives are asked to rate one another on a collection of factors.

At the end of the three days, the whole batch is put together. The staff talks over each man, using observations, peer ratings, test scores, and anything else available, and makes an assessment of his executive potential and, usually, of his development needs.

Sometimes all these data are kept confidential in the center files. Usually they are fed back to each man in a series of interviews; occasionally they are made available to the boss of the man in question.

Technically the process is probably quite effective. It uses a team approach to assessment, exploiting "soft" observational data as well as more hard-nosed test scores. It provides good training in observation and evaluation for the senior executives who work as staff members.

On the other hand, are there ethical problems that such schemes generate? Of course. May we ask the reader to ponder those broader concerns for himself? For example, is it proper to subject a man to three days of assessment, whether he wants it or not? May an executive not want it? Is refusal really possible? What about the findings? Who sees them? What are they used for? How long do they remain in the personnel file?

Day-to-day assessment of people

People directing an organized human effort must necessarily spend some of their time making judgments about the fitness of certain members for certain tasks. Some judgments can be formalized, but it is at an informal, day-to-day level that most assessment goes on. Top management informally, gradually, imperceptibly, perhaps even unconsciously, decides that Jones looks like presidential timber and that Smith is never likely to go anywhere.

The professional psychologist has surprisingly little to offer the industrial manager in this area. The social scientist has offered industry tests and measurements and forms and systems to help with the massive formal job of screening and selecting and record-keeping. But he has helped comparatively little with the job of improving the manager's personal skill in making judgments about the people he encounters in his business life. Of course the capacity to judge other people is not one that can be easily handed from one person to another. It is a skill requiring effort and practice and also requiring the absence of certain personality blocks. Parental and other early environmental influences probably have more to do with this skill than anything else. A man's capacity to judge probably correlates positively with the extent to which he can view the outside world undistortedly, i.e., it correlates with his own security and self-knowledge. For judging is one kind of problem-solving. It can be reduced to three phases: determining what information is necessary to make a judgment; obtaining that information, usually through communication with other persons; evaluating that information into a judgment. Each of these processes is likely to be as good as the judge's own internal information-processing system.

The first, deciding what information is relevant, requires also that we ask: "Relevant for what?" Is he being considered for a specific job? What kind of a job? Working with whom? And so on. If we can get a good psychological picture of the task, we may be able to isolate the kinds of psychological information that would be relevant in a personality.

But even with a clear objective, how shall we go about ordering the information we can hope to get? Many schemes are possible. The one that follows is a crude one, but perhaps it will be useful. It is made up of three categories: first, the "givens" in a personality; second, the goals of a personality; and third, the methods by which a personality uses its givens to achieve its goals. Put another way, we can say that the accuracy of our predictions of a person's behavior would increase if we could adequately answer this question: How does this person use what he has to get what he wants? This question asked in conjunction with the question "What are we judging him for?" constitutes a reasonable starting point for the assessment process.

The givens in a personality. By the time we have become adults, all of us show some relatively unchanging characteristics. Some of these characteristics are givens in the sense that they were inherited, some in the sense that they were learned early and intensely and aren't given up easily. Intelligence is such an aspect of a person; so is the general energy level of his personality—almost his biological metabolic rate; so are his skills and knowledge, his educational background, the things he can do well; so, too, probably, are his sensitivity to others, the level of concreteness or abstractness with which he thinks; and certainly his physical makeup and appearance. We can find out something about these things indirectly. When we know them and when we know what we are judging for, we begin to have some basis for making comparative judgments.

The goals of a personality. To a considerable extent people are known by their needs. We can communicate something to a third person if we can describe the dominant pattern of needs in a personality. Something imprecise, but nevertheless meaningful, is achieved by saying of another person that he has an uncommon need for orderliness, or that he is unusually affiliative, or that he has a strong need for autonomy or independence and tends to react against restrictions. Long lists of such needs can be set down, and, though they are likely to be poorly and overlappingly defined, communication about the pattern of a particular personality's needs contributes toward defining it, at least temporarily.

A personality's use of its givens to satisfy its needs. One can also seek information about a person's "habits," his manners of behaving. If personality is a dynamic but goal-directed system, then these characteristic methods of behaving must represent the personality's characteristic ways of trying to achieve what it wants. Like the computer, we can expect people to use methods that have worked for them before. At this level one is asking: How does X perceive other people? What is the nature of his social relationships? What are his relevant attitudes toward relevant issues? To what extent does he satisfy his needs through methods that conform to the culture of the organization in which he must work? To what extent does he use methods which do not conform? How does he control his moods and his areas of insecurity? Are his methods consistent or variable?

It is possible to follow out each of these three categories in some detail: to provide a list of givens, a list of needs, and a list of methods for using givens to satisfy needs. But the usefulness of such a process for this book is doubtful. Perhaps what is most useful here is to suggest that a judge order the information that he can obtain about another personality into categories like these and then compare what he finds with the purpose for which he is judging.

Getting information about a person

A good deal of information about A can be obtained by talking to B or C. A good deal more can be gotten by talking to A. If the judge has lived closely and intimately with his subject, the process of gathering additional information to make a new judgment is minimal. He probably knows all he needs to know, and his task is to order it against the problem for which the judgment is being made and to try to extricate himself from his prejudices. If one is dealing with a relative stranger, however (and it is in this category that most problems of assessment reside), then gathering information is a major part of the problem. Historical sources provide the assessor with one kind of information. He can use records, biographical information, recommendations from other people, etc., and try to infer future behavior from this second-hand knowledge of past behavior. But he will have to form some large part of his judgment in the here and now by talking with the person being judged. The conversations may be one or more formal interviews or several brief informal discussions of business problems, or they may take a social form, a cocktail party or an evening at home. In all cases, the personal evaluation process goes on, even if there is no particular job about which an evaluation needs to be made.

Such personal, face-to-face evaluation always means that information about the other person filters through the screen of the judge's own needs and prejudices. Nevertheless, the wise judge may not always try to discard his own feelings and prejudices entirely in favor of an "objective system." Discarding such feelings might be desirable if it were possible. But it is doubtful whether it is possible. The alternative for the judge is to recognize the characteristics of his own filters and then to pay attention to what comes through these filters.

For whether one tries to or not, he listens to another person at two levels: at the level of the speaker's words and the information they carry, and at the level of the listener's own feelings about the speaker's words and the feelings these words convey. For example, most people can decide quickly whether or not another person seems to be afraid of them, or angry at them, or comfortable or uncomfortable with them, whether he talks too much for their liking, whether he has what they consider a good sense of humor, etc. And yet, in most formal evaluation situations, we often try consciously to block out and ignore this fundamental source of information, preferring to deal with what we like to think of as "the facts."

This tendency to discard our own semiconscious but nevertheless valuable insights probably derives from our justifiable doubt about our own ability to make judgments. Certainly such self-doubt is warranted. Most of us would like to have something more solid to lean on than our own amorphous judgment. We prefer to draw inferences from grades in school, test scores, number of jobs the applicant has held, and any piece of objective, "factual" information we can find. Yet, paradoxically, especially outside the office, only the most insensitive of us would try to estimate another's friendliness by asking whether he has read Dale Carnegie. Instead, data about friendliness are obtained by talking and socializing and then filtering the results through our own conception of what "friendly" means. In effect, we listen with our "third ear." Of course, the third ear is only as good as the person using it is objective about himself. But the same can be said about the first and second ears.

In industry "subjective" personal assessment may lead an organization always to find new people like the old ones. "Good" people may become people that today's management likes. And the people today's management likes may well be people like today's management. Subjective, personalized assessment, with little reference to the question of assessment-for-what, may indeed ultimately yield an in-group of "all-alike" people. But since all-alike people may be able to work together better than all-different people, an organization may, under certain conditions, profit from just such prejudice. For example, one can argue that in a period of growth and youth an all-alike team has many advantages; later in an organization's life the same subjective prejudices may be stifling to the birth of new ideas.

There is another side to this picture. When people are being assessed and know it, they behave in ways they think will evoke the best assessment. If a personnel interviewer asks Mr. X, "How do you get along with people?" his answer might be, "Oh, just fine. I like people etc., etc., etc." But if a psychiatrist for whose services Mr. X was paying asked him the same question an hour later, his answer might be different: "Well, Doc, that's just the problem. Some people don't seem to pay any attention to me etc., etc., etc." This truism, that people play to their audiences, is frequently overlooked in industrial interviewing.

One method for dealing with it is to evaluate in disguised situations. This alternative immediately introduces procedural as well as ethical questions. A second alternative is to make the evaluator an ink blot. Thus the interviewer does not ask, "How do you get on with people?" but instead asks, "What are the kinds of people you like best?" By opening up his questions, by modifying them so that the "right" answers are not at all obvious, the interviewer at least provides a situation in which the subject's answers are his own and not the interviewer's. Even so, people being assessed through interviews will make some guesses about the "right" answers, but, as long as they remain guesses, they represent a valid projection of the personality being interviewed. The major assumption underlying what has come to be called "non-directive" interviewing is just that one. It is the idea that an ambiguous stimulus (an uncommitted interviewer) requires the interviewee to "project" his own attitudes into the interview. An unambiguous interviewer, for whom the "right" answers are obvious, yields only a reflection of himself.

The idea is simple and sensible. The purpose of an interview is to gather information about another person, not about the interviewer. It is appropriate also that the interviewer provide a situation free enough so that the interviewee can talk about himself and be himself. In practice, the application of this principle suggests that an information-gathering interview should be designed like a series of inverted triangles. The interviewer opens each area of information he is seeking with big, broadside queries so that the interviewee can talk at length about his perceptions of the question, raising points in the order that seems significant to him and with the intensity that he thinks is appropriate to them. If the interviewer is still unsatisfied because he wants specific areas of information in more detail, he can then proceed to narrow his questions down to greater and greater specificity. Then he is ready to open up a new area with a new broad and ambiguous question.

These thoughts about day-to-day evaluations of other people are general and incomplete. Ultimately, after all, an evaluation of one person by another is a judgment and nothing more. A good judge needs all the information he can get from all the sources he can find. To an extent, scales, forms, and categories can be helpful. But no "system" provides a means for escaping from one's own lack of sensitivity or understanding in making such judgments. There are no formulas that can rule the judge out of the judging equation.

Assessment and the atmosphere of the organization

Drawing from earlier chapters, we can predict that people in an organization will try to evoke the best assessment they can get. They will (and should) try to stack the cards in their own favor. More than that, however, we can predict that they will have mixed feelings about assessment, both resenting it and seeking it out. We should expect resentment because assessment is a threat to independence and autonomy. But we should also expect people to "want to know where they stand," to want to know whether they are loved and thought well of by those on whom they depend.

From the managerial point of view, then, the problem of assessment is more than a problem of technique. The tests, the interviews, the other ritualistic paraphernalia of assessment, are only a small part of the problem. The bigger parts raise questions like these: Shall we consciously assess our people? Shall we formalize the process? Shall we report back results? All results? Or only "good" ones? Who shall assess? Superiors only? Or peers? Or subordinates? What is to be assessed? Personality or performance? Shall we build a work environment permeated with an atmosphere of assessment?

This book can offer no pat answers to such questions. There are none. But the chapters that follow are devoted, in large part, to examining such problems of human relationships and to considering the implications of some alternative courses of action.

In summary

Three general approaches to formal assessment have been described: pencil-and-paper tests, projectives, and sociometric methods. Each has its own advantages and costs. Pencil-and-paper devices are relatively cheap and relatively standardized, but their use is largely limited to mass-selection situations. Projectives go deep and are rich in the material they dredge up, but subjective, individualistic, expensive, and poorly validated. Sociometrics are easy and relatively valid but carry serious implications for the power relationships in an organization.

Day-to-day assessing of people is a more difficult problem. It can be helped by a set of categories for thinking about personality, by utilizing modern interviewing techniques, and by increasing one's insight into oneself.

The larger questions of assessment are not "how" questions but questions of "why" and "how much."

2

**People two at a time
Problems of influence
and authority**

Introductory note

The focus of this second section shifts from the singular to the plural, from one person to relationships between people and especially to the efforts of one person to influence and change the behavior of others.

Influence is not a small problem. It is not only a problem that pervades business and industry, where people must continually devote much of their energy to trying to change other people. It is also a central problem in the family, in education, in psychiatry, in international relations, in politics, and in every other phase of human interaction.

To some extent, one can say that the behavior-change problem is growing more and more complex in America. Our technological, specialized culture has made people increasingly dependent on one another for physical-need satisfaction. And some as yet undefined psychological characteristics of our culture seem to be making people increasingly interdependent for social and egoistic need satisfactions too. One observer has called us an increasingly "other-directed" people—people who need others not only for bread and warmth but for justifying our presence and for providing us with standards to live by. The young executive finds it hard to separate good work from his boss's approval of it. The author cannot feel sure he has written a good book until the critics laud it. The housewife's new sofa is successful only if the neighbors want one too.

The behavior-change question is such a universal one that it cannot be tossed off lightly with a few clichés about hand shaking and open office doors. Another thing is clear, too. No adequate answers will be found in this book. The most we can hope for is to try to isolate some of the dimensions of the problem as it seems to exist in industry and to look at some ways that people outside industry have tried to tackle it.

This section puts a good deal of emphasis on the idea of communication because communication is the most important prerequisite to any attempt to change human behavior. But communication is a problem in engineering as well as behavioral science. Many of these pages therefore do not have their origins in psychology or sociology but in the physical and engineering sciences. I have also tried to interweave some other ideas that evolve mostly from social psychology. And I have tried to treat the whole in the light of the picture of man that was drawn in part 1.

Part 2 begins with a brief consideration of relationships and roles in our society to set the background and to show how part 1, on individuals, is related to part 2, on influence. Then we consider some ideas about communication, the basic mechanism of influence. The next chapter hits the problem head-on, describing some dimensions of influence and their implications. Then we devote four chapters to four approaches to influence: The first considers the possibilities and limitations of authority as a tool for influence; the second examines coercive power; the next looks at manipulation as a tool for influence; and the fourth examines motivational and collaborative tools for influence. The last chapter of this part, like the last chapter in the first part, picks one major applied problem of influence, the problem of money incentives, and examines it from a psychological perspective.

Relationships
The forest
and the trees

In chapter 2, in the discussion of dependency and the paralyzed brother, one important item was omitted. We treated the case as though only the paralyzed brother were dependent. The big brother was free of dependency. But is that ever really true? Isn't big brother dependent too? Clearly the child is dependent on the parents, but aren't the parents also dependent on the child? The employee is dependent on the boss, but why does the boss put ads in the paper asking, literally, for "help"?

What was omitted, then, in the first section was the emphasis on interdependency, the idea of the relationship. We can define relationships as situations in which individuals or groups seek mutually to satisfy needs. In this section, we try to broaden the spotlight to include a bit of the forest of relationships as well as the individual trees.

Interdependency

In modern American industry everyone is, to a degree, the paralyzed brother, and everyone is also, to a degree, the big brother. Modern industry is complicated, socially and technologically, so complicated that everyone from the chairman of the board on down requires the help of other people for the satisfaction of his needs.

If that assertion is true, then the next step should be the same one talked about in chapter 2—ambivalence. Anyone who lives in an organization is living in an atmosphere of dependency. He should therefore feel some love and some hate toward the organization. The intensity and direction of feelings should, in turn, vary with the ups and downs of organizational life.

The morals of this tale are simple and important ones. Don't look for psychological equilibrium in organizations (or in marriage or any other relationship, for that matter). Look for variation and change. Don't look for statics; look for dynamics. Don't look for a permanently "happy" organization; look for one that is self-corrective, that doesn't build up unexpressed grudges.

Big brother (the organization) must always be frustrating as well as satisfying. He fools himself if he thinks he can be otherwise. But what he and the paralyzed brother can do is to limit the duration and build-up of frustration by providing mechanisms for expressing and acting upon it. Big brother had better also be satisfying as well as frustrating, because the dependency is mutual.

Some categories of relationships

If relationships are cases of mutual dependency, it follows that each member is trying to satisfy his needs through the other. Each is trying to influence and modify the behavior of the other to satisfy his own needs.

Influence, or efforts to change behavior, then, becomes the property not only of ethically questionable "manipulators," politicians, militants, advertisers, and hard-selling salesmen, but also of husbands, wives, children, staff people, school-teachers, burglars, managers, and just about everyone else in our society. So much so that it is nonsense for any of us to be "against" influence.

Let us consider here several categories of relationships to see what limits they put on influence techniques and what ethical questions they raise.

The first category, the *one-shot* versus the *long-term* relationship, provides some serious, ethical-technical questions. In a long-term relationship, when A knows he must go on living or working with B after he has tried to change B's behavior, he may proceed with caution no matter what his personal ethics. His own dependency on the other in the relationship serves as a built-in governor on his influence techniques, even if his conscience doesn't. But in short-term, one-shot relationships, when A never expects to see B again—after the door-to-door sale or after A has talked B out of giving him the traffic ticket—the range of influence techniques A may use is limited only by his own conscience and his fear of the law. Incidentally, except for selling (and most of the time even there), relationships in industry are *not* of the one-shot variety. That may be why some observers see salesmen as the last stronghold of individualism and independence in industry (and why other observers see salesmen as the last stronghold of amorality).

Besides variation in duration, relationships vary along a

power dimension, too. Big brother may need little brother, but little brother needs big brother more, or at least he may think he does. If that is so, the constraints imposed by the relationship on big brother's behavior are fewer than those on little brother's. Big brother may feel free to use influence methods that outsiders might feel are exploitive and harsh, if he uses his power directly, or manipulative and paternalistic, if he clothes his power in silk.

Relationships also vary in the extent to which *rules of interpersonal behavior* and *escape clauses* are clearly specified. There are legal and religious constraints, for instance, surrounding the marital relationship, making escape from it rather difficult. The union contract, similarly, is often the umpire of union-management relationships, and the law sets other limits on the use of managerial power over employees.

The rules need not be written, however. Unwritten ones are often equally significant in controlling behavior. A death in the immediate family of an employee evokes a clause in an unwritten contract that says that he shall have time off and shall be free of undue pressure for a while. Any superior who breaks that unwritten rule may find himself facing the disapproval of his peers and superiors, as well as of his subordinates. Such unwritten social rules exist for a society as a whole, but they also differ from company to company. In some companies executives expect to have to work overtime, to call the boss "Mister," to wear white shirts, to have a cocktail at lunch, and so on. People who break such unwritten rules are punished as much as people who break written ones. But it is possible for people to break off relationships with a company. A self-selection process in organizations with numerous and well-established social rules can, therefore, eventually yield a homogeneous, "think-alike" group of personnel simply by driving out or modifying those people who are not initially willing to accept the rules.

The continuous popular and important debate on individualism versus conformity (which we shall examine in detail in part 3) centers on this problem of the depth and extent of social sanctions on individual behavior. Strong sanctions encourage homogeneity of interests and outlook, which some companies feel is good, but thereby discourage individuality and peculiarity, which many observers feel are even better. At least one question is appropriate here: Are there some stages in an organization's life at which it needs conformity and homogeneity to make for orderliness and efficiency in its operations? Are there other stages when it needs heterogeneity and interpersonal conflict, and the creativity and re-examination of assumptions that may accompany heterogeneity? Using the terminology of an earlier chapter, are there some unprogrammed classes of problems that need individuality? And some programmed, semiroutinized problems that need conformity? We shall look for answers to such questions later in this section.

Another critical issue centers around the *social roles* of the members of the relationship. For our role—our formal position in a social system—determines to a great degree the readiness of other people to accept our efforts at influence. It is "appropriate" or "legitimate" in most of our eyes for college professors to try to influence their students—in certain areas. It is appropriate for parents to try to influence children or for salesmen to try to sell. But it is less legitimate for youngsters to try to influence oldsters, or for enlisted men to try to influence officers. The power variable is especially important here, of course. Certain kinds of roles are assumed to be powerful relative to others. And generally influence is expected to flow more readily from more to less powerful roles, than vice versa.

One last category of relationships is worth mentioning here. Some relationships center on the satisfaction of *personal* needs, others center on *impersonal* needs. Salesmen, for example, usually set up customer relationships which, from the salesman's standpoint at least, are largely impersonal. The purpose of the relationship for him is to sell the goods, not to make friends per se. Occasionally, however, salesmen's relationships with customers deepen in subtle, inadvertent ways so that the salesman finds himself on "intimate" terms with a customer. Personal, social, and egoistic needs enter the scene. The relationship becomes valuable to both parties in its *own right*. Often if that happens the salesman finds himself in a trap. He can no longer use the influence tactics ordinarily drawn from his regular armamentarium. He begins to feel stirrings of guilt and conscience about goals and methods he normally uses without concern. He wants to maintain the friendship as much as he wants to sell the product.

Similarly, within the organization, managers often discover that the relationships they see as primarily impersonal and problem-oriented (as roles, not as persons) are seen by subordinates as *personal* relationships, involving vital social and egoistic needs. The boss says something about changing the method of promotion in a merchandising problem, and the subordinate feels his personal competence has been criticized or that his boss has stopped liking him.

These variations in the kinds and intensities of relationships lead one immediately to expect, quite rightly, that the problem of influencing behavior is a complicated one, varying with the internal nature of the relationship and with the nature of the external social, legal, and economic environment. Simple magical rules of thumb will have no very useful place in such a complex and dynamic set of situations.

The place of communication

The next chapter discusses communication in relationships. It is an appropriate next step in a consideration of influence for these reasons: First, it is by communication that people try to modify the behavior of others to satisfy their own needs. Second, it is by communication that the needs and perceptions of others become known. So A influences B by talking to him, and he learns about B by listening to him.

We come back then to the closed-loop notion of active learning discussed in chapter 6. Only now A is not learning to solve arithmetic problems, he is learning to solve B.

In summary

Our new unit of discussion is the relationship between A and B, rather than A or B alone.

Relationships are defined as multiperson efforts to satisfy needs through one another. Members of relationships are therefore *interdependent*. They can then be expected to hold mutually ambivalent feelings toward one another. Hence we should not expect organizations, which are structures built of relationships, to reach any lasting psychological equilibrium.

Relationships vary in duration, in power distribution, in environmentally determined rules of behavior, in degree of "personalness," and in the social roles occupied by the members. Each of these aspects raises questions about the ethics and the techniques of influence to be used by one member to satisfy his needs through others.

Communication is a basic tool of relationships. In most relationships it is simultaneously a tool for information-gathering and for influence by *all* members of the relationship.

Communication
Getting information
from A into B

People begin, modify, and end relationships by communicating with one another. Communication is their channel of influence, their mechanism of change. In industrial organizations it has become popular recently to communicate about communication—to talk and write about the importance of communication in problem solving. The talk about communication is appropriate because communication is indeed a critical dimension of organization.

Unfortunately, though, much of the talk has been either nonsensical or unusable. For one thing, the word "communication" has been used to mean everything from public speaking to mass merchandising. For another, most of the talk has been hortatory rather than explanatory. Managers are urged to use "two-way" communication, because it is "better" (what does "better" mean?) than one-way communication. The fad has extended to "three-way" communication, again without evidence or precise definition.

The purpose of this chapter is to describe some major dimensions of the communication process, to examine what can be meant by "better" or "worse" communication, and to relate the idea of communication to the ideas of interpersonal influence and behavior change.

Some dimensions of communication

Sometimes there are advantages to asking simpleminded questions. They can help to strip away some of the confusing gingerbread surrounding an idea so that we can see it more objectively.

Suppose we ask, simplemindedly, what are the things that can happen when A talks to B? What is involved in two people's talking to one another?

First, A usually talks to B *about something*. The process has a content. They talk baseball or they talk business or they talk sex. The content is what usually hits us first when we tune in on a conversation. Content of communication, in fact, is what psychologists and businessmen alike are usually thinking about when they think about human relations.

We can see subclasses within content too. We can differentiate categories of content like, for example, *fact* and *feeling*.

Other things, quite independent of what is said, take place when A talks to B. Some conversations take place in the presence of a great deal of *noise;* others are relatively noiseless. In this context "noise" means things that interfere with transmission. We can encounter channel noise like the static on a telephone line that makes it hard for B to hear what A is saying. We can also usefully think of psychological noises, like B's thinking about something else, so that again it is hard for him to hear what A is saying; or like B's being so afraid of A that it is hard for him to hear what A is saying. Language or code noise may make it hard for B to hear: he doesn't understand the words A is using in the way A understands them.

All sorts of noise can occur independently of content. We can find noisy or noiseless communications about any content. We also can usually observe that A, in the presence of noise, is likely to communicate more redundantly—to repeat his message in the hope that B will be able to hear it better the second time or to say the same thing in a different way. Redundancy is one of the most common weapons for combating noise. It is "inefficient" in the sense that repetition is wasteful of time and energy. It is "efficient" in the sense that, so long as noise exists, redundancy helps to push the content through.

Besides the content and noise dimensions of conversation between A and B, a third dimension is the *communication net*. Usually we think of A to B conversation as direct; but many such conversations, especially in organizations, are mediated through other people. One thing an organization chart is supposed to tell us is that A can speak to B only through C or D. As a later chapter will show, the structure of the net a particular organization uses can have a lot to do with the speed and accuracy of members' communications with one another.

One more dimension of the process is worth noting, especially since it has been ridden so hard in managerial literature. It is the *direction* of communication—its one-wayness or two-wayness. Again it is an independent dimension. No matter what A and B may be talking about, no matter how much static may be involved, no matter what the

network, A may talk to B this way: A→B; or this way: A
⇄ B. A can talk and B can only listen, i.e., one-way communication; or A can talk and B can talk back, i.e., two-way communication.

This last aspect of the process, one-wayness versus two-
wayness, gets special attention in the remainder of this
chapter. Is two-way communication really better? What does
"better" mean? Better for what and for whom? When?

One-way versus two-way
communication

Essentially our problem is to clarify the differences between
these two situations: (1) one person, A, talking to another, B,
without return talk from B to A; versus (2) conversation from
A to B *with* return conversation from B to A. The differences
can be clarified best by testing one method against the other.
Here is such a test situation:

The pattern of rectangles shown here is an idea you would
like to tell some B's about. Suppose you try to communicate
it in words to a half-dozen of your friends who are sitting
around your living room:

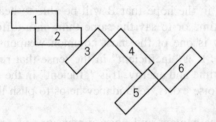

Assume that the rectangles touch each other at "sensible"
places—at corners or at midpoints along the line. There are
no touch points at any unusual places. All the angles are either 90° or 45° angles; there are no odd ones. This pattern of
rectangles is an idea comparable perhaps to a complicated set
of instructions you may have to give to a subordinate or to
the definition of a policy that you would like to pass along or
to the task of explaining statistical quality control to a sales
manager. This idea can be communicated to others under (1)
one-way or (2) two-way conditions.

If you are the communicator, these are your *one-way* instructions:

1. Turn your back on your audience so that you cannot
get visual communication back.

2. Give the audience blank sheets of paper, so that they

can listen and draw exactly what you are communicating. Ask them to try to draw as accurate a picture of the pattern of rectangles as possible.

3. Describe the pattern of rectangles to them in words as fast as you can. The audience is not permitted to ask questions, or laugh, or sigh, or in any other way to communicate back to you any information about what it is receiving.

This game is a good parlor game, if you can find some people to try it on. Try it, time it, and then check the accuracy of your communication by determining whether or not your audience has drawn what you have described. If they received what you tried to send, so their pictures match the test picture, then you have communicated. To the extent that their pictures do not match the one in the drawing, you have not communicated.

Two-way communication can be tested for contrast in the same way. The same rules apply, and here is a similar test pattern:

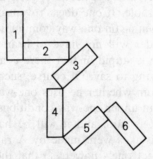

This time the basic job is the same, to describe the pattern verbally so that the people who are listening can draw it. But here are the differences:

1. This time you may face your audience.

2. They are allowed to interrupt and ask you any questions they want to at any time they want to.

Try it this way and time it. The differences between what happened the first time and what happened the second time are the differences between one- and two-way communication. (The order in which the two methods are used matters, but is not critical.)

Under experimental conditions these findings have emerged from this game: (1) One-way communication is considerably faster than two-way communication. (2) Two-way communication is more accurate than one-way, i.e., more people in the audience correctly reproduce the drawing under two-way conditions. (3) The receivers are more sure of them-selves and make more correct judgments of how right or wrong they are in the two-way system. (4) The sender finds himself feeling psychologically under attack in the two-way system, because his receivers pick up his mistakes and over-sights and let him know about them. The receivers may make snide remarks about the sender's intelligence and skill, and, if the receivers are trying very hard and taking the task seriously, they may actually get angry at the sender, and he at them. (5) The two-way method is relatively noisy and disor-derly—with people interrupting the sender and one another, with the slowest man holding up the rest, and so on. The one-way method, on the other hand, appears neat and efficient to an outside observer, but the communication is less accurate.

Such a demonstration points out both the advantages and the costs of one-way and of two-way communication. If speed alone is what is important, then one-way communication has the edge. If appearance is of prime importance, if one wishes to look orderly and businesslike, then the one-way method again is preferable. If one doesn't want one's mistakes to be recognized, then again one-way communication is preferable. Then the sender will not have to hear people implying or saying that he is stupid or that there is an easier way to say what he is trying to say. Of course, such comments may be made about him whether he uses one-way or two-way com-munication, but under one-way conditions he will not have to listen to what is said, and it will be harder for anyone to prove that mistakes were made by A rather than B. If one wants to protect one's power, so that the sender can blame the receiver instead of taking blame himself, then one-way communication is again preferable. The sender can say: "I told you what to do; you just weren't bright enough to get the word." If he uses two-way communication, the sender will have to accept much of what blame there is, and it will be apparent to all that he deserves some of it; but he will also get his message across.

If one wants to simplify managerial life, so that even a rank amateur can handle it, one-way communication helps. It tightens and structures the situation so that A only has to make decisions about one kind of thing—content of the problem. When he opens up two-way communication, he has to be professional—for now he must make many kinds of decisions at once—content decisions and also decisions about people (Whom shall he recognize? How long should he work to make sure Joe understands while everybody else waits?), about personal strategies (When shall I cut off the discussion? Shall I accept sarcasm or fight it?), and about lots of other things. Like some formations in football, two-way communication is too powerful a device for safe use by people who are amateurs at management. But skilful use by a competent professional can be as beautiful and impressive as the work of a good **T**-formation quarterback.

Those are the major differences between one- and two-way communication. They are differences that most people are aware of implicitly. If a person gets a chance to ask questions, to double-check what he might have missed, then he can make sure he has gotten exactly what he is expected to get. On the other hand, if he must only sit and listen, he may or may not get the word, and he is likely to feel frustrated and uncertain about what he does get. Moreover, that bit of frustration and uncertainty is likely to grow because he has no way of making sure of things he isn't sure of.

To put it another way, one-way communication is not likely to be communication at all. It is more likely to be talk. One can talk by passing words out into the air. Those words don't become communication until they enter meaningfully into somebody else's head.

Of course, it is simple for a communicator to claim that his responsibility is only to pass a message along, that the receiver's responsibility is to make sure that he understands it. But this is not a very adequate claim. If one really were to argue through the question of who is responsible for the success of communication, one would certainly conclude that communication is largely the communicator's responsibility. For if the communicator's job is to communicate—and if to communicate he must get his message through to the receiver—then his responsibility cannot end until the receiver has received. And he cannot be sure that the receiver has received until he gets confirming feedback from the receiver. On the other hand, the location of responsibility becomes a far less significant issue when one perceives communication as a two-party process to begin with.

A partial definition of communication is now possible. First, to communicate is to shoot information and to hit a target with it. Shooting alone is not communicating. Second, to have more than chance probability of hitting a target requires that the sender get feedback from the target about the accuracy of his shots.

If an artilleryman had to fire over a hill at an invisible target, he would have to fire blind and hope that by luck one of his shells would land on the target. He would spray the area with shells and go away, never being certain whether he had or had not destroyed his objective. But by the simple addition of a spotter standing on the hilltop, the likelihood of accurate shooting can be greatly increased. The spotter can feed back to the gunner information about the effects of the gunner's own shots. "Your last shot was a hundred yards short. The second was fifty yards over." And so on. The advantage is obvious, and it is precisely the advantage of two-way over one-way communication—the communicator can learn the effects of his attempts to communicate and can adjust his behavior accordingly. Like the learning machine we discussed in chapter 6, the decision-maker needs inputs as well as outputs to correct his own behavior.

*One-way and two-way communication
are really different methods*

By this definition two-way communication is not just different from one-way in degree but also in kind. For when one switches from one-way to two-way, a great many changes take place, changes not only in the outcomes but in the inputs. For example, one-way communication usually calls for and gets much more planning than two-way. When you tell a sender in these experiments that he is to send one-way, and you show him the diagram and tell him he can take a few minutes to get ready to start, it is almost always true that he uses more minutes getting ready to start than he does in the two-way system. The reason is probably obvious. The sender needs to choose carefully the code he will use, even the precise words he will use. But in two-way communication he is apt to start out much more quickly, not worrying too much about a general plan or strategy, because he knows that the feedback will provide him with opportunities to correct himself. The first system is like a phonograph record. Once it starts, it must be played through. Hence it must be planned very carefully. Two-way communication is a different strategy, a kind of "local" strategy, in which the sender starts down one path, goes a little way and then discovers he is on the wrong track, makes a turn, discovers he is off a little again, makes another turn, and so on. He doesn't need to plan so much as he needs to listen, and to be sensitive to the feedback he is getting.

There are important differences associated with these two kinds of approaches. Planfulness, order, systemization: these are associated with one-way communication. The two-way method has much more a trial-and-error, "let's make a stab at it and see what happens," kind of flavor. It is understandable, therefore, that certain kinds of personalities tend to favor one of these or the other because one method or the other is apt to be much more consistent with one's personality.

With our definition of communication, the issue of one-and two-way communication in industry can be cast somewhat differently than is usual. For now one encounters apparent conflict between the short-run efficiency of two-way communication and the long-run need to maintain power and authority at various levels of the hierarchy. Two-way communication makes for more valid communication, and it appears now that more valid communication results not only in more accurate transmission of facts but also in reorganized perceptions of relationships. Authority, for example, may under ideal conditions of two-way communication cease to serve as a sufficient protection for inadequacy. The dictum that a well-informed citizenry is democracy's protection against autocracy may also be applicable to the well-informed staff or the well-informed employee. And though "democracy" may connote things desirable in government, its connotations for industrial organizations in our society are far from clear.

Barriers in the communication process

In our experiment we set up two-way communication simply by telling our subjects that we wanted them to talk back to the sender, to ask any questions they wanted to, any time they wanted to. Moreover, the experiment was just an experiment anyway, and nothing really rode on it. So there wasn't any reason why people shouldn't talk back—apparently. But, in fact, in almost every case, it turned out that some people in the two-way situation did not get complete and perfect answers. And it was also true that most of these people knew they were wrong—*yet they did not ask questions.* Why not?

When we asked people why not, we got a variety of answers. Some of them didn't ask questions because they were bored; they didn't think much of the experiment anyway. Some of them didn't ask questions because they didn't want to occupy the group's time. Sometimes they were just plain mad at the sender because of the way he was encoding the material. They wouldn't give him the satisfaction of asking him a question. Sometimes they were scared. They had noticed that when Joe Blow asked a question earlier, the sender had given a curt and nasty answer. So they just quit asking questions. Some people said that they had wanted to ask questions, but so many other people were talking all at once that they couldn't get in.

So even in this gamey little experiment, where nothing

much rode on what was going on, where the sender was not the boss—even in such a situation, there were lots of things that kept people from saying what they should have. Lots of barriers to two-way communication remained even after we had tried to set up a situation in which no such barriers would exist.

In the real world, of course, the barriers are likely to be greater and much more numerous. In the real world the boss's statement that his office door is always open has much much less meaning, probably, than the experimenter's statement that people should feel free to ask any questions they want to, any time they want to.

There is, then, a moral to this tale. The moral is that if someone wants two-way communication in his organization, he had better plan to work for it. It does not come naturally or by issuing a proclamation. If a sender wants to make sure that two-way communication will in fact occur, he will need to be extremely sensitive to what the people in his group are thinking and feeling. He will have to have his eye open for the man who wants to talk but doesn't dare. He will have to be alert to the extent to which his own behavior is deterring people from asking the questions that need to be asked. He will have to worry about some degree of order or discipline in his group, so that people can get in questions they want to ask. He will even have to worry about the interpersonal relations among the members of the group, for sometimes people do not ask questions of the sender because they are fearful of one of their colleagues. He will have, in other words, to take many new kinds of responsibility.

Communication about novel and routine problems

In chapter 6, when our focus was on individual learning and problem-solving, we pointed out that people learn; they use their memories of past problems to solve similar present ones.

Correspondingly, it is obviously true that if the problem in the experiment on two-way communication had been a familiar instead of a novel one, the results might have been quite different. A, for instance, could probably have communicated the English alphabet accurately and rapidly through one-way communication alone. In fact, it has been shown that if we use two-way communication on these rectangle problems again and again with the same group, communication soon becomes one-way anyhow. People stop asking questions. They don't have to. They have learned the code; so A and B understand one another.

From the point of view of speed and accuracy, then, one could make this tentative generalization. Two-way communication improves the accurate communication of previously uncoded or insufficiently coded ideas. But two-way communication contributes considerably less to accuracy after the code has been clarified—after new problems have been programmed and routinized. Coupling this generalization with the notion that new unprogrammed problems tend to occur more frequently in upper organizational echelons, we can also tentatively conclude that two-way communication may be generally more useful for problem-solving within the management group than further down the line—except when the problems are people problems, and those are unprogrammed everywhere.

What gets communicated?

One aspect of the content problem deserves mention here, although it will be dealt with more fully later. The problem is that people usually communicate more than information to the target; they communicate feelings as well as facts. Suppose the artillery spotter, instead of simply announcing where the last shell had landed, decided to add a few typically human comments of his own. Suppose the spotter said to the gunner: "Look, you stupid s.o.b., your last shot was three hundred yards over. Where the hell did you learn to shoot?" That kind of communication of unsolicited information will complicate the psychological picture, just as will the communication of inaccurate information, sometimes causing the now frustrated gunner to change his target from the farmhouse to the spotter.

These problems of the content of communication are the subject matter of the next few chapters of this book—the chapters on (communication as a tool for) influencing people's behavior.

In summary

Communication is a primary tool for effecting behavior change. We can isolate at least four independent dimensions of the communication process: content, noise, network characteristics, and direction.

One-way communication has some advantages in speed over two-way. It also has the advantages of protecting the sender from having to recognize his own faults and protecting him from some more complex problems of managing. Two-way communication has the advantages of greater accuracy and greater feelings of certainty for the receiver. But two-way communication involves some psychological risks to the defenses of the sender. Two-way communication also means less *planning* work for the sender as far as the message itself is concerned but opens up a whole new series of managerial problems in maintaining and expanding the two-way system.

Influencing behavior
Some dimensions
of the problem

The purpose of this chapter is to scan panoramically some things that happen when one person, A, sets out to communicate with another person, B, for the specific purpose of changing B's behavior.

The problems under consideration here are largely tactical ones, like these: A sets out to get B to quit smoking; or A sets out to "discipline" B, who has again shown up late for work; or A sets out to stimulate his passive staff into more energetic activity; or A sets out to get B to like him better or to respect him more. When we watch A's undertaking such tasks, several common aspects become noticeable; some seem to center in A, others in B, and still others in the interactions between the two. Let's begin with a clear code. A is the chang*er*. B is the chang*ee*.

The changer's motivation

One oddity about people who seek to change others is their readiness to undertake the job without thinking much about their own objectives or their own motives. A friend of mine told me a story recently about his extended efforts to get his daughter to stop sucking her thumb. He had been worried about it for a long time and had seen the family doctor about it. The doctor had examined the child, found no physical damage, and advised the father to forget about the problem.

But when the child got to be about three years old, Papa began to worry about it again. He was worried, he said, about what thumb-sucking would do to her teeth and jaws. This time he took her to a psychiatrist who talked to the child at some length and came up with the same advice the family physician had given: forget about it; it would take care of itself.

Six months later Papa decided on his own to try some of the popular methods for stopping thumb-sucking. He put some nasty-tasting stuff on the thumb; he spanked her; and he made her wear mittens. But these methods didn't work either. Now he had come to me.

His objective *seemed* clear enough: it was to stop the child from sucking her thumb. But when pressed, he agreed that there were some secondary objectives that were perhaps not so secondary when he thought about them. He wanted the child to stop sucking her thumb, but he was not willing to pay any price to accomplish it. He was not willing, for instance, to exchange thumb-sucking for stuttering or even for nose-picking. Moreover, when we talked more generally about what he was trying to accomplish, he finally admitted that what he really wanted was to start making an adult out of his daughter, to start socializing her. He was disturbed because this three-and-a-half-year-old extension of himself was behaving in a way that he considered childish and shameful. He thought that other people disapproved of little girls who sucked their thumbs and that their disapproval reflected on his capacity as a parent. He finally decided, after thinking a good deal about himself, simply to stop the whole attempt.

Such confusion of motives is not at all unusual, even in business. A supervisor, under pressure from his own superiors, starts pushing discipline without thinking much about its effect on production. If an observer raises these issues, the foreman will argue that his goal is to get more work, purely and simply. But his behavior may suggest that some of the needs involved are personal and emotional, e.g., to get the approval of his boss.

A personnel manager tries to get his staff working hard on a suggestion system. His objective is to build a system that will help the company. But under a microscope one can see other objectives that the personnel manager may not admit very readily. He received a copy of *Business Week* from the president the other day with a note about an article on suggestion systems: "Joe, please let me know what we are doing about programs like this one."

Perhaps the most common form of unclarity about motives for changing others stems from conflicts between immediate and long-term needs. In most industrial situations, no matter how simple and specific the case, a secondary, long-term factor is likely to be lurking in the background. It is the factor of the continuing relationship. Any time a supervisor performs some specific act to get more or better work on a specific job at a specific time, he is acting like the big brother of chapter 2. He is influencing his long-term relationship with his employees. Unlike the big brother's, the supervisor's acts almost always have a large audience. And every specific incident in a supervisor's handling of his people can be thought of as one frame in the long movie which determines his people's general willingness (or unwillingness) to work, their optimism or pessimism, their approval or resentment. The difficulty is that work-a-day pressures tend to push executives, like parents, toward the short-term problems and toward the satisfaction of short-term personal and egoistic needs, at the expense of long-term objectives.

It isn't always easy to take the long view in the face of short-term pressures. Since every superior in an organization is usually a subordinate to someone else, each is likely to be intensely concerned with the short-term problem of doing what his superiors want him to do. And if the foreman feels squeezed by his superiors, he cannot simply ignore his own tensions in order to work for the long-term good. But, perhaps, if he can recognize for himself the several motives that may be relevant to an effort to change someone else's behavior, he can select a course of action that can better accomplish all the ends he wants to accomplish.

So if any generalized rule of thumb exists for the prospective behavior changer, it might be this one: Let him examine his own reasons for wanting to effect a particular change before plunging into the effort. Let him examine his own motives. If he does, he may be more likely to effect change successfully because he will be more clearheaded about what he wants to do; or he may alter or give up his efforts altogether if such an examination brings the realization that changing other people would not satisfy the needs he most wants to satisfy.

The changee is in the saddle

No matter how much power a changer may possess, no matter how "superior" he may be, it is the changee who controls the final change decision. It is the employee, even the lowest paid one, who ultimately decides whether to show up for work or not. It is the child who ultimately decides whether to obey or not. It is the changee who changes. A can exert more or less influence on the situation. A can cut capers before B; he can cajole, threaten, or punish; but B (and he may be an irrational and unreasonable B) makes the ultimate decision about whether or not he will change. Moreover, it is A who feels the tension, whose needs are unsatisfied. So it is A who is dependent on B.

B, after all, is a whole person; and A's activities in trying to get B to change constitute just one set of forces in the multitude of forces that affect B's behavior. B, in effect, sits behind the solid fortifications of his own history and his own personality, integrating A's activities into all the other forces that act upon him and coming up with a new behavioral pattern that may or may not constitute what A wants.

Greater power in A's hands, greater control over B's vital needs does not necessarily give A greater control over B. B is never completely dependent. So the industrial worker finds numberless ingenious techniques for evading, avoiding, or retaliating against changes imposed by his superior.

Change is uncomfortable

Still another thing that commonly happens during the process of behavior change is that changees get disturbed. B, during the course of a significant change in his own behavior (whether the change results from A's actions or not), gets upset and anxious. A, the changer, may mistakenly interpret such action by B as a sign that his change efforts are a failure, that he has gone too far.

In fact, however, some disturbance seems to be a necessary accompaniment of change. The absence of signs of disturbance may, therefore, be a more negative warning than their presence.

Signs of upset in the process of change are visible in many situations. The child is likely to get upset when switching from diapers to the toilet. The bachelor suffers from sleeplessness and loss of appetite as he wrestles with the idea of marriage. The executive somehow feels anxious and upset, as well as happy, when he learns of his promotion to greater responsibilities.

Moreover, these upsets are likely to lead the changee into aggressive and hostile activity or into moodiness and withdrawal. A is often the logical target for tensions created by such disturbances; so B is likely to become aggressive and hostile toward A.

The explanation of these upsets takes us back to chapters 4 and 5. We have introduced frustration and conflict into the situation. People change when their present behavior begins to appear inadequate, either because they have been frustrated—something in the world has thrown a block across a previously open path—or because some new path has become visible and looks as if it *might* (conflict) be a better one. In either case a kind of behavior that had in the past been adequate has now become less adequate. If the present path is now inadequate, but no alternatives are immediately available, we have a classic frustration situation—and hence manifestations of aggression are to be expected. If one's present tack does not look as good as it did because another has begun to look better, we have conflict between the safety and security of the old path and the risk of an uncertain new one. Once again we should expect some emotional disturbance, the particular nature of which should be grossly predictable from our knowledge of the individual.

What does A need to know about B?

Different changers in different change situations have different ideas about the importance of "diagnosis," of gathering information about B.

As who use force as a prime device to effect change usually do not worry much about diagnosis. The effects of a whip, after all, are fairly predictable even if one doesn't know much about the psyche of the particular person being whipped. But at the other extreme one can find As (and many psychiatrists are among them) devoting a large portion of their effort to finding out a great deal about the changee—about his background, his childhood, and his personality down to the finest detail.

In industry the whole range of changers are represented, with most exponents of "modern management" favoring the diagnostic side. One finds, for example, the common supervisory dictum "Get the facts before you act." That seems to mean that diagnosis is a useful predecessor to change.

A great deal can be said here, as elsewhere, in favor of gathering information about a problem before trying to solve it. But three easily overlooked points are worth considering. First, who most needs the information thus gathered, A or B? Second, what kind of information does A (or B) need? Third, how much information is worth chasing after, especially if the chasing process costs time and effort?

Behavior-change problems may be somewhat different from some other problems in this regard. Often it is more important for B to understand the problem than for A to understand it. If the ultimate control for change lies with B, and if it is for B to fit A's efforts into the larger framework of B's own perceptions, then B can best make a reasonable change decision when he, not A, understands what is going on. A may understand B inside out, but he may not be able to communicate that understanding to B or even to plot a very effective course of action. Somewhere along the line B has to line up the facts in a form *he* can understand and utilize. This is the problem with giving advice. A looks over B's situation, thinks (often correctly) that he sees it more clearly than B, and says: "What you ought to do is. . . ." B thereupon feels that his defenses have been violated or that A's advice represents poor understanding; or he takes the advice literally and utilizes it poorly and finally rejects both advice and adviser. Perhaps if A spent less time diagnosing B and more helping B to diagnose himself, the likelihood of successful change would be enhanced.

The second problem involves two kinds of information that are available to both A and B—information about facts and feelings. Facts in the usual sense of observable phenomena are likely to be much less important than feelings in change situations. Fears, doubts, feelings of confidence, inadequacy, ambition—these are much more likely to be significant information for behavior changers than the cold facts of duties or salary bracket. Moreover, these feelings may be hard for A to get at, even if he needs them. This is so partly because our language and our culture make verbal communication of feelings so difficult and partly because feelings often touch on people's psychological defenses.

An A who wants to know how B feels needs to have a sharp third ear. He has to be able to pick up information from such cues as the tone of B's voice, or the raising and lowering of B's eyebrows, or the secondary emotional connotations of B's words. Any A who sets out to find out why a B is doing what he is doing had best think of the job as something considerably more than a simple fact-finding expedition. He had better recognize that he will have to listen for some subtle cues and that, because they are likely to be subtle and indirect, they may be easily misinterpreted. Market-research people are struggling with just this problem as they worry through the concept of "motivational research" into consumer attitudes.

One of the best of many good things to be said for a serious effort by A to understand B's feelings is that those As who undertake such diagnosis often end up changing their own objectives. An A who takes time to find out about an employee before disciplining him may end up changing his attitude toward the employee and hence changing his own behavior instead of B's. The guy isn't a lazy bum after all; he had reasons.

The "how much" question is an important one, too. In chapter 6 we pointed out that if we demand perfect information for a decision, we may never get to the decision. In the kind of human decision-making we are talking about here, the same statement holds. To what extent must the manager be the psychiatrist of everyone in his department? To what extent need he know their sex lives to improve their working efficiency? Most managers implicitly recognize the diminishing-returns aspect of this problem. "Counseling," listening to people's personal problems, is tricky, for one thing—it has a way of changing the focus of a relationship from its value for business problem-solving to its value in its own psychological right. More than that, after a while it costs a good deal more than it brings in in improved performance. If A needs to know about B, he needs to know the factors immediately relevant to the problem at hand. More might help, it is true, but it might cost far more than it is worth in the total business picture.

The location of responsibility in change situations

In watching As trying to change Bs one may also notice that the responsibility for effecting the change seems to settle in different locations on different occasions. Sometimes A takes all the responsibility, and B none of it. Both A and B tend to see A as the person in charge and B only as an actor. On a road gang, for example, each laborer often seems to be saying to himself: "It is not my responsibility to work, it is the boss's responsibility to make me work. Therefore it is perfectly proper for me to do as little as possible, to do only what the boss can directly manipulate me into doing."

The location of responsibility in A is not limited to labor gangs, and it does not always occur against A's wishes. If anything, many As accept the idea that it is their responsibility to change B and to see that he stays changed. Sales managers sometimes take this view in an extreme form. They properly consider it their job to stimulate salesmen but mistakenly assume that what is their job cannot also be the salesman's job. Since the effects of such stimulation seem to wear off, they feel it must be periodically reinforced. Hence one finds a great deal of emphasis by many sales managers on incentive gimmicks, on "inspirational" sales meetings, and so on. Very often even managers who talk a lot about "delegation" take such a view and succeed too well. Their salesmen end up taking the same view, i.e., that it is not their job to sell so much as it is the manager's job to use magic and gadgetry to get them to sell.

Clearly, the responsibility for change does not have to lie

solely with the changer. It can be shared by changer and changee or even be taken over altogether by the person being changed. From the changee's viewpoint change is equivalent to learning, and learning, we agreed in chapter 6, is an *active* process. If teachers want to motivate their students to learn, one thing they can do is to try to get the student to take the responsibility for his own education, to come to want to learn on his own rather than to sit passively while the teacher pumps learning into his head. Many psychiatrists and counselors will even argue that there is no real hope for effecting much "deep" change in clients unless the clients take such responsibility. But in industry, organizational pressures and ideas about authority tend to make As feel that the responsibility is theirs. They thereby encourage Bs to take the easy, non-responsible course of action.

The advantages of shared responsibility are great for both A and B. For one thing, a B who feels that he wants to change is more likely to change effectively and lastingly than a B who feels no such internal tension. Moreover, no A is likely really to understand the subtleties of B's position better than B himself. No matter how successful A's communication with B, there are probably significant things left uncommunicated. So that if A takes sole responsibility, he may find himself trying to solve a problem, working with less information about the problem than is available to B. If, on the other hand, B takes some of the responsibility for changing, he can take some of his own peculiarities into account, and perhaps A and B can find a new behavior that fills the needs of both.

In summary

In this chapter the spotlight has been on a few common aspects of many behavior-change situations.

The changer, A, has the serious problem of knowing what he is doing. Often As literally do not know what they are doing or why they are doing it. Their motives may be partially unconscious and unperceived and their objectives equally so. Advance thinking through of one's purposes may lead to a reorientation of objectives or even to the abandonment of a change project.

Changees ultimately control the decision to change or not to change. A can influence that decision but he cannot make it. For the decision that B makes represents the integration of the forces imposed upon him by A along with a whole multitude of forces over which A has no control.

Some As try hard to understand B's reasons for his present behavior before attempting to change that behavior. Others make no such effort but depend instead on observed similarities in all people. There are advantages to some degree of diagnosis of B. But if B ultimately controls the decision to change, then perhaps it is more important that B make the diagnosis of himself than that A make it of him. Moreover, the diagnostic process can be conceived of as a fact-finding or a feeling-finding process. The position is taken here that feelings are as important, if not more important, than facts in behavior-change problems.

Final responsibility for changing can rest with A or B, or it can be shared. Behavior changers, especially when they occupy superior positions, are wont to feel that the responsibility for change must lie exclusively with them. But if B can be made to accept some of the responsibility for changing himself, the resulting change may be more lasting and more generalized.

13

Authority
One model for
influence

From the previous chapter's discussion of dimensions of the influence process, we turn now to means and tools, to models for influencing behavior. In this chapter and the three that follow, we shall consider several such models, examining each against the background of chapter 12.

This chapter focuses on the use of authority as the key tool of influence. Authority is worth a whole chapter because so many people in industry feel it is the *only* useful tool for modifying the behavior of other people.

Industrial organizational structures seem even to be designed with authority in mind. We build organizations in the shape of pyramids because that shape makes the exercise of authority easier. Pyramids create differences in rank and status, and the people in higher ranks can use their authority to influence lower ranks. Superiors in industrial organizations almost naturally turn to authority whenever a change problem arises with subordinates. The very idea of *delegating* authority rests on the assumption that authority can help people who have more of it to change the behavior of those who have less of it. In fact, we usually even define the "superior" in a relationship as the person with more authority.

Like other tools, authority can be used expertly or blunderingly. And like other tools, it must be used by men. Top managers have long since unhappily recognized that the delegation of large quantities of authority to middle and lower echelons is no guarantee of effective supervision. If anything, some executives seem to supervise better with less authority than with more. And, contrarily, some supervisors function better with more of it than less. The issue is not only how much authority but how it is used and by whom.

The several meanings of authority

Let's start with some definitions, not to be academic but to try to clarify an important but fuzzy concept. Sometimes when we talk of authority, we are thinking about something formal, like *rank*. Authority can be defined by one's military rank, for example. The captain may not know exactly how much authority he has or even what it is, but he knows he has more than the lieutenant and less than the major.

Authority also has something to do with power, sometimes formal power, again like military rank: power that can be formally changed or delegated. "They," the "top brass," somebody up above, can change one's rank and thereby one's authority and thereby one's power.

Sometimes, however, we relate the words *authority* and *power* differently. We talk about someone with an "authoritative" (synonymous with "powerful") personality. Here we mean something like "influential" or "respect-evoking," but we do not mean formally delegable. We mean something the person carries around *inside* himself, not something he wears on his shoulders.

Besides this mix-up between formal and personal authority, another confusion results from the word. Sometimes we talk about authority from the perspective of the manager who uses it, sometimes from the perspective of the managed on whom it is used. When we identify with the user, authority looks like a mechanism for coordination and control. When we take the perspective of the subordinate, authority looks more psychological; it is a mechanism by which we are rewarded or punished for our behavior.

Once we have clarified and related these different meanings, we can go on to consider the uses of authority and the advantages and disadvantages attached to them. First, however, more clarification is in order.

Formal aspects of authority

Suppose we start defining authority by calling it one kind of power. There are other kinds which we shall discuss in the next chapter. We can narrow it further by defining it as formal, delegable, worn-on-the-shoulders power. By thus restricting it, our picture takes on this form:

Authority is power that enters the two-party relationship through the organization. It is an institutional mechanism that aims to define which of two members of a relationship, A or B, will be the superior. Authority is potential extra power, given by a third party (the organization) to some of its members in order to guarantee an *un*equal distribution of power; in order, in other words, to make sure that some people are chiefs and others Indians.

Sometimes the power thus delegated has nothing to do with relationships. For example, the organization may assign to A the power to spend some of its money for supplies. But very often authority does include power over other people, power to restrict or punish, and power to reward. Thus the president announces to the superintendent, in the presence of the foremen: "You are permitted to decide to fire foremen or keep them; you are permitted to decide to raise foremen's pay to this limit or not to raise it." Now the superintendent has some authority—some additional, formal, potential power over and above any other power he may have carried into his relationship with foremen.

A difficulty arises at this point. An organization (or a powerful person) cannot delegate all the power it possesses, even if it wants to. A president can delegate only certain kinds of power by calling it authority. The forms of power over the satisfaction or frustration of another person's needs are legion. In industry, power may take the form of control over income—a form delegable as authority. Or it may take the form of control over the terms of the relationship. That, too, is delegable as authority. It may be power to provide status or prestige. That, too, may be partly delegable.

But other sources of power are not so readily transferred; for example, the power deriving from an individual's competence and skill or from a member's sensitivity to the needs of another. Sensitivity cannot be delegated. One's name, or one's social standing in a community, or one's whole personality may constitute significant forms of power in a relationship, and they too are nontransferable. In fact, only a fraction of the ways in which one person can control another's needs are readily delegable as authority. The delegable forms include mostly external, nonpersonal kinds of power.

This analysis suggests that a superior who turns immediately and exclusively to his authority is either ignoring many other kinds of power he may possess or else he derives all his power from his authority. In either case his effective range of control over other people will be narrow.

Authority as seen by those who hold it

If we ask a manager if authority is useful to him, he will have some ready and reasonable answers, among them these: Authority is indeed useful because authority is a mechanism for coordination and control in organizations. People have to be gotten to work on time. They have to spend some of their time working, rather than telling stories or visiting the men's room. They have to carry out policy and make appropriate decisions. They have to do all these things if the organization is to move toward its goals in some kind of coordinated fashion.

Certainly if authority is used as a tool for influencing behavior, it is not for influence's sake but for the sake of the organization. Moreover, if it is used most often to restrict and limit individual behavior—and thereby it blocks or frustrates people—that is because organizations are what they are. Industrial organizations are places where people cannot do what they please, where people are required to submit to certain restrictive rules and standards. If people came to work when they felt like it or said what they felt like saying, no industrial organization could survive.

Given this view—and it is an extremely reasonable one—authority is a tool to restrict behavior (even if restriction frustrates), to create necessary homogeneity by leveling out individual variations. It is an important and efficient tool because it has the advantages of the shotgun over the rifle. We can broadcast restrictions, rules, and limits, and then use our authority to back up the rules when someone steps out of bounds. The mere presence of authority (precisely because it can be used to frustrate nonconformists) will keep most people within the rules most of the time.

The legal structure seems a fair analogy. Laws, in a sense, constitute a threat of frustration for anyone in the population who steps outside the bounds. We need laws even though most people obey without threat. However, to carry the legal analogy a little further, even the threat of frustration can become insufficient when a specific law is seen by too many people to be too restrictive. The issue here is much like the issue of frustration versus deprivation (chapter 4). Restriction that only deprives is tolerable, especially if it has accompanying rewards; restriction that frustrates can backfire.

Authority as seen from the underside

We cannot observe authority in action just by observing the boss. Whether A has or has not blocked or frustrated B is determined almost entirely by B's interpretation of A's actions. The perceived world, we said in chapter 3, is the world that determines behavior. Thus the mere presence of the company president in a department may constitute a block for some people in that department. Or an extremely insecure employee, with a distrustful set of attitudes toward superiors, may interpret *any* act by a superior as a threat of frustration, even if the superior is busy patting him on the head. In fact, a superior almost always has to work harder than an equal or a subordinate in order to be seen as a rewarding, nonrestrictive force. The reason again is the dependency of the subordinate on the superior. No matter how nice Papa may be, he is still Papa, and the belt of authority around his middle *could* be used as a whip.

Even though the boss's position carries continual implications of potential frustration, the intensity of such implications depends on the boss's own behavior. Certainly many organizational superiors use their authority in ways that obtain a great deal of confidence from their subordinates. Limited and consistent restriction can be seen by most of us as "reasonable," if the atmosphere of a department is generally satisfying of our social and egoistic needs.

Basically, then, most subordinates probably see authority in the same way superiors do, as a tool for restricting and controlling their activities. But though they may see the same thing, they attach different meanings to it. While the boss interprets restriction in organizational terms as control and coordination, the subordinates' interpretation may be far more personal. Authority is a mechanism for satisfying or frustrating their personal needs in a dependent relationship.

Recently some impressive research has been carried out demonstrating just how much many of us have come to accept authority and to obey it almost without question. The experiments were typical psychological ones in which volunteer students were paid to serve as subjects. They were asked to help as trainers in a teaching experiment designed to test the effects of punishment on learning. They were given an electric shocking device and told to push the shock button every time the "learner" in the next room gave a wrong answer. They were also told to increase the intensity of shock with each wrong answer, if necessary, up to a point on the machine scale marked with danger warnings. The "learner" in the next room was actually part of the experimental team. His job was to groan and on occasion scream in pain as the shock got stronger. He would, in late stages of the experiment, beg to be released, and warn the trainer that he suffered from a heart ailment.

The disturbing outcome was that a very large number of subjects put in the trainer's role continued to give shocks up to the maximum, obeying the experimenter, who simply kept telling them to go on despite the pleas and cries of the tortured learner.

Some pros and cons of
the use of authority

From the manager's viewpoint the advantages of authority, especially restrictively used authority, are huge. We have already cited one of them, the control and coordination advantage. There are many others too.

For one thing, one doesn't have to know much about any particular Joe Doaks to be fairly certain that firing him or cutting his pay or demoting him will strike at some important needs and thereby keep him in line. But one might have to know a good deal about the same employee to find out how to make work more fun for him.

A corollary advantage, then, is simplicity. Authority as a restrictive tool does not require much subtlety or much understanding of people's motives. How simple it is to spank a child when he misbehaves, and how difficult and complicated to distract him or to provide substitute satisfactions or to "explain" the situation. Given a hundred children, how much easier it is to keep them in line by punishing a few recalcitrants than to teach them all to feel "responsible."

No matter how "improper," we cannot ignore the fact that exerting authority is often personally gratifying to superiors, and therefore attractive. The exercise of discipline can be reassuring to those who need reassurance about themselves. Moreover, authority fits neatly with a superior's needs, if he has any, to blow off aggression deriving from his own frustration. When the father spanks the child, not only does he change the child's behavior, he also provides himself with an outlet for tensions built up in him by his own boss, or by his wife, or by the irritating, troublesome child.

Similarly, authority is sometimes seen, perhaps properly, as a way for a superior to guarantee his superiority. If his subordinates know that a superior can and will punish readily, they are likely to behave respectfully and submissively, at least in his presence. The reassurance derived from these demonstrations of respect may constitute a great distortion in feedback channels, but it can be helpful to the superior's own uncertain psyche. The superior who takes an essentially supportive approach has no such reassurance. Like the good big brother of chapter 2, he may be complained to and complained against. He may get true feedback, even if it is unpleasant. He may have to tolerate emotionally upset people telling him stupid, even insulting things.

Restrictive authority has another kind of advantage: speed. A do-it-or-else order eliminates the time-consuming dillydallying of feedback. But speed, as chapter 11 pointed out, may cost accuracy or morale. Where those issues are not critical, speed may be worth its costs.

Restrictive authority, we have said, also has the advantage of imposing orderliness and conformity upon an organization. By a threat to reduce some opportunities for need satisfaction, large numbers of people can be made to conform to fundamental regulations. A manager must make *sure* that his people stay through the required eight hours of the day. Even though the great majority may conform without external threat, the superior has to guarantee minimum conformity by all employees. The job of obtaining willing or self-imposed conformity without threat just looks too big to handle.

Moreover, this restrictive authority is efficient because it can be used on large numbers of people at the same time, even when one doesn't know much about the people.

If those are the pros, here are some cons worth thinking about. First, restriction may have some by-products. When A's activity interferes with B's efforts to satisfy important needs, B may not sit still very long. A often finds he has caught crabs instead of lobsters. He has changed behavior he had not intended to change as well as (or instead of) behavior he did intend to change. The child who is spanked every time he puts his hand into the cookie jar may learn to keep his hand out of the cookie jar, or he may learn to go to the jar only when Mama isn't looking. He may also learn (irrationally) that his parents are out to keep him from getting what he wants. Employees who expect to be censured whenever they are caught loafing may learn to *act* busy (and *when* to act busy) and also that the boss is an enemy. They are thereby provided with a challenging game to play against the boss: who can think up the best ways of loafing without getting caught—a game in which they can feel that justice is on their side, and a game they can usually win.

Restrictions, then, can be effective in changing specific *actions* in the direction A wants (B will *act* busy), but often only to the minimum that B can get away with. It is less likely to change B's attitudes, and when it does it may change them in the wrong direction, in the general direction of distrust and hostility.

Moreover, the circular element described in chapter 2 often enters the scene when restrictive authority is called upon. Restriction includes the possibility of a downward spiraling relationship. A begins by trying to change B through threatening frustration. B changes to the extent that he feels he must, but because he has been frustrated he will feel aggressive and in one way or another he may try to retaliate. A uses more restriction, this time to control the retaliation. Again B is frustrated, and wants even more to retaliate. And so it goes.

It might seem that a serious downward spiral can occur only in relationships between equals. If B is extremely subordinate, he should not have enough power to retaliate effectively. But subordinates do have power in relationships, even though the power may be considerably less than the superior's. As long as B has any power, and as long as the relationship exists, he can retaliate. Sometimes he does it by joining together with other Bs, perhaps to form a union. Sometimes he does it by cutting down or distorting the flow of feedback on which the superior depends so heavily. Often several Bs work together informally. I know, for instance, of a group of middle-management people who succeeded very well in defeating a superior they had come to dislike. Their method was passive resistance. They simply did everything the superior asked them to do—*and no more.* For every problem that arose, each of the three went to him for a decision. They took no initiatives, solved no problems by themselves. The superior was soon forced into the impossible position of trying to do every job in the department by himself.

The tenuousness and the self-defeating weakness of reliance on restrictive authority becomes apparent right here. When his authority has been "undermined" by the "sabotage" of subordinates, the superior who has depended on authority is likely immediately to assume that what he needs is *more authority,* because authority is the only tool he knows how to use. But can the president, in fact, delegate any authority by which the superior can coerce his subordinates into doing more than they are told? More likely the president simply begins to view the superior as the person on whom it is now appropriate to exert his (the president's) restrictive authority.

Such cases are many, and they are understandable. It is a serious error to assume that the *greater* power in a relationship equals the *only* power. As parents we may start out feeling that power lies exclusively in our hands, only to change our minds radically when one of the children runs away from home or gets hurt. It is also a serious error to think that delegable power—authority—is a useful weapon in *all* conflicts.

Still another difficulty with restrictive authority is its relative irreversibility. It is just not so easy to pat a subordinate's head after spanking him as it is to spank him after patting. For human beings have memories, and since restriction tends to reduce feedback loops rather than to build them, a series of restrictive experiences for B may destroy the possibility of further communication between A and B. Once A has lost communication contact, *no* tools of influence are useful.

In fact, the irreversibility of restrictive methods sometimes creates difficulties even for those who preach a supportive, "human relations" approach to these problems. A restrictive industrial manager, exposed to human-relations propaganda, will sometimes suddenly see the light and change his methods completely. The scowl turns to a smile; the office door is thrown open; a ration of grog is distributed to all hands. Then comes the rude awakening. Subordinates don't behave right. They don't dance in the aisles. They get drunk on the grog. They "take advantage" of their new freedom. A then decides he was taken in by the longhairs. He reverts to the "right" way, the way he had been using to begin with.

Obviously this kind of sudden reversal from frustration to satisfaction is silly, just as it is silly to leave a candy-starved child alone with five pounds of chocolates. The child is likely to stuff himself. His behavior is then taken as proof that letting children have their own way does not work.

Added together, the pros and cons of restrictive authority lead toward the conclusion that, in general, restrictive methods may be effective in situations that meet some or all of these conditions: (1) the change that A is trying to bring about is a change in specific overt action, rather than in generalized action or attitude; (2) the restrictions are seen by B as depriving rather than frustrating; (3) the balance of power is such that B's power is minimal and A's maximal. One might add a fourth condition: restriction can be effective when speed and/or uniformity are critical.

In a way, industry has already learned some of these lessons, mostly the hard way. Authority as a direct and open restrictive weapon is, in fact, used more consciously at lower levels than at higher ones. Lower levels are (or once were) the levels at which B's actions, more than his attitudes, are the targets. They are also the levels at which employees have generally already retaliated against frustration by organizing, so that restrictions, openly imposed, are now depriving more than frustrating. And lower levels were also the levels at which the power difference between A and B used to be greatest, though those conditions, too, obtain less clearly today than they used to.

At higher levels we have tended to be more interested in changing attitudes than actions, and we have perceived that Bs have power, too. So, broadly speaking, we lean less heavily on restrictive authority as we move up the pyramid. A vice-president who shows up a half-hour late is not likely to be "disciplined."

Key ideas in the authoritarian model

Consider now the relationships between this discussion of authority and our discussion in the preceding chapter of the dimensions of the influence problem.

First, what kinds of motives is the user of authority likely to be working from? Toward what objectives? Usually when we label someone with the word "authoritarian," we intend to connote domineering, power-seeking motives. And certainly many of us are motivated by needs for power and dominance when we order our subordinates around. But many of us also use authority for less emotional, more rational reasons. Authority, in any complex social system, is a means to orderliness. We use authority as a mechanism to coordinate complex, multiperson activities, as well as a mechanism of control.

Second, what kinds of assumptions about B's motivations are made in such authoritarian views? One may be the old white-man's-burden assumption: the assumption that other people, like our children or our subordinates, are too dull or naïve to understand anything but the direct use of authority or too lazy to work without a push. Another very different assumption that more rarely underlies the use of authority is that B perceives the world as we do, as far as authority is concerned; that he perceives our use of authority as reasonable and *legitimate*. It may not be that B is stupid at all. He may be quite intelligent, intelligent enough in fact to recognize the need for legitimate authority in this realm of activity.

By the first view, the commanding officer gives the orders because the troops can't or won't make their own decisions. By the second view, the CO gives the orders because the situation demands some single center of control; because the CO's role is legitimate and necessary.

Third, what assumptions do the authoritarian models make about the relations between A and B? First, they assume that the responsibility for change lies with A rather than B. In fact it is precisely out of authoritarian models that the idea that "authority requires responsibility" has emerged. When I give an instruction, by this view, its outcome is *my* responsibility. Responsibility is the burdensome but legitimate price I must pay for the right to give such orders.

Clearly, then, authoritarian motivation may range from needs for self-aggrandizement or protection of the status quo to needs for efficiency and achievement and orderliness. Notice, however, that these motives do not involve social needs for affiliation or love, nor is there very much emphasis on A's drive for personal success or upward movement. These latter two sets of needs show up much more strongly, as we shall see, in other models.

Notice, too, that the use of authoritarian means is usually quite direct and open. There is no slipperiness or circumlocution about an honest-to-god authoritarian boss. He gives his orders straight, clean, and, perhaps, nasty, too. Moreover, there is an impersonal quality to authoritarian influence. It is rules and contracts that are called upon for justification, rather than personal emotions like affection or hate. The authoritarian father takes his son to the woodshed—or he believes he does—because the boy has broken known rules, or because the boy "has to learn." He does not consciously take him there out of hate or vindictiveness. Conversely he does not offer rewards out of love or personal esteem, but rather because B has lived up to the rules, won the race, carried out his "duties."

It is these ideas then that prevail in the authoritarian model; the ideas of order, efficiency, system in a world full of people who are at best basically lazy; the idea of legitimate "rights" to use authority; the idea of impersonal, rational "contracts" between employer and employee.

Let us contrast these ideas now with the ones we shall encounter in the next three chapters on other approaches to influence.

In summary

Formal authority is a delegable kind of power. Power to influence behavior may also derive from other sources, largely from the skills, personality, and possessions of the changer.

Restrictive authority is seen by managers as a tool for coordination and control. It has advantages in simplicity and speed and in personal gratification to powerful changers who feel unsure of themselves. It also helps to establish a minimum level of conformity by all subordinates to the superior's standards.

A major difficulty inherent in restrictive authority is the probability of secondary changes in attitude along with desired changes in act-behavior. Restriction may constitute frustration and may consequently be followed by aggression toward the changer. Restriction may then incur only a minimal amount of the desired behavior change while also incurring significant increases in hostility and decreases in feedback. Restriction may thereby destroy relationships.

Authority, as a restrictive mechanism, seems to be most useful in short-term, specific situations, where B's retaliatory power is minimal, where the change sought is change in specific overt action, and where the restrictions are perceived as depriving rather than frustrating.

The authoritarian view of influence is likely to be motivated in part by needs for order, efficiency, and control. It assumes either that B is less competent than A or that A's role legitimizes A's use of authority on B. And it assumes a kind of B who will accept and live by impersonal rules and social contracts.

Pressure and coercion
A second model
for influence

The power we considered in the last chapter was largely institutionalized into a quasi-legal system of roles. Everybody
knows that majors can give orders to captains. Indeed, the
extent of that major's authority may even be quite clearly
specified. But the kind of power we consider in this chapter
isn't that bounded, legitimated kind. It's the power that one
picks up where one finds it, and uses for his own or his
group's ends only so long as it works. In this chapter, then,
we focus on coercive power—on blackmail, pressure, threat
—the power tactic almost all of us despise, and almost all of
us use. In 1972 such a chapter seems to this writer to be
necessary. Indeed, I wonder now how I could have been so
naïve as to ignore it in previous editions.

This will be a short chapter because, psychologically speaking, we don't know very much about blackmail and pressure
and other more raw forms of power.

Power as reduction

In this chapter, then, we remind the reader that much of the
influence practiced in the world takes the form of blackmail,
terror, threat. Such coercive power tactics usually depend on
the *reduction* (or threat of reduction) of other people's means
to need satisfaction, accompanied by a demand for behavior
change.

The powerful nation masses its troops at the border of the
weak one and says, "Unless you return that territory (which
is, of course, historically rightfully ours) we will invade you."
The gunman demands, "If you want your life, give me your
money."

But notice: "Come to work on time," says the foreman, "or
you'll be fired." That's reductive use of power, too, isn't it? But
for a foreman to threaten to fire a worker is just a legitimate
use of authority, isn't it?

So one of the big issues that arises here is that issue of social *legitimacy.* When is such reductive power considered by the relevant group, or by the larger society, or by the world legitimate or illegitimate? When is such behavior within the rules and when isn't it? And who makes the rules, and how are they changed? That foreman could have "legitimately" threatened to fire that worker in 1920, but because workers used some then illegitimate power tactics, they were able to change the game rules, so that that foreman's behavior may not be legitimate today.

We are thus dealing with a great big floating crap game in this chapter, with the changing borderland of social rules and social values. But we are also examining the psychological issue of the reductive uses of power.

Let's consider that psychological issue a little more before returning to the broader social issue.

Notice that the attempt to influence by reduction may not work for several reasons. The foreman may have misjudged the relevance of his threat. This week B may be developing a new life style that doesn't call for a job at all. The foreman may also have misjudged B's vulnerability. Our B may have enough support from his buddies so that he's willing to test the foreman's ability to carry out his threat. B organizes other Bs, for example, and sometimes discovers that the foreman may be very scared of having his whole department aligned against him. Now carry the same conception along to areas not quite covered by the rules of the game and we are in the realm of this chapter. "Give me an exclusive interview," demands the columnist of the senator, "or I will publish a story about your weekend with your secretary." "Give up those defense contracts," demand some students of the university president, "or we'll sit in in your office." "Convince your people to work at our rates," says the company president to the small-town mayor, "or we will move our plant out of town."

Power and dependency

Notice, too, how closely associated power is to the problem of dependency we discussed in part 1. If B is more dependent on A than A is on B, then A has the potential for exerting power over B.

But we come now to the difficult question: how does one decide which member of a relationship is the more dependent? Most of the time the answer to that question appears more obvious than it really is. It is obvious that the lieutenant has power over the sergeant. Or is it obvious? It is obvious that the teacher has more power than his student. The teacher can fail the student or discipline him. But if you have lived around a university during the last decade, you know that the balance of power in the teacher-student relationship has become much less clear. Students fill out faculty rating forms these days, and the dean reads them. Or they write letters to the campus paper or stand outside the classroom singing songs about the teacher. Who's really in charge? Who's influencing whom? The reader surely can go on and cite other examples from his own experience. They may range from the father's discovery that his son is no longer willing to do what he's told (and may be able to back up his unwillingness) to the panic of the young officer when he discovers that his men are just going to stand there deadpan and not do what he has ordered them to do.

There is another kind of dependency which for most of us has been so implicit and so pervasive that we are seldom even conscious of it. It is the dependency involved in our relationship with the aggregate of persons we call society. It is our dependency, in effect, on law and order, our expectation that other people on the street, *all* other people, will obey minimal social rules in their interactions with us. When that dependency is violated, when one of us is mugged or someone smashes a window of our home, we begin to appreciate both the extent of our dependency on societal rules and the fragility of these rules. If we consider the other side of that same coin, we can empathize with what must be the exhilarating discovery of power that comes with a successful breaking of the social rules. How exhilarating it must have been for students to discover the vulnerability of the university, to discover, as it were, the power of their own muscle.

Power and the rules of the game

The important point is that A may appear more powerful than B, but may in fact be more powerful *only so long as both A and B play the game within a particular system of social rules*. Those rules, implicit or explicit, may range from the acceptance of the hierarchy of authority in the organization to mutual respect for private property and to a mutual agreement not to use physical force. One important way to influence other people is by unexpectedly violating the rules of the relationship. Those violations can range from captors torturing prisoners, despite the regulations of the Geneva Convention, to students breaking classroom windows, to the politician making up and broadcasting the big lie about an opposing candidate. Notice that rule-breaking is not the property of underdogs alone. It can be done by those at the top of the relationship, by a peer, and by those at the bottom. In the short run it is an infuriating and often terrifying experience for its recipients and a most difficult tactic to defend oneself against.

In this chapter, what we mean by coercive power is power used outside or at the very edges of the rules.

Some sources of coercive power

If the reader is interested in the techniques of using coercive power, we can refer him to a whole variety of handbooks. They include a tactical manual on guerrilla warfare by Che Guevara, police handbooks, some tactical statements made by the Students for a Democratic Society, and the military interrogation techniques of the Chinese or, for that matter, the U.S. military. Man's skillfulness in coercive persuasion is as old as man. We've been extraordinarily creative in developing everything from torture racks to isolation cells. Man is expert in the techniques of extortion and blackmail, riot and political pressure.

But this chapter is not intended as a treatise on the tactics of coercion. It is intended rather as a discussion of that power which makes it possible for one person to coerce another.

Most of the sources we shall discuss supply "legitimate" power, but they can also be used as sources of coercion. Clearly, one such source is ownership. If I have the Bomb and you don't, I can coerce you. If I have money and you don't, I can coerce you if your needs are susceptible to manipulation by money. That last qualification brings up the issue of relativity again: I can coerce you only if the resources I have are useful in reducing your possibilities for need satisfaction. If your needs are irrelevant to my resources, I have no power over you. If your needs change so that they are no longer relevant to my resources, I no longer have power over you.

Another traditional source of rule-breaking power lies in numbers. Throughout the history of man, from the uprisings of the slaves to the organization of workers and the massing of armies, numbers have been one of the great sources of coercive power, modifying the behavior of kings and college presidents and even, on occasion, of generals. But numbers are not always, let us remember, used in the interest of the good guys. Crowds carry out lynchings, too.

We must not forget still another extremely large and important power source of a very different and much more direct kind, anonymity. This time we are talking about a

source which is seldom legitimate, almost always directly coercive. If you've ever had a burglar stick a gun in your ribs,
you have experienced one manifestation of power that rides
on anonymity. If you have ever received an anonymous
threatening phone call or have had a cross burned on your
lawn, you have been exposed to this source. Once again, notice that this kind of rule-breaking, coercive behavior is not
necessarily limited to the underdog. On many occasions it is
used by those in authority: from leaking anonymous stories
to the press to having agents start revolutions. And notice
that such coercive behavior is almost never officially sanc-
tioned by society.

Business organizations and rule-breaking power

Here is an assertion we are ready to defend: American business organizations are now among the most civilized institutions in American society. *Civilized* in that assertion means
working within the rules.

That assertion is both descriptively defensible and behaviorally understandable. Businesses generally influence within
the rules these days, though occasionally they break them.
Within the organization there are still plenty of examples,
too, of the use of power tactics by one group against another,
very much in the tradition of power politics. Certainly there
are conflicts within the executive suite. But outside-the-rules
coercive behavior has become very rare indeed within the organization itself. Executives don't strive for power in the
same nefarious ways that dukes and princes used to. They
don't assassinate one another or kidnap one another's
children. Nowadays they don't even—very often—set torches
to their own shops in order to collect the insurance, or to a
competitor's in order to put him out of business.

But they are by no means clean either, particularly in their
relationships outside the organization. Private businesses
have been known to bribe city officials. And certainly private
organizations, particularly in the financial and marketing
sectors, have been extremely creative in using tactics just
barely within the rules in order to get what they wanted.

Of course, it wasn't very long ago that the tactics of coercion were widely used by American business, internally and
externally. Private businesses hired armies to beat down
union organizers. They engaged in physical combat with
other businesses for territorial rights, as in the days of
railroad construction. They have used (and continue to use)
espionage mechanisms.

But they are cleaner than many other institutions in our society, cleaner than businesses in many other countries, and cleaner than they used to be.

But if so, why? Because they are run by beautiful people? Perhaps because they've made it, because they have achieved legitimate power. They have created enough of the rules so that they don't need to break them very often. They have become the establishment.

By this line of analysis, we should expect the greatest use of outside-the-rules power, either by groups on the outside looking in, or by groups on the inside when they feel their kinds of rules are seriously threatened. It follows, doesn't it, that if we are in a period of social upheaval, we should expect more coercive pressures from weak groups trying to make their way to legitimate power, like unions a generation ago and militant black groups now, and more coercive pressures from powerful groups which feel their power is threatened, like southern whites and business organizations.

In summary

This chapter is about coercive power tactics as mechanisms of influence. Such tactics, ranging from torture to the torch, have been around for a long time. A major protection against them has been the evolution of social rules and humanitarian values. Those rules and those values, of course, depend heavily on social consensus. Coercive tactics are periodically used, however, by deviant members or by legitimate organized authority to keep underdogs in line. They are also widely and understandably used by underdogs, who justify them as the only feasible means to the ends that they desperately seek. No society in history has ever developed foolproof protection against the use of such coercive tactics by other societies, by recalcitrant members of their own society, or by their own institutions under threat. Our society is no exception. Business organizations have perhaps come as close to moving beyond the need for such extreme coercive tactics as any institution in society. One might have guessed a decade ago that universities had come even closer. It is now clear that they have not. It behooves the business manager, even now, to look to his organization's defenses against such tactics and even more to the capacity of his organization to deal with them without resorting to the same tactics.

So this is a red alert chapter. Its message: Watch out! Coercive power is not dead. The rules of the societal game can crumble more easily than most of us had thought.

Manipulation
Another model for influence

If we were to ask a military officer how he gets his subordinates to do things, he would talk about issuing orders and commands. But if we ask a salesman how he gets people to buy things, or a politician how he gets people to vote for him, or a successful courtesan how she gets mink coats from men —all these are apt to give different answers, but answers that have some common elements. The kind of things we would expect to hear are things like these: "You've got to make them think it's their idea." "You've got to make them like you." "You've got to sell yourself." "You've got to be sincere." "You have to pay attention to their interests and the things that are really important to them." "You've got to make them think they're in charge."

Just how are these answers different—as they obviously are—from the kinds of authoritarian ideas we talked about in chapter 13 and the power tactics of chapter 14?

One of the biggest differences, of course, is in the fact that the quotations we just listed pay a great deal of attention to human emotions and human needs. They recognize that human beings are their objects of influence, and that human beings are complex systems with needs for affection, for dependency, for support, for approval and recognition, and all the rest. In this respect they contrast sharply with the authoritarian model, which assumed a kind of rational, hardheaded man who obeys rules and understands abstract justice.

But those quotations have another distinct flavor too. They have a quality of surreptitiousness, of slipperiness, at least in their implications. "You've got to make them think it's their idea," implies, of course, that the idea is really yours, not theirs.

We notice a third quality, too. These are the kinds of ideas or beliefs that any of us might spout in talking about dealing with peers or superiors; but we would be less likely to pay much attention to them when dealing with our subordinates.

They differ from the authoritarian ideas in another way too. The person using an authoritarian model is likely to be fairly open and direct. When your boss tells you to do something right now there's nothing very secret about his motives or objectives. He says clearly what he wants. But when the salesman, or the courtesan, or the politician sidles up to you, then you begin to suspect some unannounced motives, some hidden purposes.

This last point probably gets at the heart of the manipulative problem. It is the reason that so many of us want to reject it and retaliate against it. For this kind of attitude, the I-will-make-you-think-it's-your-idea attitude, is seen by most of us as an effort to degrade us, to play us for suckers. If A succeeds, then B never realizes he was manipulated and A wins. But if A fails and if B realizes suddenly that he is being manipulated, then B is apt to retaliate rather violently.

The growth of the manipulative models

The manipulative models have been with us for a long, long time. They show up in the writings of Machiavelli and even earlier. Since 1930 or so modern versions have become especially popular in selling and sales training, an understandable phenomenon. For the salesman enters into a relationship of his own initiation with customers who are usually at least as powerful as he is. Authority isn't a very useful tool for him. On the other hand, the salesman has a rather clear and precise objective, which varies very little from day to day or customer to customer. He doesn't want his customers to buy an automobile, he wants them to buy a Ford. So the salesman's problem is very clear. It is to get that man to do what A wants him to do, but to do it without resorting to power tactics.

Out of this specific problem—the problem of trying to get someone else to do precisely what I want him to do, without using authority or other direct power—there has emerged a series of sophisticated manipulative models for influence. These models all share five key ideas, although they vary considerably from one to another in other respects. The five ideas are these:

1. A's motives should not be made fully known to B. A wants to sell magazine subscriptions, but he starts out to convince B that A is really not selling anything at all, just offering free samples. The mistress really wants a mink coat, but the motives she communicates are love and nurturance.

2. Second, the manipulative models usually use the relationship between A and B as a tool for influence. Most of the manipulative approaches are essentially two-step processes: step 1 is to develop the relationship with B so that B comes to value it; step 2 is to use the now-valuable relationship itself as a bargaining weapon in bringing about change. The magazine salesman tries to develop in his customer feelings of sympathy and support because he is working his way through barber's college; and having thus developed nurturant needs in the housewife, he offers his magazines as a means for her to show her support. The politician offers favors-jobs, little services to the people of his ward, and then asks of them only the little personal favor of their votes. The paternalistic manager takes a deep personal interest in his people, buys them gifts at Christmas and in other ways develops personal feelings between himself and his employees; and then, consciously or unconsciously, he uses that relationship, with its implications of loyalty and friendship, to get what he wants.

Just for contrast, it is worth pointing out that the complete authoritarian we described two chapters ago does not move in the same direction at all. The personal relationship is set aside for him. The world is a world of rules, not of men. The complete authoritarian sells the product; the manipulator sells himself.

This manipulation of the A-B relationship can be thought of as an effort to create the kind of dissonance we talked about in part 1. First we make another person feel love and loyalty toward us, and then we demand of him that he change the beliefs he now holds dear. Thus we set up an imbalance. For B to love us and keep his contrary beliefs places him in a dissonant state. So he must choose between his beliefs or his feelings toward us. If we're clever, he changes his beliefs. But if we fail, it is understandable that the failure can be explosive, with the possibility of B shifting from extreme love to extreme hate.

3. A third and related characteristic of the manipulative models is the exploitation of dependency between A and B. While the authoritarian exploits dependency, too, he does so directly and always downward in the hierarchy, demanding that subordinates perform or get fired, that children obey or get punished. But the complete manipulator exploits dependency differently. He exploits it in both directions in the power hierarchy, using psychological power rather than legalistic authority. The manipulative executive, for example,

may make his way upward in his organization by becoming dependent on some higher-level executive, and by trying to make that dependency reciprocal. He searches for a sponsor, someone with whom he can develop a son-father kind of relationship. Then, he feels, as the father's star rises so will his. If he can be successfully dependent on some superior, then the superior reciprocally will be dependent on him. Certainly women, in Western society, have learned to manipulate dependency skilfully, even though they seldom have the greater official authority in relationships.

The manipulative executive is likely to exploit dependencies downward, too. He will not count on his impersonal role as the boss, but rather on personal dependency on himself as an individual. He may seek personal, intimate relationships with his people, and then use these deep personal attachments as a base for effecting change.

If he is a really consistent manipulator, he will try to have his superior and/or his subordinates develop very strong attachments to himself, but he will always hold back on the reciprocal end of the deal. A good manipulator never exposes himself completely. Some of his personal motives are always undisclosed. He must never become so entangled either with subordinates or superiors that he cannot abandon them if he needs to.

4. A fourth characteristic of the manipulative approaches is that they are apt to be extremely sophisticated about the psychology of the individual. While the power user ignores matters of feeling and emotion and is apt to be quite insensitive, the manipulator is extremely sensitive to people's humanity, fallibility, and emotionality. The good manipulator exploits people's needs for approval, support, recognition, dependency, participation. Aware of the potency of these needs in his two-step process, he makes great efforts to sell himself by satisfying other people's needs for recognition and attention. This awareness of widespread psychological starvation in our society is of course precisely what the over-the-line manipulators—the con men—exploit so successfully in old widows and teenagers. But within the law, it can be these same kinds of needs that a manipulative wife can exploit in her husband; currying favor with him, flattering him, providing him with satisfactions that may be hard to come by elsewhere in the world. She thus increases the value of the relationship and the extent to which she may use it as a bargaining weapon. But she is also giving him what he needs.

5. A fifth related general characteristic of these models, a

characteristic that is really just an extension of the two-step process, is gradualness. The manipulator does not move precipitously, nor directly, nor completely. He influences in bits and pieces. Unlike the coercive holdup man, the con man moves slowly, establishing a relationship with his prey, letting him win a few hands of poker, and only gradually moving him along to where he wants him. If he is a good con man, he even "cools out the mark" after he has taken him; he takes steps to make the widow feel good after she has been bilked of her funds, so that she will not go to the police or retaliate against him.

Finally, it is worth pointing out that manipulative models not only exploit the relationship between A and B, but also *the relationships between B and other people*. There is a step beyond the process of developing a relationship between you and me so that I can later press you to do what I want you to do. That next step is the use of group pressures, pressures by other people, Cs and Ds. The early primitive stages of the human-relations movement represented such a transfer from the exploitation of the A-B relationship to the exploitation by A of the relationship between B and others.

Much of the early talk about group participation, and many of the early experiments on group decisions, represented such an extension of the manipulative models. A still wanted to get people to do what he wanted them to do. And A still kept some of his motives to himself. But now A used group discussion as a tool, and he did not work hard to develop the relationship between himself and the group. Rather he tried to develop cohesiveness and rapport *within the group*. Then when the group began to move toward a particular direction of behavior, the individual member was pressed by the group to conform to the group's wishes. This device was not new, of course, even several decades ago. Any good rabble-rousing politician knows how easy it is to keep someone from saying "no" in a public meeting after 90 percent of the crowd has already shouted "yes."

So group participation as a tool for influencing behavior had its problems, too, especially in its earlier forms. One got workers to accept a methods change (a *predetermined* methods change) by holding group discussions and by getting group commitments to a decision to change. But in our next chapter we will consider some more recent developments on the participative side: collaborative methods for trying to effect change that make large use of groups, but which try to escape from some of the ethical and technical difficulties of manipulation. As we shall see, this fourth model differs quite distinctly from the authoritarian, the coercive, and the manipulative models.

In summary

The manipulative models for effecting change have grown up mostly in settings wherein the use of authority was impossible, settings in which A is a peer or subordinate of B. The several manipulative models share some basic ideas: Manipulative As withhold some of their motivation from public exposure. Manipulative As tend to develop close relationships with B, often dependent relationships, and then to use that relationship as a tool. The manipulative models tend to take two steps in the influence process, the relationship step and then the influence step. Manipulative As are sensitive to human needs and emotions, and they tend to work in bits and pieces, by indirection rather than by direction.

One wonders sometimes whether the industrial game really is played the manipulative way, as most novelists about business like to describe it. If it is indeed such a game, need it continue to be?

16

Collaborative models Influence without power

If power is such a lethal tool and manipulation such a questionable one, what are the alternatives?

Some readers may already have discerned and perhaps been disappointed by the absence of rules of thumb in this section. The absence will continue, not wilfully, but because the nature of the influence process obviates magical little rules. The process of influencing behavior does not reside in one person. It resides in the *relationship*. If Bs stood still, As could indeed devise rules for influencing Bs. But Bs move, respond, retaliate, change. So if we are to come up with any rules at all, they must be rules governing the behavior of the A-B relationship, not just the behavior of one of the elements.

It is true that we could play probabilities. We could say to our salesmen: "This is your spiel. Run it off like a phonograph record. Seventy-five percent of your clients will throw you out. Twenty-five percent might be influenced." But if a manager takes that view about influencing his subordinates, or his peers, or his superiors, he is in for trouble.

Without expecting rules for answers, then, we can ask: What are the alternatives to the use of authority or manipulation?

The AA model

Consider Alcoholics Anonymous. That organization effects deep and difficult influence with considerable success. Their objective is to cause drinkers to stop drinking. What are the methods by which such a goal can be achieved?

Many people have tried many methods on alcoholics. Wives have threatened to leave their drinking husbands. Churches have warned drinkers of everlasting punishment for their sins. "Conditioned reflexers" (I put the phrase in quotes because such views of conditioning do not do justice to conditioning concepts) have added cathartics to the alcoholic's drink so that he gets nauseous and sick.

All these are essentially restrictive methods, using power or manipulation to restrict. They are concerned with symptoms rather than causes. They aim at changing overt behavior rather than the more fundamental need or attitude.

AA approaches the problem quite differently. Essentially, their procedure is the following:

They make the availability of their services (and their motives) known to the alcoholic (and he may choose not to avail himself of them).

If he chooses to attend a meeting, he listens to testimonials from ex-alcoholics (and he may be impressed by none of them—in which case he is again free to leave).

If he decides they know what they are talking about, he asks for help (but he doesn't have to).

He is given one or more "buddies"—once alcoholics like himself. The buddies make themselves available (if he chooses to call on them) to talk over his problem or just to hold his hand.

If he decides to try to quit drinking, it is not easy. So he calls on his faith in God, if he has any, and on his buddies. They provide help with support, with hand holding, with a supply of knowledge of the future—i.e., "Sure it's tough, but if you hold on a while longer, you begin to feel different, and then it gets easier, *and we know*." They also provide the knowledge that real change requires a really new way of looking at the world.

When AA is successful, the alcoholic stops drinking. Often he then helps others to stop drinking as one way of handling the new void in himself.

One finds no threat, no command, no surreptitiousness in the process. The alcoholic stops drinking; he is not stopped. He is helped to change himself. He is helped by being shown alternative means, substitute behaviors, new sources of faith —by anything that will fit his needs. This is a predominantly augmentative, supportive process in which responsibility never leaves the changee.

Is management different from AA?

The businessman will point out several differences between the problems faced by Alcoholics Anonymous and the ones he faces. First, AA can afford to wait for people to recognize their own problems and to seek help. The businessman often cannot. He must bring about change even when people don't come to him seeking to be changed. Second, AA can let each man solve his own problem in his own way at his own pace.

The business organization requires conformity to certain standard behaviors and to the pressures of time. Finally, the businessman will complain of the risk in this method, the lack of control over the changee. In AA's approach any alcoholic can just walk out the door any time he feels like it without changing at all. In business we have to be sure that people will do what needs doing; we cannot allow them to decide whether they would like to or not.

The alert reader will add still another objection: Where is the diagnosis, the understanding of causes so heavily emphasized in the preceding chapters of this book? In this AA situation effective behavior change seems to occur without any attempt to look into the source of alcoholism, into the frustrations and the conflicts that probably led to it.

These are partially valid objections, both to AA's method and to the whole-hog applications of the AA model to business problems. But before considering the modifications that need to be made to fit business requirements, it might be useful to consider the similarities between the AA method and those used by some other behavior changers.

Similarities between AA and other approaches

The AA pattern, in its broadest outline, is a pattern that has independently taken hold—for good or evil—in a great many segments of modern American life. It shares with the manipulative models a strong sensitivity to human needs, but there most of the similarity stops. It showed up in chapter 6, with the emphasis on learning as an active, responsible process in the learner. It shows up in educational thinking, in the position that a student's education is an active function of the student as well as of the teacher. The teacher's role is to provide help and knowledge as the student requires it and as he can integrate it. The teacher's job is not to make the student a passive sponge to soak in a pool of pedagogical wisdom, but to help him to help himself.

Child-rearing practices have gone the same way. Today's pediatricians talk to mothers about "demand" schedules, easy toilet training, affection and support. Rigid discipline, even great emphasis on personal cleanliness, have gone by the boards.

Counseling and psychiatry have moved rapidly in the same direction, with "nondirective" therapy and most present-day psychotherapy. Similarly, penology and criminology, with their emphasis on rehabilitation through new skills and new adjustments, have moved in the same permissive, supportive direction.

Some may argue that these methods are precisely what is wrong with present-day America. They make us weak and soft and heaven knows what else. Perhaps they do. But if any businessman feels that these methods will be our ruination, he had better look over his shoulder at his own plant. Related ideas have probably crept in disguise into his own operations. His first-line supervisors are probably practicing manipulative versions of "human-relations" techniques all over the place—especially on him. His market-research people are going motivational. They are using nondirective depth interviews and projective tests in dealing with consumers. Ditto his employment interviewers. His industrial-relations people are probably trying to apply essentially the same ideas to their relationship with the union. And his advertising people certainly are not using whips on the consumers. Even the businessman himself is probably saying things like: "To learn to swim, jump into the water," or, "Experience is the best teacher," or, "You can lead a horse, etc." All these are just other ways of saying that men must at least help to change themselves; others cannot do it all for them.

Applicability of the AA model to management

We said earlier that three major obstacles block the use of the AA approach in industrial problems. Let's examine these difficulties one at a time to see whether or not they really are difficulties and, if they are, to see what modifications are needed.

Here is a simple, but perhaps typical, industrial behavior-change problem:

> A new manager of a staff department grows increasingly concerned about the "weakness" of many people in his group. They seem stolid and unchanging, unimaginative and uncreative. They go on doing things as they have always been done, though it is obvious to the manager that many methods and procedures could be simplified, many new services could be rendered to line people. How can he make them less resistant to new ideas? How can he get them to take a new outlook toward their jobs? How can he get the lead out of their pants?

Getting people to see a problem

Alcoholics Anonymous, for the most part, simply waits for the alcoholic to become unhappy with his alcoholism. Only then do they undertake to change him. Similarly, psychiatrists wait behind their office doors for the patient to feel bad enough to visit a doctor. But the social inefficiencies of such a process are obvious. Many people may be psychologically sick for a long time before the sickness becomes painful or crippling enough to make them look for help. And it doesn't make much sense in education for a teacher just to wait for children to want to learn arithmetic or in business for an executive just to wait for his secretary to want to be more careful of her spelling.

And yet, although the manager cannot wait for people to see a problem, theoretically his people will not change very significantly unless they do see a problem, until they feel the tensions of relevant, unsatisfied needs. So the manager's first problem becomes: How do I make these people feel dissatisfied with their present behavior?

A variety of methods exists. Just waiting is one, and we should not discount it too quickly. Certainly many a young man in industry will notice by himself that a new superior is different from an old one and, apparently out of the clear blue sky, will come voluntarily in search of help, say, in learning how to write better reports. He may already have felt uncomfortably inadequate as he compared other people's writings to his own. Now he has his first opportunity to try to do something about it. The manager who had been wondering how to get this subordinate to improve his reports is now in a superb influence position. So, just waiting for B to encounter problems, to recognize his inadequacies, and to screw up enough courage to ask for help should not be thrown out altogether. Moreover, the very act of *not* acting, of waiting, especially by a new superior, may be seen by subordinates as a sign of tolerance and hence of accessibility.

But there are other possibilities besides waiting. One is to throw the subordinate into situations which will make some inadequacy obvious to him. The superior takes an active part here, but an impersonal part. The subordinate begins to see a problem because of the trouble he gets into with other people; the superior has simply caused these encounters to occur. Thus, a manager may cause one of his people to recognize problems by increasing his responsibility, by sending him out on difficult assignments, by exposing him to meetings with people who make no bones about their attitudes toward his staff. Such behavior by managers is unusual, for managers are wont to reduce the responsibilities of "ineffective" people much more frequently than they are to increase them, thereby reducing risk but also reducing the opportunity for learning.

Again, a superior can get a subordinate to recognize a problem simply through his assertion that a problem exists. Thus, a staff group which has been perfectly happy about the way things are going can be made to recognize a problem if the manager simply announces that the group's work is unsatisfactory. The teacher can do the same for a student by giving him a low grade on an exam. The difficulty here is obvious. Although the manager will probably succeed in getting the group to recognize a problem, he will also succeed (though he may not have attempted it) in having the group blame him for it. The group may decide that its work doesn't need to be changed but that the boss does. And sometimes they can do it. To get people to see a problem by threatening, directly or by innuendo, that if they don't change they will endanger their bread and butter is, of course, straight restriction and carries with it all the dangers inherent in reactions to frustration. The danger is especially great when the source of the threat is the same individual who later wants to "improve" B's behavior.

This is the point at which a third party becomes useful. Parents are often abashed at how easily a new teacher can accomplish what they themselves have been unable to accomplish. Some of the credit given the teacher, or the family doctor, or Uncle Joe, does not belong to them as individuals so much as it does to their roles in the relationship. Anomalous as it may seem, a position of lesser power may often be a better position from which to effect a behavior change than a position of greater power. Our manager may try to start a change with a threat, but then he may have to turn over the rest of the job to the personnel department. The third party can often do much more to effect change from there on out than the manager himself can do. In a sense the manager's action has made personnel's job easy. For now personnel, like AA, receives a knock on the door from a B who has already decided he needs help.

There is something paradoxical in this line of reasoning. This chapter is about methods for effecting change without authority. And yet it seems that one cannot effect change unless some restriction has been going on, so that B feels unsatisfied.

But that is only half the picture. It is true that people are likely to start wanting help after they find out that their present behavior isn't as good as they think it is. But there is a second possibility, too. People can want to change because they learn to want more or better or higher goals. We may start looking for a new car when the old one stops performing. We may also start looking because Detroit has put out some shiny new ones. The manager can add new information to his staff's picture of the world. He can open new promotional avenues, new opportunities for learning, for socializing, for satisfying all sorts of needs that can often stir even the most stolid of old-timers into activity.

This is the problem of raising levels of aspiration. It is a difficult problem. It requires the changer always to keep such opportunities for growth and development open—always new ones, always better ones. For as long as B can foresee new, better, and achievable means to the satisfaction of his needs, he will be ready to change his behavior in the direction of those better means.

The alert reader will notice that many of these techniques for getting B to see a problem are not very easily distinguished from some of the techniques labeled "manipulative" in the last chapter. A's motives aren't always fully disclosed, for example. And many of the suggestions call for indirection if not surreptitiousness. In this respect, as in the case of sensitivity to human needs, it is just plain true that manipulative models parallel part of the collaborative approaches. The differences between the two become clearer when one moves on to the way A uses his relationship with B, and in the locus of control over what will happen.

All this is to say that people don't change unless they get uncomfortable. One may use AA's method of standing by until the world makes the person uncomfortable; or one may do it by trying to raise levels of aspiration so that B himself finds his present behavior inadequate and awkward; or one may get a third party to use his power to make B uncomfortable. Some one of these methods or a combination of them is a theoretical requirement for getting B to think seriously about changing his behavior.

Diagnosis: Why is B doing
What he is doing?

The second objection raised to the Alcoholics Anonymous method is that AA seems to ignore the causes of B's alcoholism. A good deal of emphasis earlier in this book was placed on the importance of understanding the reasons for B's present behavior, either the factual or the emotional reasons. Now a model shows up in which relatively little emphasis is given to such diagnosis.

The problem really is this one: Who must make the diagnosis? In many cases, it is more important for B to understand the causes of his own behavior than for A to understand those causes. In the AA model the buddy provides the alcoholic with an opportunity to communicate any facts or feelings that may be relevant. If they are communicated aloud, it is true that the buddy may come to understand them, but, much more important, the alcoholic may also come to understand them. And if one already has a man who wants to change, then it is far more important that he understand what he is gaining or losing from his present behavior than that someone else understand it.

This is not to say that A needs no understanding. It is only to say that A's understanding of B's problem is often not nearly so important as B's own understanding of it.

Let us return here to the problem of the new manager of an ineffective department. His job is to revivify the department—without changing personnel. How much does he have to know about why his people are unimaginative, unenthusiastic, unproductive?

He has to know more about *how* they feel than *why* they feel that way. He does not need a case history on every man so much as he needs enough understanding of feelings to estimate the meanings his actions will evoke. He has to know whether his people have just been waiting for a break and are all ready to grab it or whether they have settled firmly into a path of safe stolidity. He has to know something about their dominant needs and dominant fears. He has to know these things primarily in order to know how to communicate his conception of their inadequacies to them. For to suggest great new responsibilities to people who are fearful even of their small old ones may not get them to recognize a need for change but only to deny it more completely. *What's behind these feelings is usually better left as B's own business.* The present feelings, more than their causes and origins, are the most important working materials of the industrial behavior changer.

Who controls the change situation?

The third objection to the AA method is that AA seems to have so little control over the alcoholics' behavior. At any step along the way B is free to reject the whole process and to leave the situation without changing. In industrial situations, allowing B such opportunities would seem an extremely risky process. But those risks are worth thinking about.

Consider again the new department staff manager. First, as manager, he can always veto what his people decide to do. He can give his subordinates opportunities to change themselves, and, finding that they fail to change in accordance with his wishes, he can then still resort to his authority. So the only risk added by giving B more leeway is the possible loss of time if the method fails.

On the other hand, if the kinds of behavior changes sought were only changes in overt behavior, then there might be a good case for tight control. If all the manager wanted was his people's putting their shovels into the ground and lifting them up full of dirt at specified intervals, and if the manager could afford to stand over them to make sure they carried out the ritual, then obviously he could actually exercise pretty close control. But in practice the kinds of changes the manager usually seeks are changes in brain as well as muscle behavior. He wants his people *to make decisions differently* than they did before, and he knows perfectly well that many of the decisions will have to be made in the manager's absence. Though he can watch to see that a man uses his shovel right, he often cannot watch to see whether he is using his brain right. Since that is the case, is it actually riskier to let subordinates decide they want to change and then to make decisions that fit their changed perceptions of the world? Or is it riskier to force them to change, so that when they face a new decision they face it with a mixed feeling of wanting to do it and of resentment against having to do it?

The answer seems clear. The manager's control, in the sense of his ability to foresee his subordinates' behavior, is far greater if he has given them an opportunity to accept or reject change (and knows where they stand) than if he has required change without obtaining "honest" feedback.

Even self-imposed change is uncomfortable

AA does not have an easy time changing people. And people do not even have an easy time changing themselves. Since any behavior change usually represents giving up some previously adequate behavior in favor of some new and untested behavior, any behavior change will be accompanied by some degree of tension and anxiety. So it is with the switch from one job to another—butterflies in the stomach on the day or two preceding the first day on the new job.

Although he uses a permissive, augmentative approach in trying to effect a change in his subordinates, our manager must still expect B to show this kind of tension and anxiety. The changer probably cannot prevent anxiety in B, but he can help to alleviate it by encouraging and supporting B's efforts to change.

A generalized pattern

So the AA method has some limitations and some difficulties for industrial use. But perhaps by making some modifications we can set up a general set of conditions for effecting behavior change in continuing relationships:

1. *B perceives a problem.* AA waits for people to perceive a a problem. In industry one must often take action to get them to recognize that a problem exists and that consequently a change is necessary. We suggested several possibilities, all the way from simply telling B that his present behavior is inadequate to manipulating the world so that he runs into inadequacies in his own behavior. But the changer must always beware lest the problem B perceives is the changer himself.

2. *B takes responsibility for considering alternative ways of behaving (and if possible seeks A's help in discovering additional alternatives).* When B has decided he has a problem calling for change, it is for him to consider the possibilities for change and for A to provide help.

3. *A and B mutually communicate the implications for both A and B of one new method of behavior versus others.* Since A is the person who is seeking the change, and since the change that B selects is important to A, A must have an opportunity to feed back to B the implications of one alternative or another. Thus possibly B may decide to change, but to a behavior that is *still* unacceptable to A. This unacceptability is one real factor in B's deciding whether or not the alternative is feasible.

4. *B selects an alternative which A can accept.* The responsibility for deciding what B shall do and how he shall do it still remains with B. Especially if A is a superior, B's selection will have to be acceptable to A, although *acceptable* may not be the same as *ideal*. This is a little like collective bargaining but even more like a discussion between husband and wife about where they shall take their vacation. If a location can be found that is entirely acceptable to both, all to

the good. If the location is only a satisfactory compromise to each, that is still pretty good. If no compromise is possible, then A, if he is in a position of authority, can always revert to the simple use of the veto.

5. *B tries to change. A supports.* It is at this point that A's role shifts from that of provider of information to helper and supporter and reassurer. For it is here that tension and anxiety may show up in B. After taking a few baby steps in the new method, he may decide that this new behavior is hopeless or ridiculous. A can help by providing knowledge of the future, reassuring, making B feel that he is progressing (if he is actually progressing). It is here, too, that A can expect to come under overt or covert attack. It is A after all who has "forced" B to try this new, awkward, and inefficient way of behaving. The great mistake that A can make is to insist he is not to blame and to argue the facts of the case. What B needs is help, not argument.

6. *B finds the new method successful and integrates it as part of his behavior; or he finds the new method unsuccessful and abandons it.* After being nursed along in his attempt to behave differently, B's skill may increase and he himself may find the new method serving his purposes better than the old. B can then be said to have changed. But if B finds that the new is not so good as the old, he may revert to the earlier method, if that is still possible, or he may move to a third method. If the latter is his choice then the whole process begins again.

These six steps constitute a crude and incomplete set of conditions for behavior change in continuing relationships. It is a difficult set of conditions to bring about. But the important question is whether it is more difficult and more time consuming than the beguilingly simple use of authority or the strategic planfulness of the manipulative ones. If the time and energy that must be devoted to the unforeseen by-products of other methods are added to the total, the restrictive and manipulative processes may be even more difficult than the supportive one. Moreover, one of the most important advantages of supportive methods is that they tend to become easier with time. For Bs who have "been changed" by this method are likely to develop feelings of confidence in A that make future changes in the relationship easier. Such feelings of confidence may even allow A to use authoritarian methods effectively because they are no longer seen as frustrating.

In later chapters we shall try to show how these approaches have generalized to groups and large organizational policies.

In summary

Alcoholics Anonymous seems to do a good job of changing people without much call upon authority and without the guile of manipulation. Its method appears to be uncontrolled and uncertain, but with modifications it may be much more applicable to industrial problems than one might guess.

The basic assumption underlying the AA approach is that people must take most of the responsibility for changing themselves, and changers therefore must be helpers rather than manipulators. A superior's authority thus becomes a supply of means by which to help subordinates satisfy their needs through work rather than a supply of ammunition with which to threaten, reduce, or seduce them.

Money incentives
One effort to influence

Managers, acutely conscious of the paycheck, have tried to turn their control over it into a mechanism of influence. They have devised all sorts of rules for trading money for work, incentive systems among them.

In fact, of all the ways of setting up a work situation that encourages hard work, the one that industry has formalized most is the money-incentive system. Money incentives have come to occupy a central place because money is a common means for satisfying all sorts of diverse needs in our society and because money may be handled and measured. Money is "real"; it is communicable. Many other means to need-satisfaction are abstract and ephemeral. Moreover, money incentives fit with our culture's conception of what work means, with the definition of work as non-satisfying and restrictive activity given by people in exchange for means like money. The means thus earned allow the earner to satisfy his idiosyncratic needs off the job.

In this chapter we shall look at two kinds of money incentive plans—individual and multiple incentives—to see how they fit with the preceding chapters and to see how and when they ought to be useful tools for influence. The first step in such an analysis is a consideration of money as a motive.

The place of money in the hierarchy of motives

Most readers are probably familiar with some of the many surveys designed to find out what workers want from their jobs. Social scientists and personnel people have been quick to point up the results of such surveys—results showing that workers rank money only fourth or fifth among the variety of possible rewards obtainable from their jobs. Workers, including supervisory and research personnel, are likely, in these surveys, to place things like "fair treatment" or "good working conditions" well above money.

It seems to the writer that these are misleading findings. Where management once may have overrated the significance of money (sometimes feeling that this was the only reward due a man for his labors), these rank-ordering surveys directly suggest that money is somehow less important than some other things. The difficulties with this reasoning are two: the presumption that man's motives can be broken down into a static order representing his permanent and unchanging attitudes and the fact that we live in a society which approves the expression of interest in working conditions and supervision and disapproves the expression of interest in money. No "good" supervisor in today's industry will easily admit that his primary motive is money even if it is.

People's wants are neither static nor clear-cut. Instead they are dynamic and conflicting, as part 1 emphasized. Money is important to most people only in relation to the current state of other needs that money cannot satisfy. Any manager would be foolish to accept a list of his employees' rank orderings of motives at face value and try to "do something about them." For wants are seldom permanently satisfiable, even if the ordered list correctly indicates people's current motives.

Money is an important potential motivating force in industry, but not because of its rank on the "most wanted" list. Money is important psychologically for the same reasons that it is important economically: because it is a symbolic substance, a common basis for the exchange of goods and services that are differentially required by different individuals.

One psychologist has proposed a useful scheme into which to fit the motivational power of money. He argues for two gross classes of motives associated with work. One set, which he calls "hygienic" factors, are the aspects of work which do not in themselves provide challenge or incentive, but which are essentially supportive, background factors. These more or less necessary, but not sufficient factors include things like physical working conditions, hours of work, satisfactory working relationships with others, and money. All such aspects of work, by this argument, become important only when they fall below a critical psychological level. Raising them above that level does not contribute positive additional incentives to work.

It is my guess that money is a somewhat more complex factor than the other hygienic factors, serving as a symbol, a surrogate, and an instrumentality for many other needs. Hence the view that money may be a positive incentive, or it may be only a hygienic factor, depending upon—you guessed it—the way it is perceived by the recipient.

A couple of examples: You and I are bright young executives competing for advancement. We were hired at the same time, at the same pay. Our boss must by company merit-rating rules differentiate between us at the end of the year. Also by rule, the one rated higher will get a larger raise. Won't that larger raise motivate both of us to put out? But not of course, for the money itself: just for the symbolic acknowledgment of being the winner. Or try the man at the machine, on a piece rate, just before Christmas. Will he work a little harder to buy a few extra presents?

Individual incentives as tools for influence

Let's start by granting that individual incentive systems have, in fact, frequently increased production in American companies. Let's also grant that they frequently lead to trouble. Our purpose here can be to consider why they sometimes work and why they sometimes cause more trouble than they are worth.

The two assumptions underlying individual incentive systems are these: (1) people want money, and (2) people will expend more effort to obtain more money.

There is nothing wrong with these two assumptions except that they are usually not enough. If a *directly perceivable,* positive, and causal relationship can be arranged between a man's productivity and money, the man's productivity will be greater than when no such relationship exists—other things being equal. The trouble, of course, is that other things are not always equal.

Perhaps by specifying these "other things," we may be able to make them equal. Experience with individual incentives suggests that the other things center on interdependency. We can, for discussion purposes, break the interdependency issue down into these three factors: (1) other people around B; (2) other needs within B; and (3) unrecognized needs within A. Let's look at them one at a time.

B plugging away at his machine is usually not alone. He is in a social environment. B's activity has some effects on other people around him. And he is, in a different way, as dependent on these other people as he is on the boss. He does not shed his group membership when he goes on incentive. So the direct incentive path to money, though desirable, may be partly blocked by the counterinfluence of other members—members who, out of "obstinacy" or "irrationality," do not trust or like the incentive rate. It is no easy task for any of us to put up with the label of "rate-buster" or in other ways to bear the sanctions of the group we need to live with.

But even if workers are working alone, when we tie money rewards directly to individual performance, the individuals involved frequently find themselves in conflict. They now have a new and simple path to more money (which they want); but the path takes them away from some other things they also want, like taking it easy, socializing with the boys, and so on. These other social and egoistic needs, unlike money, are not easy to see and measure, which is probably why early industrial engineers missed them.

The third "other" thing, management's own motives, shows up very often too. It shows up best when an incentive system works too well. When the girls begin to produce at 300 percent of the standard and their premiums make their take-home pay out of line with other departments, then managers are likely to recognize that they did not want just to influence every individual to do his best. They wanted individuals to do their best within limits and according to the total pattern of the company.

Let's take an example that is not unusual. Consider eight girls removing casings from skinless frankfurters. The frankfurters are molded in cellophane-like casings which must be peeled off after chilling. The girls stand alongside a conveyer, pick up the frankfurters, hook a fingernail under an edge of the casing and strip it off. This is the kind of straightforward, repetitive job that is almost ideally suited to an individual incentive rate. So the industrial engineers work out a standard, succeed in getting union and employee approval, and put an incentive rate into effect.

The rate works well for a while until one of the girls hits upon the idea of taping a small razor blade to her finger. The "other people" factor shows up at this point. This creative technological improvement is immediately adopted by all the other girls (who are not, for good reason, as "resistant to change" in this case as they are purported to be in many others), and productivity per girl increases several hundred percent. Now the take-home pay of the girls is far out of line with the pay of other employees doing comparable or even more skilful tasks in other departments. Management's motives now need reexamination. If management changes the rate, the union will accuse it of reverting to rate-cutting practices and of reneging on its contract to pay for productivity. And so on.

The logic and illogic of individual incentives

Psychologically speaking, the example shows how the logic of individual incentive pay is wrong as well as right. It is right in the sense that it usually ties meaningful rewards to the kind of effort that the rewarder wants. It is wrong in what it omits: other people, other worker needs, and managerial needs. In its failure to take interdependence into account, the incentive system is not based on the assumption that the workers are independent individuals. The assumption is that the total job of a company can be broken down into individual subparts, each subpart just the right size for one individual in the organization. The work of the organization will be accomplished best (this argument runs) when each man does his job as effectively as he can.

Many psychologists like to point out the fallacy in such reasoning. The whole is not the sum of its parts, they argue, but something much more, because the parts are interdependent. A tune is more than the notes that make it up; the bicycle remains a bicycle even after every one of its original pieces has been replaced. Contrarily, all the parts are not a bicycle, not until they are put together in one particular way. If every man looks at his own small task alone, ignoring its relationship to other tasks, the greatest total productivity will not be attained.

It is easy to show the same phenomenon in experimental situations, just as long as intercommunication and interaction are required. For example, suppose we give each of five men several pieces of a puzzle. No man has enough pieces to complete his own puzzle, but among the five there are enough pieces to complete five puzzles.

Suppose we set up an individual incentive system. We say to each man: "You will be paid in accordance with the speed with which you can put together your puzzle. The man who makes his puzzle first gets first prize, the man who makes his last gets the booby prize." Under these conditions, with each man concerned about his own immediate productivity but necessarily caught in the trap of having to give up some of his pieces in order to get others he needs, the total productivity of the group in X minutes is usually less than five completed puzzles.

Change the incentive system now so that each man is given an equal share of the prize money, the prize money being determined by the total number of puzzles they can complete in X minutes. Five completed puzzles are the likely result.

But it is only when there is such interdependency, such a need to trade off pieces with other people, that this disadvantage of the individual incentive system shows up so clearly. For if we give to each man all the pieces needed to complete his own puzzle, it may well be that he will complete it fastest under conditions of individual motivation. If management can indeed faultlessly divide and plan the parts of an operation so that each part is actually independent of any other part, then management can truthfully say, "All that we want this worker to do is to produce as many of these pieces as he can produce."

Such conditions are rare in the industrial world. We still find them occasionally in home work situations, and they are sometimes approximated at lower levels of industrial organizations. But only approximated, because most managements, when they reflect on it, want people to do more than their jobs. They do not really want the individual employee to go on blindly punching out blanks when his machine needs lubrication; they do want him to take a few seconds off to show the new employee at the next machine how to cut down his enormous scrappage; they do want him to report a fire when he sees one.

In the puzzle experiments just mentioned, an interesting thing may happen. Subjects often refuse to accept the individual incentive rules of the game. Many of them simply don't serve their own "best interest"; they insist on trading pieces they know will produce puzzles for two other people, even if they can't complete their own. Moreover, they begin to look sheepish and unhappy if they sit with a completed puzzle before them, being stared at balefully by the others they are blocking.

As one goes up the scale in an organization to higher levels of responsiblity, these points become far more obvious. At higher levels we seldom say, "Do this—and don't do anything else." For at higher and more technical levels more and more decision-making must be left to the individual. He must define for himself more of what a good day's work is.

Although we cannot very well rank people's wants, we can be fairly safe in assuming that money is not all they want all the time. Even as early as 1927 the Western Electric researches were pointing out that the introduction of individual money incentives could create psychological conflicts by forcing people to choose between money and the important social standards of their own group: between cooperation and competition; or between the need for approval of one's group at work and the approval of one's wife when she sees the paycheck.

Like most conflicts, these too may be solved by unexpected means. One compromise for a person caught in such a conflict is to work out some way to beat the system and yet maintain or even improve his relationships with others. The development of a new jig hidden from management can satisfy both needs. Aggression is another way of working off the tension evoked by such conflicts. And who is the ideal target?

Moreover, the control of individual incentive rewards is perceived by employees to lie almost exclusively in the hands of an unpredictable and not always beloved managerial big brother. One should therefore expect to find ingenious and powerful forms of resistance. Incentive plans then may become pawns in games of strategy, with management seeking always to plug potential loopholes in the system while employees, in ways that can be unbelievably imaginative and creative, drill new holes in "impossible" places. As a consequence, I think, many industrial engineers find themselves caught up in a frustrating, never ending, and unpopular holding-action strategy. If the socially determined production ceiling has become a commonplace in plants with individual incentives, so has the unhappy, slightly embittered industrial engineer.

In two ways, then, the simple maxim "A good day's pay for a good day's work" becomes hard to implement. First, we have to specify, as managers, whether we want a good day's work from *every* man, or a good day's work from *all* the men. The two are not the same. Second, even if we want a good day's work from every man, money isn't always enough to get it, especially if the means we provide for getting money conflict with other available means to social and egoistic satisfactions.

If this picture of the individual incentive seems unattractive, the reader should keep the alternatives in mind. In many, many situations, when the alternative is a flat rate, the individual incentive can and does yield significant improvements, both in productivity and morale. When employee confidence in management's integrity is high and when the "atmosphere" of an organization is cooperative and friendly, the addition of an individual incentive may do much good and little harm.

Unit-wide multiple incentives

Consider the profit-sharing plan as an extreme contrast to bare individual incentives. Consider, for example, a small company of, say, three hundred employees which chooses, instead of individual incentives, one of the many varieties of such plans. Assume it chooses the Scanlon plan, which is itself an extreme within the profit-sharing group. In a sense such a plan does not properly belong in a chapter on money incentives, for though it begins with money incentives and though money incentives derive from it, it can be better thought of as a plan for the psychological reorganization of a company.

The elements of the plan are these: (1) A monthly bonus for everyone in the plant based on an index of the overall productivity of the plant—an index that is a satisfactory measure of improvement in the organization's efficiency. (2) The introduction of production committees. If every man's take-home pay is tied not to his individual productivity but to the productive efficiency of the company as a whole, then the production committee becomes the mechanism for tying everyone's efforts to the goal of productivity.

Notice that this plan includes the same assumptions made in individual plans. But profit-sharing plans also add two others: interdependency and social and egoistic needs.

These two additions are surprisingly important. The underlying proposition of individual incentives reads something like this: Individuals will work harder if they are individually rewarded with money for harder individual work. The profit-sharing modification is of this order: Organizations will work harder if they are organizationally rewarded for harder organizational work.

The two propositions do not even contradict one another. The second is an extension of the first. We do not have to prove one right and the other wrong; we have only to decide whether we are dealing with *independent* or *interdependent* individuals and with simply motivated or multiply motivated ones.

The second proposition assumes that individuals in industrial organizations are both socially and economically interdependent. It therefore defines an individual's job differently than the first. His job is no longer to punch his press as productively as possible; it is to punch his press in a social environment, to think about ways of improving the operation of his press and the company, to help whenever helping other people in the plant will contribute to the overall efficiency of the organization, and finally, when faced with unusual decisions, to try to make those decisions which will contribute to total efficiency.

One result of such a plan is an increase in feelings of responsibility for the total operation on the part of all members of the organization. For now it is harder to make management the scapegoat for all problems. If production, and therefore the bonus share, drops, there is no tight rate to blame it on. If some people work too slowly or stupidly, it costs everyone something. What should everyone, not just management, do about it?

This increase in employees' "ownership attitude," however, is not an unmixed blessing. Even though most managers insist they want their people to develop one, an ownership attitude in each employee means that each employee may take a serious interest in things management considers its private property. It may mean, for example, that the machine operator now expresses interest in the sales manager's decisions. He may question such decisions. He may want an accounting for the sales department's failure to bring in a large order. At this level secondary and tertiary changes in atmosphere and organizational structure are likely to occur. Notions about secrecy, about prerogatives of one group or another, are likely to be battered down.

If profit-sharing plans succeed in developing what they set out to develop, a strongly active desire on the part of everyone in the plant to improve the plant, what then? Where individual incentives so often sharpen the line between management and employees, these profit-sharing plans tend to obviate it. They tend to push the whole organization in the direction of oneness, in which everything is everybody's business. The new control problem may not be how to get people to work on time but how to keep them from henpecking management.

When a management is struggling for productivity, when employees appear obstinate, inconsiderate, and entirely insensitive to management's needs, the development of an ownership attitude in employees may seem wonderfully utopian. But the reality creates difficulties. The senior officers of more than one small company that has adopted such plans have spent some sleepless nights and gone on even blander diets precisely when they have achieved what they sought—a working force intensely and creatively motivated to help the organization to succeed. Management feels the pressure when it has to face up to the reality of long-sought honest feedback. They find that they are hearing not only the happy news of dollar savings but the unhappy public exposure of past managerial inadequacy. For as every phase of production is examined in the bright light of joint committees, almost any management team is bound to discover case after case in which its decisions were not quite so good as they had seemed to be. Yet the fact remains that the multiple incentive system has paid handsome dollar dividends to management and worker alike. Its cost is that management and everyone else must operate in a glass house.

The words "multiple incentives" were used advisedly in the subheading of this section. Although the money incentive is central to the development of such plans, they also encompass changes in the whole organizational structure. Incentives in the form of greater opportunities for independence and for greater participation in planning and decision making are other outgrowths of these groupwide systems. In these ways, they represent an almost total rebuilding of the relationships among members of an organization.

Several of these plans have been tested in many small companies, with variable success. Psychologically they make sense in that they open channels of communication and create a situation in which at least one goal, the goal of greater productive efficiency, is spread more widely through all levels of the organization. They move people toward an ownership attitude by the simple expedient of providing a kind of ownership.

But they are no panaceas. Sometimes, even an ownership attitude cannot outproduce technically superior people or equipment. They create new, difficult psychological and organizational problems while solving others. They lead us into the pervasive problems of working groups. It is one thing to find a group of people with common goals. It is another to find them working together efficiently toward those goals.

Incentives and methods of influence

This chapter started out to relate money incentives to the ideas about influence and behavior change outlined earlier. What are the relationships? There are several.

Neither individual nor multiple incentives make direct use of restrictive authority. Both offer rewards for work rather than punishment for non-work. Both seek some impersonal, measurable, objective criteria on which to base rewards. Both give up, thereby, some of the control that management often says it wants.

But at that point the two plans part company. Earlier we

argued that shared responsibility between A and B encourages broader and deeper change in B than responsibility kept by A alone. Multiple incentives share responsibility. Individual incentives do not. They keep the responsibility for behavior change in the hands of the changer rather than the changee.

Second, individual incentive systems call first for A to take the responsibility and then paradoxically to give up some managerial authority by setting impersonal, open-for-inspection incentive rates. They, in effect, contradict the dictum that authority should equal responsibility. Even if that dictum is not too meaningful, the fact remains that management takes responsibility for the incentive and then lets go the reins of control, sometimes thereby getting unintended results. Multiple incentives, though also giving up control, are more flexible, allowing for change by encouraging feedback and by emphasizing the mutuality of influence. Moreover, multiple incentives implicitly accept the idea that the changee is in the saddle in that they say to B, in effect: "Here are the rewards of productivity, if you want them. Our job together is to find a mutually satisfactory way of getting them." Restrictive authority plays a minor role. Productivity is the focal point of the problem, not the conflict between manager and employee. They also, like AA, lay more emphasis on the whole man, taking his social and egoistic needs into account far more than individual incentives.

Finally, multiple incentives recognize the interdependency of members of modern businesses. They try to deal with, rather than deny, that interdependency. They encourage direct communication and cooperation. They try to set a common goal. And herein lies the hardest problem of all—the problem of trying to get all the members of an organization to operate like one good man.

Multiple incentives (and individual ones) can, of course, be set up manipulatively; designed by A to promote A's interests and to increase B's dependency. The amount of reward, for example, may be privately decided by A, rather than publicly known in advance. Those designs often work, and they often end in explosion.

Money, cognitive balance, and equity

The reader will remember, hopefully, our discussion in part 1 of cognitive dissonance. And earlier in this chapter we pointed to the peculiarly symbolic nature of money, its tendency to serve as an index for many other needs.

Let's now put these two ideas together. One thing money can symbolize is the justness of one's treatment. You get as much as Joe Blow for doing the same job. That is just; it is equitable. You get more than Henry Smith. That is just, too, because you work harder, or have a more dangerous job, or whatever.

Now suppose something changes. Joe Blow and you are on the same job at the same pay. He gets a raise. You don't. Dissonance. So you search for a dissonance-reducing solution. Maybe Joe has seniority. No. Maybe Joe has ten kids. No. Maybe Joe produces more. No. Somewhere along this list, you may find a satisfactory dissonance-reducing answer, or you may flip the other way—reducing dissonance by swearing at the company or quitting.

But push it a step further—to something less obvious. Take it from Joe's side. He wonders why he's being paid more. He looks at seniority. No. At productivity. No. He's a cognitive balancer, too, isn't he? Except that he's on the high side, not the low side. He feels overpaid. Does he swear at the company? Not likely. What are his other alternatives? One is to work harder because he feels overpaid—to justify to himself the overpayment.

Some experiments on these issues have turned up just such results. But think about the dynamics. Suppose you feel overpaid, but you're on a piece rate. More production will increase the overpayment and therefore increase the dissonance. In the experiments, overpaid piece workers didn't increase production, but they did increase quality.

Now we make an experimental switch. You're put on an hourly rate—still feeling overpaid. Now you do produce more, using the greater productivity to justify for yourself the greater pay.

In summary

Money remains a significant but not exclusive incentive to work in our society.

Individual money incentive systems are most appropriate where workers can operate independently of one another and where their jobs can, in fact, be designed so as to permit independent operation. Difficulties begin to arise when individual incentives are applied to interdependent people on interdependent jobs. Then productive work by each person on his special job (even if it could be attained) may not add up to productive accomplishment for the whole organization.

Company-wide multiple incentive plans are psychologically different from individual plans. Individual plans tend to isolate the individual and his work from the organization and its work. Company-wide plans tend to focus everyone on a common organizational goal rather than his own individual one. This common concern for the organizational goal makes for basic changes in worker-management relationships, for increases in the range of satisfactions available to people in an organization, and for new and difficult problems of interaction.

As influence mechanisms, individual incentives are more likely to effect overt actions than basic attitudes. Multiple incentives, closer to the AA model, may have deep and wide effects.

Wages and salaries are not just money. They are also indicators of progress, worth, and status. And they are equity measures, too, telling us whether our treatment relative to others and to our own performance is right and proper.

3

**People in threes
to twenties
Efficiency and
influence in groups**

Introductory note

In part 3 we change our perspective in two ways. First we shift again in breadth, changing focus from the A-B relationship to the group—the A-B-C-D-E, etc.—relationship. And, second, we simultaneously shift our observation point outward, so that instead of observing B through A's eyes, we look at groups from the outside, trying to account for the things that happen in them.

In the last section we saw that influencing behavior is difficult enough when we are dealing with just one B. But it is clear, too, that most organizations cannot deal with people one at a time. The essence of organization after all is people many at a time. This section is concerned with interdependent people, five, ten, or twenty at a time, trying to operate efficiently.

This intermediate range is worth a separate section for several reasons: First, the small group is an incomplete but simplified model of the large organization. Second, we have a good base of research on small groups to draw upon. Third, the small group, in its own right, is playing an increasingly important, but problematical, part in modern business.

Staff meetings, problem-solving committees, informal planning groups, work groups—all seem to have multiplied and gained importance in the last couple of decades, and for good reasons. Businesses have been growing in size, for one thing, many past the point at which one person can keep his finger on everything. They have been growing technologically, too, so that the specialist has come into the picture. Where buying, manufacturing, merchandising, and selling were once all common-sense operations, often all performed by one person, they have now become technical specialties, each requiring specialists and subspecialists.

Size and specialization have forced the individual manager to give way in part to the group, to recognize his dependence on his subordinates. One head is no longer big enough to get all the facts, to analyze them, to decide, and to act—hence the information-gathering staff group and the problem-solving planning group and all the others, each made up of many brains trying to act like one superbrain.

It therefore seems fair to say that "problem-solving groups" are a new managerial tool. True, business has used committees and other small groups for a long time, but it is only recently that the small group has been consciously singled out as a major problem-solving tool.

Two more comments are in order here, this time about the place of small groups in industry. First, people in business often express intense feeling about committees and group meetings. The majority seems to be on the antigroup side, the same majority that grudgingly accepts the necessity for some kind of committee meetings but holds out as long as possible against them. But they are counterbalanced by a vanguard of "group-thinkers," people with an almost mystical faith in the potency of groups. Groups, for them, can do anything better than anybody.

But size and technology dictate the use of the group, whether we like it or not. So the problem is a "how," not a "whether or not," problem. The "how" issue can be divided into two subproblems. The first is how to make groups work. The second is how to fit them into the hierarchical design of most organizations. The first subproblem, how to make them work, is considered in this part.

The problem of how groups fit into the organization involves *intergroup* relationships. As organizations grow more complex and more differentiated, they also grow more groupy. But the groups must interact, correlate, cooperate. Yet, as we shall see, solid groups tend to view other groups as competitors as often as allies—competitors for power, for resources. So with the multiplication of groups comes the growing problem of intergroup conflict. In chapter 22 we focus on that extremely important organizational problem, and we return to it in part 4 for a further discussion of organizational power politics.

This part accepts groups as facts of industrial life. It considers, first, some alternative structural designs that affect the efficiency of small groups (chap. 18); then some operating problems that arise in trying to lead and participate in them (chaps. 19–20); and then two key problems, the problems of conformity to group pressure (chap. 21) and the problem of relationships among groups (chap. 22). Finally we take one applied managerial problem, management development, and look at it from the perspective of the small-group psychologist (chap. 23).

One general purpose in this part is to shed some light on conditions that affect the problem-solving efficiency of groups. In so doing we will come up against some controversial techniques that are being tossed around in industry these days, like "sensitivity training." We will take a quick look at these techniques, trying to fit them into the contemporary scene.

Once again, as the reader will see, the problem is complex. Although we can understand a good deal about groups, no neat formulas work very well for controlling or influencing them. But some mapping out of the processes that go on in groups may be helpful to people who spend many of their working hours trying, in groups, to solve problems, while maintaining their integrity as individuals.

18

Communication networks in groups Designs for getting the word around

Like the relationship between two people, the relationships among members of a group are limited by the kinds of communication that occur. In the chapter on two-person communication in part 2, we pointed out that communication has several dimensions, only one of which is the content of what is said.

The same holds for groups. Group members can talk about all sorts of ideas, but they can also use one-way or two-way communication no matter what they talk about. They can, moreover, carry on more or less noisy and redundant conversations. And, the reader will recall, group members can communicate over different *networks*.

These networks, it turns out, do indeed affect the ways groups solve problems. By experimenting with networks, we can tell a good deal about the efficiency with which a group will operate on a problem and a good deal about how individual group members will feel. So an analysis of communication nets can serve as a good bridge between problems of individual behavior and problems of organizational behavior.

Experimental research in the field has only a short history. Many of the findings are highly tentative and not subject to ready generalization. But students of industrial organization should be aware of the history, despite these inadequacies, because it points to the accessibility of organizations as subjects for quantitative experimental research. In fact, studies of group communication networks are just one phase in a body of research, as yet unintegrated, concerned with organization for decision-making and action. The scope of these larger researches goes beyond industrial organization into the nature of "systems" in general, whether the system be the single cell, the single person, the machine, or the organized human group. It promises, in this writer's opinion, to produce some extremely useful results.

What we mean by communication nets

Communication nets are a *structural* aspect of a group. They tell us how the group is hung together. Consider, for instance, the difference between a boss who sets himself up with his staff like this:

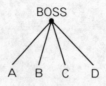

and one who prefers to divide his four staff people into two seniors and two juniors:

The lines here represent lines of communication. These diagrams are structural. They tell us nothing about the people involved—just something about the "system." What differences might such different setups make in the boss's flow of information? In his flexibility? In the originality of the ideas he gets?

Consider also the effects on subordinates of being in one communicational position or another—like B in the two charts. In one case he can talk to his superior directly, in the other he must go through channels.

The issue here is not whether the several channels in these group networks are one-way or two-way channels but whether the problem of existing channels affects the performance of the group. For example, suppose that for a group of five men all channels are two-way channels. Then this question still remains: What system of channels will be the most effective system for these five men? Will such a group solve problems best when everyone has an open two-way channel to everyone else? Like this:

Or is *this* system better?

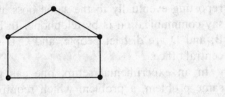

Or this one?

Even though each of these networks provides enough communication channels to permit intercommunication, the arrangements and numbers of channels differ, and so, therefore, may the effectiveness of the group as a problem-solving body. Moreover, some of these networks fit better with the usual company organization chart than others; some would look very strange indeed on an organization chart.

In practical terms the question now is this one: How does the communication network affect the efficiency of a group's performance?

Testing communication networks

The best way to answer such questions may be temporarily to strip away the complications found in real life. Then one can set up small experimental committees and put them to work in one or another of these different networks. By providing each experimental group with some standard problems to solve and then measuring performance, one can get some ideas about the relative efficiency of one of these networks versus another. In the past two decades such experimental work has been carried on, and the results have been both consistent and interesting.

The reader might like to try to decide for himself, on a common-sense basis, just what results one should get with one of these networks or another. So, for illustrative purposes, consider these two networks of five people each:

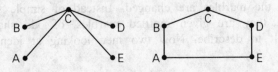

Such groups might be analogous to groups of field staff people, each located in a different branch or district but all reporting eventually to the same boss at headquarters. Let's say communication is by telephone. In both networks, A, E, B, and D are district people, and C is someone back at the central office.

In an experimental setup, one can give each group the same problem, a problem which requires some information from each man before it can be solved. Usually it is some sort of puzzle, in many ways analogous to a pricing problem in a rapidly changing supply-and-demand situation.

Which of these two groups will solve this kind of problem faster? Which group will have the higher morale? Will there be a leader in no. 1? In no. 2? Which particular positions in group no. 1 or no. 2 will be high morale positions? Which will be low morale positions?

Here are the answers that have come out of experiments like these:

Network no. 1 will be the faster of the two.

On the whole, the morale of group no. 2 will be higher than that of group no. 1. People will be more enthusiastic in group no. 2.

Only one person in group no. 1 is likely to get a big bang out of the job, and that man is C. The others, A, B, D, and E, will probably feel bored and left out of the center of things.

Man C in no. 1 will probably be the leader of that group. Everyone in the group will be likely to turn to him. In no. 2 the leader (the one who gets the answer first and sends it out to the others) can be almost anybody. In fact, there may be a different leader each time the group runs through a problem, or else no identifiable leader at all.

Another finding in these researches is most intriguing in its implications for industry. Two groups are put to work in the circle (no. 2) and star (no. 1) patterns. Their task is as follows: Each man is given five solid-colored marbles of which one color is common to all men in the group. The group must find the one color that all 5 members have in common. They then write notes to one another over the available channels, saying things like this: "I have red, green, yellow, blue, and brown." Eventually they discover that all have red marbles. After playing this game several times, the groups in both networks become proficient and fast. At this point, the marbles are changed. Instead of simple solid colors, they are given mottled marbles, of odd shades, difficult to describe. Now two men looking at identical marbles may describe them quite differently. One may use the term "greenish yellow," the other may call it "aqua." "Noise," in other words, has entered the system in the form of a semantic problem.

The interesting finding is the difference between these two networks in their ability to adapt to and meet this change. The circle handles it nicely, so that after ten runs or so it is back to high efficiency. The star can't seem to cope with it, still making a large number of errors after many trials. This result certainly suggests that the structure of an organization influences its adaptability as well as its other forms of efficiency.

Communication structure, then, does affect a group's efficiency, at least in this kind of situation. But much depends on the definition one gives to the word "efficiency." Some communication networks allow for faster operation than others, but the advantage of speed may be gained at the cost of accuracy and/or morale. People are happier in some networks than they are in others, and some networks therefore are more likely to keep going longer without blowing up, but these networks may be slower or less accurate than some others. This conflict between "morale" and "efficiency" may indeed turn out to be a generalized conflict in industrial organizations. Some networks have fewer errors than others. Some are more flexible than others. All these words may have something to do with what we mean by "efficiency."

Why different networks cause people to behave differently

If we look at these results in the light of parts 1 and 2, they are not hard to understand. Why is network no. 1 faster than network no. 2? For one thing, no. 1 is like a one-way communication system. Although people can talk back individually to the central man, they cannot talk to one another. No. 1 imposes an orderliness on the group that wipes out extra messages. In no. 2 no such clear organization is imposed. People can send messages to two people; they can get around more and thereby spend more time.

But in sending more messages, members of no. 2 also are taking advantage of more checkpoints of the kind provided by two-way communication. Thus, they can locate and correct more of their errors.

They also have in no. 2 more chance to participate and take responsibility. They are less dependent on one person since they can check with one other person. So they are more satisfied and happy, just as people were in the two-way communication example in chapter 11.

On the other hand, the central man in network no. 1 is quite happy—and for the same reasons. He has responsibility, he has several sources of information and several checkpoints. He is independent and powerful.

In these ways, then, the mere mechanical fact of *structure* can act upon individuals by making them more or less dependent, more or less certain of where they stand, and more or less responsible. The same fact of structure can also act upon the total operational efficiency of the group, causing it to work faster or slower, more or less accurately, and more or less adaptably.

Once again, though, it is worth pointing out, as we did in chapter 11, that structure seems to affect people's feelings in one direction and their speed and accuracy in the other. No one has yet found a structure that maximizes speed and accuracy and, at the same time, morale and flexibility.

Networks in industrial groups

One may argue that these laboratory findings, though interesting, are not particularly relevant to the problems actually encountered in industry. In most face-to-face industrial groups only one communication network seems possible, and that is a fully connected network in which everyone can communicate directly with everyone else.

But the argument that this is the only actual network, even in committees, does not hold water. A clear, albeit informal, notion about who can talk to whom exists in most groups. In fact, in face-to-face meetings, although the *official* network is a fully connected one, the *actual* network may be some other one altogether. Communication networks are much like organization charts: there is likely to be a formal, officially charted organization, and there is likely also to be an informal, uncharted organization that nevertheless plays a significant role in the functioning of the company.

In a committee meeting, for example, a chairman can usually manipulate the communication setup so that in practice each person talks only to him and not directly to other people. And even if the chairman tries to be "democratic," the same result may occur unintentionally because of differences in rank or power among members of the committee. Privates don't interrupt generals whenever they feel like it, no matter what the official communication network.

In continuing work groups, the possibilities for changing communication nets are better than in meetings. Almost any network is possible if the group in question is the continuing membership of a particular department.

However, the members of a great many industrial groups seldom meet face to face. Where there is physical separation, one would expect the structure of the communication net to have far more direct effects.

"Good" and "bad" networks

What, then, are the characteristics of the "best" communication networks? That question demands another: Best for what? If the question is what is "best" for small meetings and conferences, where everyone's ideas are worth something and where the same people will probably get together again next week, then the answer seems clear. The best networks are likely to be the ones with at least these two related characteristics:

First, equalitarian networks are probably preferable to hierarchical networks. That is, networks like the circle, where everyone has access to about the same number of channels, are preferable to networks like the star, where one person has many neighbors and the rest none.

Second, those networks that provide everyone with at least two direct communication channels are probably better than those that give some people only one channel to the rest of the group.

Several different networks meet these criteria. And there are real differences even among these. But as a group, networks that meet these standards seem—in experimental situations—to yield higher morale, greater willingness to work, and a series of other advantages over networks that do not meet them.

But if by "efficient" we mean fast in getting started and fast in its operations, our conclusions about the best network must be quite different. Then differentiated, nonequalitarian networks like the star look better. For they impose a clear-cut organization on the group, defining each person's job and leaving little leeway for wandering away from that job. As a consequence, those groups get started faster and work faster once they have started.

Similarly, the experimental findings would lead to other predictions. For instance, consider a superior, A, who puts himself in the position shown here:

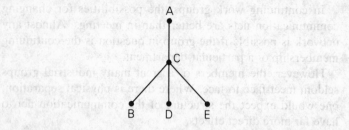

Any superior who does this may be leaving himself in serious danger. And his assistant, C, may find himself in a very powerful spot. For the assistant has more and faster access to internal organizational information than his boss or anyone else, and by being a little selective in what he transmits (purposely or by oversight), he can end up controlling the organization. Sometimes one sees this situation with the president's private secretary. By being in a position to screen all incoming and many outgoing messages, she can be a formidable personage.

Preferential access to information, after all, is a major source of power in any organization. In experiments in the star network, any man in the central position, C, is likely to become the functioning boss. His personal characteristics do not matter much. He learns more, faster, than anyone else. In real life, his communicational power may be balanced by someone else's authoritative power. Curiously, one will often find groups so organized that the position of greater authority is not the key communicational position, even where power maximization in the hands of authority is the objective sought.

These ideas are related to some ideas about feedback talked about in chapter 11. Information is transmitted more broadly and apparently more accurately, and people are happier about sending and receiving it, when the people involved have some degree of control over what is happening, that is, when they have some feedback, or when they have checkpoints to help them increase their certainty about what they are getting, or when they have opportunities to contribute to what is going on. Free feedback clearly helps in this direction, and now one can add that "equalitarian," "multichannel" communication networks seem also to help toward the same end.

A word of warning may be appropriate here. It may seem to follow from what has been said that the very best network is the fully communicating one, wherein everyone can talk directly with everyone else. Although this is probably true for certain types of problems in relatively small groups, it may not be true as groups grow larger. Purely practical considerations, like how much one person can send or receive at one time, might require limitations in the number of channels to be used in larger meetings, or even in small meetings for special kinds of problems.

Another warning: To date the research on communication has not dealt much with "real" situations. Problems of authority and responsibility that exist in industrial organizations clearly complicate real-life situations. So we must necessarily be cautious about jumping off into generalizations from such experimental research. Nevertheless, the very fact that some aspects of organization can be dealt with quantitatively in the laboratory seems a promising advance in a field so recently limited to experiential, "clinical" examination.

Unfortunately we do not know much about the networks that will or will not work for large organizations. Some of our little ones "look" centralized, some decentralized. But we can't put a thousand people in a laboratory, or at least we haven't yet.

Although it is probably true that many of the results would hold up if we could test them on large groups, many of them would not. We would run into the problem of oversupply of information if we expanded the star network to even twenty-five people with only one central man in position C. We would probably need some intermediate people to absorb irrelevant information and organize the remainder for C. Similarly, if we had a hundred men in a fully connected network, we would probably get chaotic results, at least until a good many channels had been voluntarily closed off. And we cannot even draw some networks for larger groups. Some,

like this one,   are unique to

a particular number of people. How does one draw that same net for ten people?

Self-defense and the design of networks

If these notions hold, one may ask why work groups are not more often of equalitarian, multichannel design in industrial organizations. One good reason is that these designs conflict, as do many aspects of small-group operation, with the pyramidal, highly individualized structure of most industrial organizations. Another good reason is that speed and control are often more critical than morale or even creativity.

There is also a not-so-good reason that may be worth special mention. Two-way communication in equalitarian networks is often dangerous and threatening to some people in the group. For instance, people in higher positions in an organization may prefer hierarchical communication networks like the star pattern because it helps to maximize their power in the group (assuming that a superior will put himself in a position like C's). Patterns like this one serve the same purpose as one-way communication. They keep a boss off the psychological hook. His weaknesses are hidden better in a position like C's in the center of the star than in any position in the circle. He can screen information from others. He can blame errors on others, and maybe he can get away with it. The other people in such a group may have no way of checking on the real source of either an error or a bright idea. Often people argue for the star pattern over the circle on grounds of speed or businesslike efficiency when an underlying reason for the preference is the protection of someone's self-esteem. The same reasoning may hold for subordinates. It is easier for them, too, to hide in a hierarchical network.

In summary

The simple structure of the communication network in a group, independent of the persons in the group, seems to set limits on the group's performance.

Groups whose problems require the collation of information from all members work faster when one position is highly centralized and the others relatively peripheral. But the morale, the self-correctiveness, and perhaps the creativity of such groups may be better when the communication network is more equalitarian and when each member has more than one source of information.

Highly centralized groups may often be used for their consistency with general organizational designs, their speed, and their controllability; but they are also used as psychological defense devices to protect superiors' "weaknesses" from being exposed to subordinates, and vice versa.

19

The content of communication in groups Getting valid words around

The *structure* of communication in a group is one thing, the *content* another. In this chapter, content is the issue to be treated. What information ought to be transmitted over any particular network? What information is or is not relevant to the solution of a problem? When a group sets out to solve a problem, after all feedback and network questions have been resolved, it still must decide what should be sent through the network.

This may seem a simple problem. Yet anyone who has ever been on a committee must have noted how discussion can bog down into argument, name-calling, and storytelling; how some points are stated and restated and others never get heard. Are arguments, name calling, funny stories, and redundancy relevant or irrelevant to the solution of a problem that people have come together to solve? If they are not relevant, how can they be kept out? What is relevant? And how can what is relevant be kept in?

Noise and redundancy

Information theorists, we said in chapter 11, use the term *noise* when talking about things like the static one may find on a telephone connection. Some things that get communicated in group meetings are much like telephone or radio static—the wind, the argument, the *noise* that gets stirred up and interferes with communication of "really relevant" information.

Besides being noisy, the content of group communication tends to be redundant. The same information is communicated again and again. In meetings, the same point may be made half a dozen times in half a dozen ways in the course of a single discussion.

Noise and redundancy look like signs of inefficiency in the communication process. Ideally, we would like to see groups solve problems like intelligent individuals. They should do the things described in the chapter on problem-solving in part 1. They should search, systematically, for alternatives, using an appropriate set of categories; then they should follow a set of reasonable decision rules for dealing with the alternatives. They should use their memories. And they should *learn*, so that they can deal with new problems better than they did with old ones.

Those things do not always happen. Or at least so much committee activity seems devoted to noise and redundancy that those orderly problem-solving processes are obscure and even secondary. It is understandable, therefore, that most business people would like to see noise and redundancy cut to a minimum as quickly as possible, so people can get on with solving the problem at hand. The difficulty is procedural. How does one minimize the sound and fury of day-to-day life in an industrial organization: the boasting, the credit-seeking, the boot-licking, the kowtowing, the blustering?

Minimizing noise in a group

Two general approaches have been used to minimize noise, and the two are at almost opposite extremes. The most obvious and most common procedure is simply to set up rules disallowing most noise. The rules may be formal parliamentary ones or informal ones. The chairman says, "We will stick to the facts in this meeting. We will keep personalities out of this. We will cut off people who talk too long or too much." His purpose is to eliminate noise, and his weapon is his authority to enforce organizational rules. This seems a sensible, businesslike approach to the problem, but it needs more consideration.

Another not so businesslike method for handling noise is to take the position that noise should not be kept out of meetings but let in and identified. Here the chairman says, "If you want to blow off, blow off. If you want to boast, boast. If you want to deal in personalities, deal in personalities. But when anyone does any of these things, let him or anyone else point it out so that everyone will know what he's doing." This second method also deserves serious consideration.

Noise-making behavior by people in groups, like all other behavior, is goal-directed. People boast because they feel that boasting will get them something they want—recognition, or power, or status. People lick boots for reasons, too; perhaps they think boot-licking will make someone they need like them a little better. When several people join to try to solve a problem through committee action, there may be one central problem that is common to everyone on the committee, but there are also individually perceived problems that each member brings in with him. People, we said in part 1, perceive the world in relation to their operant needs. If other members of a group are in a position to help or hurt a particular member, that member is likely to be alert to their power. The noise in a group may therefore be made up, to a large extent, of efforts of individuals to satisfy their personal needs in the presence of the group. Thus, this kind of noisiness can only be considered wasteful or irrelevant when the group problem is defined as the only real problem. Such a definition is simply unrealistic. This second level of individual problems exists, and attempts to solve them—although irrelevant to the group's problem—constitute, so far as individual members are concerned, a perfectly relevant use of the communication system.

We may object to persons using a group for their own ends, or we may object to the methods that some individuals use to solve their personal problems—methods like name calling or yessing. We may also feel that the methods people sometimes use are not effective methods even for accomplishing what those individuals want to accomplish. Nevertheless, those methods are attempts by individuals to solve problems, and to rule them out by authority may be to rule out the individuals as well as the noise. For if these "irrelevant" needs are so important to a person that he tries to use the group as a sounding board for them, then to deny him that opportunity can only do one of two things: it can make him lose interest in the group and the group's problem, or it can make him disguise his communications so that they sound relevant to the common problem.

Authority or parliamentary procedure or social pressures may drive individual motives underground, but such methods do not necessarily eliminate them. Instead of open argument and open emotion, one now gets calm, seemingly rational discussions, but discussions which somehow manage indirectly to discredit opponents or to defend positions beyond any point of reasonable utility.

Everyone who has served on a committee has seen this kind of velvet-glove activity many times. Sometimes it takes the "it's an excellent idea but . . ." form, or, "Well, of course we *could* go about it your way but. . . ." Such tacks are much harder to handle, much less likely to contribute to honest unanimity (or honest disagreement), than an open haggle.

It is quite impossible to exclude individual noise from

group discussion by force or by parliamentary procedure. If these devices eliminate noise, they eliminate it as ear plugs do—at the cost of much relevant information. Problems may appear to be solved in such restrictive situations when the "solution" is actually a hodgepodge of compromise and half-truth. As in the feedback example in chapter 11, if we want the information, we may have to bear the emotion.

Hence, the other choice: let the communication channels carry whatever people want to communicate. Let everything in, but tag the different classes of information, so that everyone knows what's what. Seek out the causes of noise and get rid of the causes. When people don't need to make noise, they will stop and get down to the problem at hand.

Such a policy need not be as chaotic as it sounds. Perhaps it is more orderly to convert chaos to system than to cover it with system. The question is not anarchy versus order so much as the orderly handling of anarchistic factors in a group. Getting groups to say what they feel is not easy, however, especially if time is limited. But patience and some respect for people's ultimate willingness to accept responsibility can help a good deal. Post-mortems and bull sessions devoted to what was right or wrong about the last meeting are useful techniques for this purpose if the group meets periodically.

I remember one group of six men working on a research project full time. The project called for the six to break up into pairs and travel to some field locations for a few days. The group spent hours trying to decide who would go where with whom. Afterward, in a bull-session review of the day's progress, someone pointed out that it was silly to have thrashed around so long over this trivial point. This stimulus finally brought a previously hidden issue out in the open. Everyone liked Joe, and everyone wanted to be the one to travel with Joe. But nobody would admit it; so they had used all sorts of "rational" arguments all day about why one pairing arrangement or another wouldn't work. Of course this recognition came several hours too late, but it helped to prevent occurrence of similar stalemates later. Post-mortems like this become easier with time. In fact they can often be worked in as part of the meeting itself, so that people are always watching for and pointing up underlying feelings contemporaneously with their discussions of content problems.

Groups that operate with fairly free expression and recognition of feelings follow a somewhat different pattern from more carefully controlled groups. They start slowly, characteristically with considerable hodgepodge and disturbance and little measurable progress. But they can accelerate fast once the air is cleared. Controlled groups, on the other hand, show steadier, step-by-step progress that seems more orderly from the outside.

Barriers to communication in groups

It may be profitable to examine the same problem from the other side. Instead of asking, "What causes irrelevant noise?" one can ask, "What blocks the communication of relevant information?" This is the same question we asked in chapter 11. What blocks feedback?

Looking at the problem from this perspective can be useful; for, while it is true that too much is often said in groups, too much may also be left unsaid. The subordinate says, "Yes, I understand your instructions," but later it turns out that he did not understand. The salesman does not think it important to tell the sales manager about the change in the customer's attitude. The production worker does not report that his machine is acting oddly because he forgot to lubricate it. The patient says, "You're the doctor; you tell *me* where it hurts." These kinds of relevant information left uncommunicated are the opposite of noise. The atmosphere of a group may be too quiet—too quiet in the sense that problems do not get all available information brought to bear upon them.

Sometimes the barriers that limit communication are simple mechanical ones. Thus, when the communication system is a one-way loudspeaker, the simple absence of channels in one direction makes it mechanically impossible for the receiver to send relevant information back to the sender. Letter writing is another process that includes at least a partial mechanical barrier. People can write letters in two directions, but the process necessarily involves a time lag that constitutes a partial barrier to the communication of information that may be useful only if it arrives quickly.

Such mechanical barriers, however, are probably the least important barriers to communication in human groups. The most significant barriers are the more ephemeral psychological ones like these examples:

First, there is a *status barrier* between superior and subordinate that limits communication in either direction because of fear of disapproval, on the one hand, or loss of prestige, on the other:

"If I ask that question these people will think I don't know enough to be boss, so I'll act like I know the answer already."

"If I admit this to the boss, he'll be wild. He'll think I've lost my touch."

Then there is the *interpersonal-hostility barrier*. This is the one that goes:

"I won't give that guy the satisfaction of admitting he's got a good idea. And I certainly won't let him in on my idea."

And there is the *parliamentary methods barrier*. It sometimes takes this form:

"I can't speak until I'm recognized by the chair; and if the chair never recognizes me, my information will never come out. If the chair does recognize me later, I'll still say what should be said now—even if it's irrelevant later."

We need not elaborate on the way parliamentary procedures, which were intended to promote and simplify communication, have been used in social and political affairs selectively to prevent and complicate communication.

These kinds of barriers are troublemakers in human groups. They cannot be dammed up or set aside at will. They do not even have the saving grace of remaining stable and fixed. Instead they move and change with moods and feelings of group members, so that now one set is in operation and now another.

The answers to such barriers may be the same as the answer to too much noise. They could be circumvented if they themselves were communicated. If two people, for example, can reach the point where they can tell one another what they think of one another, they may be able to work out an understanding that will allow them to communicate successfully. But ordinarily they do not communicate these feelings—they do not especially in the industrial culture. Instead, they say, "Stick to the facts! Don't get emotional! Let's be business-like!" This cultural attitude is probably the biggest communication barrier of all because it prevents the communication of interpersonal feelings, and uncommunicated interpersonal feelings, in turn, complicate and sometimes prevent the communication of facts.

Sensitivity training: One assault on barriers to communication

Back in the late forties, when serious research into group dynamics was getting started, a team of social scientists made some interesting discoveries. They put heterogeneous groups of a dozen people out in the country for three weeks, asking the members to meet for several hours a day with a "trainer."

But there was no agenda, no announced purpose, no assignment for the meeting. Each group was simply to meet and
talk. The trainer's job was nondirective.

Two discoveries were made: First, such groups showed
considerable uniformity in their behavior, group after group
going through what seemed to be very similar stages over the
three weeks. Second, a large percentage of the people involved found the experience extremely exciting, often
reporting that it had significantly changed their lives.

That was the birth of T (for training) groups, or sensitivity
training, a set of techniques still controversial and still
growing in its organizational applications.

With time and exploration, sensitivity training began to
show two important tendencies. First, the program seemed to
give participants a deeper understanding of group psychology
and hence, it was hoped, the ability to lead or participate in
groups more effectively. Second and conjointly, it provided
members with a mirror in which to observe themselves, a
chance to get feedback from others about the way their behavior came through. Both of these tendencies can be
thought of as underlying aspects of the group process, likely
to be present, but not readily discernible, in actual, work-
oriented groups.

It may be worth pointing out, too, that much of the feedback, indeed much of the total communication in T-groups,
is in the form of feelings and emotions rather than facts. And
the language is often the iconic language of empathy, rather
than the symbolic language likely to accompany more task-
oriented discussions. Indeed, for many trainers one prime
purpose of sensitivity training is to do what that phrase suggests, to train sensitivity; that is, to train people's skills in
feeling other people's feelings—a highly iconic, sometimes
enactive process.

An outcome of this self-examination of a group turned out
to be increased "openness," an increasing tendency, as the
group progressed, for people to feel free to say what they
thought without embarrassment or fear. From this comes the
notion of more valid, more authentic communication, as a
consequence, says the theory, of reduced interpersonal barriers to communication or, conversely, an increase in mutual
trust.

Several questions then arise, and much of the controversy
about sensitivity training in organizations centers on them:
Does it follow that groups whose members trust one another
and communicate easily and openly will do better work? If

you feel, as many social scientists and others do, that restricted communication leads to distortions in problem-solving, the answer is yes (at least for problem-solving groups). But doesn't that kind of free and easy communication move counter to the idea of the hierarchy of rank and authority, which, after all, rules that subordinates should speak when asked, not when they feel like it? Again, the answer is yes. Hence, again, debate and conflict arise about what will happen to our organization if we go the sensitivity-training route. And a third issue: Isn't it psychologically dangerous to play these games? Isn't it emotionally stressful to have others finger your weaknesses and inadequacies in a quasi-public situation? Yes and no. Some psychologically fragile people have a very tough time in T-groups. Most people feel psychologically better off.

Another important qualification: Sensitivity training is a great big bag. Since it values openness and individual autonomy, its rules and controls aren't very tight, though they are abuilding. All kinds of leaders lead T-groups. In recent years some of them have surged forward (or backward) into a whole host of "encounter techniques," some of which press members very hard indeed, and some of which wave a mystical, near-religious ideological flag. Others, more earthy and establishment-oriented, have worked in the organizational context, developing techniques for more effective organizational teamwork.

In their myriad forms, these techniques retain the two elements that have caused us to include this brief discussion of them in this chapter: They always involve small groups, in organizations or out; and they are always concerned with knocking down barriers to communication among group members. In addition to those two aspects of the technique, there is also a theory, or better perhaps, a faith, that more open communication will make for healthier individuals and a more satisfactory organizational environment.

The short and the long

Sometimes when we think of a committee we are thinking of a group that meets three or four times and is then finished. For these committees we can ignore much of what has been said here. There probably is not time for people to work off feelings, anyway. But if the committee is a continuing one, these issues become important. Then some time spent lubricating and adjusting the mechanism may be well worthwhile, and so too may be the usable storage of results.

So we need perhaps to separate these two kinds of groups in the way we separated one-shot from continuing relationships in the chapter on influence. In a one-shot situation A need not look far beyond his nose; his job is to make the sale. In a one-shot committee, members need not look far ahead either. They can concentrate on the solution of the problem at hand and put on the perceptual blinders of parliamentary rules to block off the irritating intrusion of human emotions. They don't even have to remember *how* they solved the problem.

But if they are going to work together for a while, a wider perspective is required. Such groups need to develop a general program for solving many problems. They must, like individuals, pay attention to their own processes; they need to search out and learn *ways* of solving classes of problems even more than they need a quick and good solution to the problem at hand. Sensitivity training is one major tool for achieving this goal.

In summary

It may be a mistake to equate orderliness with efficiency in group processes.

The "irrelevant" noise made by people in groups may represent attempts by members to satisfy personal needs. If that noise is forbidden expression, it may go underground but continue to distort the group's operation.

Conversely, there may be too little noise in a group; that is, available relevant information may not be forthcoming because of barriers in the communication system. Some of these barriers may be mechanical, but many of them are psychological, like barriers created by status differences or interpersonal jealousies.

In either case, too much noise or too little, the preferred course would seem to be to promote rather than limit communication, that is, to accept and deal with information about personal feelings and personal needs as well as with information about pertinent facts.

Sensitivity training is a diverse package of techniques aimed at that issue. It is a way of trying to increase openness and validity of communication in groups.

For short-lived groups, the solution to the problem at hand may take top priority. For longer-lived ones, programs and processes for solving classes of problems deserve precedence.

**Operating problems
of groups
Getting words around
efficiently**

When an executive must chair or participate in a committee, he is usually up against an influence problem calling for careful strategy and tactics. He comes into the meeting with some objectives he would like to achieve, either personally or as a representative of some faction. If he is a salesman he would like the interests of salesmen to prevail over the interests of production people. If he represents industrial engineering it is that group's purposes he is serving.

Under such circumstances an executive may sometimes conclude that his ends will best be gained by sabotaging the committee on which he is participating. Sometimes an analysis of the situation will lead him to compromise some of his objectives, and sometimes full cooperation with the committee may seem the most promising course. No matter what his objective, and none can universally be labeled more right or wrong than any other, he can probably plan and execute his strategy best if he knows his own strengths and weaknesses and the strengths and weaknesses of committees.

This chapter attempts to outline, for the use of the committee participant, some characteristic operating problems of committees (and other small groups). These problems, insofar as they are problems of influence, have much in common with those considered in part 2. They raise questions about the strategic use of authority, about the mutuality of responsibility, and about AA types of influence.

Although committees may differ radically in size, purpose, design, membership, and procedure, they have some problems in common. The similarities are divided here into four categories: problems of objective; personnel problems; problems of navigation; and problems of decision-making.

Problems of objective

If a committee of executives starts out to decide whether or not to institute selection tests, their objective seems, at first, perfectly unambiguous. Then someone discovers that one member has quite a different conception of selection tests from other members of the group. Ten minutes later someone raises these questions: "Is our objective to decide on selection tests only? Or are we really here to revise all our selection procedures? Are interviews and application blanks tests, or are they outside our scope?"

Ten minutes later still, someone wants to know: "What does the boss really have in mind when he asks us to look into this? How much money is he willing to spend? Is he willing for us to do a major research job? Or does he want us to buy a packaged product even though it may not be very good?"

And still later someone with an irate note in his voice asks: "What are we trying to decide anyhow? Is it whether or not tests are a good idea? Or is it what tests to buy?"

And so on at intervals throughout the meeting. What seemed precise and unambiguous turns out to be diffuse and shadowy.

Defining objectives becomes more or less difficult with the nature of the problem the group faces. But almost every time we find a decison-making committee in action, we also find periodic difficulties with the definition of objectives.

Moreover, we find another sort of difficulty involving objectives. Besides these overt questions, a series of covert problems is often present. A major one is the problem of subgroup objectives versus group objectives. Thus, in collective bargaining everyone may overtly agree that the objective is to work out a best solution to common problems. But everyone also knows that other major objectives are in operation and that they are in conflict. The union wants to get the best deal it can get, even at the expense of management. And management wants the best deal it can get, even at the expense of the union.

Similarly, in a meeting in which several departments are represented, we often find unverbalized objectives lying just below the surface. The sales department wants to make sure that it doesn't lose any of its control over pricing. The production people do not want the salesmen to be in a better position to dictate production schedules after the meeting than they were before. And so on.

A third level of problems also exists. This is the level of the individual operating as an individual. "How does the boss really feel about this issue? What decisions will please him most? Is my objective really to take the direction that I think is best, or the direction that will most please the boss?" Or, similarly, "Where does this particular proposal fit into the larger political picture? Who will get hurt if we take one direction or another? Who will be helped?"

Clearly the "right" way to cope with these problems will vary with the motives of the coper. Sometimes an individual or subgroup can profit most by blocking the definition of objectives. One can hardly find a better way to keep a meeting from going anywhere than to raise a new specific issue every time the committee gets close to clarifying its purposes. On the other hand, one can equally well befuddle a meeting by overemphasizing objectives—especially if a member chooses so to broaden and complicate them as to take the meeting altogether out of the range of possible accomplishment. The problem is that objectives create difficulties for groups so long as they are differently understood by different people in the group and so long as some of them are not out on the table. Once everyone in the group has a reasonably good feel for the limits of the problem and for the variety of objectives present, something can usually be done about them.

Helping to clarify objectives, perhaps by restating someone else's statement, can help a group to get started and can also put the restater, the clarifier, in a position of strength in the group. Similarly, conscious efforts to talk about covert objectives (as we pointed out in the last chapter), if one suspects their presence, can help a committee to function more efficiently; although the person who does this job takes more risks with covert than with overt issues. If one member suggests, for example, that someone else's personal needs are predominating, guards will be quickly thrown up, and the discussion may thereby be led into fruitless defensive argument. So a group member or chairman who feels that someone in the meeting has ulterior motives had better word and time his suggestion carefully. If he himself is the person with ulterior motives, he may do himself and his cause some good by expressing them—if his cause will be helped by an efficient meeting.

The point is that groups are not likely to go anywhere unless they know where they are going. Even a single human being may have trouble defining his own objectives, and the problem gets much more complicated in a group. Whether it is advantageous for a group member to clarify objectives in the group or to confuse them, to express his own personal objectives or to hide them, these are questions each member of a group must weigh for himself.

From the perspective of the whole group instead of any individual member, the problems to be solved are these: (1) to have every man in the group know where the group is going; (2) to have every man in the group either want to go where the group is going or say where he wants to get off; (3) if there are people who want to get off early, either to change objectives so these people can go along or to let them off and start over; and (4) to take another look every once in a while to see whether objectives need to be changed or modified.

Several actions can help a group in these directions. If people try to communicate about objectives, both personal and official, then at least the problem is out on the table where it can be seen and dealt with. Objectives are likely to be communicated readily if they are not jammed down people's throats by chairmen, if they are treated as a normal part of the agenda, and if the general atmosphere of the meeting encourages this kind of feedback. If, in other words, they operate more like Alcoholics Anonymous and less like the old-time, iron-pants boss.

A census of ideas about the group's objectives taken early in a meeting can also help get these issues out on the table quickly. Often, in meetings, the first idea raised becomes the take-off point for discussion, thereby eliminating expression of some other possibilities. Since the first highway may not be the best one, it can be useful to map out several alternatives before starting the trip.

Problems of personnel

Another class of obstacles that seems to block small-group operation centers in the personalities of the participants. Such personnel problems include factors carried into the group by the members, like the leader's personality, his dominance or submissiveness, the intensity of his desire to be liked, and so on. They also include problems of individual members' talkativeness, shyness, argumentativeness, and defensiveness.

There are problems of communication, too, stemming from differences in rank, age, expertness, and prestige in the company. And certain problems may arise within the group —somebody's idea is ignored, somebody else's is laughed at, somebody else says absolutely nothing and just smiles, thereby frightening some of his colleagues and encouraging others. Finally, this general personnel category includes problems of group mood: elation, depression, and regression into dirty stories or golf or anything except the subject at hand.

No way of avoiding such problems has yet been found, but there are ways of minimizing them. From the group point of view, they are problems only if relevant ideas and information are omitted or distorted as a consequence of them. Often, of course, such problems do affect both the kind and degree of communication. The quiet man who sits and smokes his pipe may seriously affect the rate and even the nature of the ideas that are contributed. For out of the corner of his eye each member may be watching him for some sign of approval or disapproval. Depending primarily on any member's own feelings of security or insecurity, this point or that may be modified, withheld or overemphasized because of the quiet man.

Or shy man A offers a suggestion which is ignored. He offers it again and it is again ignored. Like the adolescent in the chapter on frustration, one can see A gradually withdraw, thereafter to come out of his shell only infrequently and only in order to jab at someone else's ideas.

What, then, can be done, not so much to prevent such problems as to deal with them? Again the answer seems to lie in the communication process. For if a group can communicate about its personnel problems, the problems may be resolved. But they cannot be resolved so long as they remain hidden and uncommunicated. This again is the problem of dealing with noise. These issues can be opened for group discussion, or they can be denied entry. If a group chooses to deny them, if it chooses to cut off argument, to require that emotionalism be kept out of the meeting and that dirty stories be excluded, then the group is ignoring data relevant to its own operation. And data about itself are as important to the solution of a group's problem as they are to the solution of any individual's problem.

Discussion of such personnel issues need not mean that the group has to examine the remote causes of people's feelings. As in the case of A trying to influence B, the original causes of B's feelings are often irrelevant, but the feelings themselves need to get aired. Thus, when some members of a group leave the field by going off into jokes or gossip or pipe dreams, it is not absolutely necessary to find out why they are doing it. It may be necessary, however, to recognize that such digressions are not accidental. They represent attempts to satisfy needs, to get rid of tension. It may therefore be wise to permit time to be "wasted" in the release of such tensions, instead of forcing the needs to find outlet through the medium of "rational" discussion. Recognition and acceptance of people's feelings and encouragement of an atmosphere of permissiveness seem to be sensible directions for a problem-solving group to take.

A group that operates this way may seem strange sometimes. It does not progress steadily, but in bursts, with periods of highly concentrated work interspersed with periods of digression or argument or laughter. If a superior should happen to walk in on such a group meeting, the chances are about even that he would be impressed or disturbed by what he found.

As it is for problems of objective, the census is a handy device for getting personnel problems out on the table. It is useful for a group to stop once in a while just so that people can say how they feel—how they feel about the group's progress, how they feel about the methods the group is using, how they feel in general. Periodic stops to examine feelings need not be formally instituted; in fact, they occur quite naturally if we let them.

A third method for coping with personnel problems is, surprisingly, to de-emphasize pre-meeting preparation. It seems, at first, to make sense to urge group members to think about the committee agenda in advance and to come "prepared." But preplanning can also be a source of serious personnel difficulties. For "preparation" may mean that each man works out his individual position before the meeting and then comes into the group to try to sell his position to the rest. If that is what preparation means, every member of the group now has a position to defend. If his position is rejected he may feel he has suffered a personal, egoistic defeat.

Group leaders especially are given to overpreparation. They often feel that the responsibility for success rests solely with them. Consequently, a new chairman is likely to go home and think out alternative answers to the problem before the meeting and to select the answer that seems best to him. He then comes into the meeting with the wrong expectations about the right answers. Whereupon a whole host of reactive personnel problems arises.

"Preparation" can have other more useful meanings, too. A leader can plan a group meeting without creating much difficulty for himself or his group. It is one thing, for example, to come armed with all the information one can muster to feed into the hopper and quite another to come armed with conclusions. Moreover, to be prepared with a general procedural plan for conducting a meeting is different from coming with a specific step-by-step outline. Group members are likely to accept information or a general plan but to resist the imposition of conclusions or tight, inflexible procedures. Moreover, if a problem is big enough to call for a meeting, a chairman who has the answer in advance is often incorrectly prejudging the complexity of the issue.

This whole personnel question involves one of the issues talked about in the section on influence—the location of responsibility. Groups are likely to function with a minimum of personnel difficulty when the responsibility for action and procedure lies with all the members rather than with any particular individual. The responsibility then remaining for the chairman or the leader is to help provide and police a communication system that will evoke all the information the group needs to make its decisions.

Problems of navigation

Groups get lost in the problems they try to solve. Often they have difficulty locating their position after they have decided where they want to go and have started out to get there. The problems here include timing, meeting deadlines, laying out sequences. They are programing problems. They can be called problems for two reasons: First, they represent sources of inefficiency in a group. Once a group has decided on a destination, it can get itself so involved in going there that it gets lost. It doesn't notice the wrong turn or the circularity of its movements. Second, navigation is a problem because of the relationship between people's self-orientation and people's feelings. Group members feel uncertain and anxious if they don't know where they are. They may feel they are making no progress when in fact they are. Or they may feel that they are drifting purposelessly. These feelings are often direct consequences of poor navigation.

Skilful navigation is something of an art. A chairman (or any member of a group) who begins to feel that his group is getting lost has several ways of trying to do something about it. He can just wait and hope the group will find itself. He can ask the members to stop and go somewhere else. Or he can ask them to stop and try to find out where they are going. If they then decide they like where they are going, they can pick up where they left off; if they don't like it, they can change.

This third alternative is a sensible one for several reasons. Failure to do anything includes the possibility that people who begin to feel lost may also begin to withdraw from the scene. Simply vetoing the present course is bound to create some kind of debilitating emotional reaction, either further withdrawal or aggression. But just asking for a pause to reconsider is likely to yield few side effects and may actually enhance the group's progress.

Any navigational act, however, especially if it comes from a leader, involves some risks for the actor. For navigational interruptions constitute restrictions on the group, and restrictions may make the restricter unpopular. But periods of unpopularity, after all, are the fate of a group leader. He must choose between the long-term gain that will come from overall efficiency and the short-term popularity he can invite by abdicating his leadership and ignoring uncomfortable problems like deadlines.

What this navigational problem amounts to, then, is that somebody—the leader or anyone else—has to keep his eye on the group as well as on the problems the group is trying to solve and has to report back what he finds.

Decision-making problems

Another source of difficulty in groups arises at those points at which a decision seems appropriate. Discussion of a point has been more or less completed, and the time to come to some conclusion has arrived. Sometimes groups block impossibly at these points. They seem unable to recognize them or unable to make any decisions if they do recognize them. And sometimes the decisions that do get made do not seem to be meaningful. People don't pay much attention to them, or they don't act upon them once they leave the meeting.

The problem is to get decisions made when they are ready to be made and to get them made in a way that will lead to follow-up action by the people in the group after they leave the group.

Group leaders may approach this problem in one of two extreme ways. Sometimes a chairman will push hard for decisions, allowing a specified period for discussion and then asking immediately for a vote. At the other end of the scale is the leader who never gets to decision-making points, either because he doesn't recognize those points or because the discussion of an issue just never seems to be fully completed. Like the individual problem-solvers in chapter 6, in other words, groups may fail to search for alternatives long enough or may demand an optimum solution well beyond their realistic level of achievement.

Most businessmen favor the limited discussion and vote method of the parliamentary variety. They recognize that the best is too hard to get; so they are satisfied with a brief search. The primary weakness of that method is that, although the decision finally reached may be a satisfactory solution to the problem, it may be a decision in appearance more than reality. When a decision is forced quickly and when the method of deciding is by vote, what is left for the minority except psychologically to reject the decision? If they were "rational" human beings, of course, they would accept the majority wish and carry out their part in it. But most of us, even though we may try consciously to accept a decision with which we disagree, have trouble getting very enthusiastic about it. In a sense the minority is challenged to prove that the majority decision is wrong. Such a challenge is easy to meet when the time comes for individual action, simply by acting in ways that "prove" the decision cannot be made to work.

Moreover, if decisions come too early, before people feel that they have contributed what they have to contribute, before they have organized and clarified the issues for themselves, then the decisions reached may indeed be superficial and unsatisfactory. They are therefore likely to be forgotten quickly or passed over lightly once the meeting is over. Vague feelings of hostility and resistance may also follow, feelings that may lead consciously or unconsciously to sabotage or denial of the decision.

A good deal of research evidence shows that decisions are carried into action most effectively when they are group-consensus decisions, when all members of a group can somehow settle by their own efforts on a choice with which they all agree. On the other hand, decisions imposed from the outside or decisions imposed on a minority by a majority or decisions imposed by the leader are not likely to be lasting or effective, for the same reasons that restrictive authority is a poor tool for effecting important changes in attitude.

Consensus decisions are not easy to achieve. People in groups have an unhappy tendency to disagree with one another, either overtly or covertly. And yet, if the group's problems require that every member carry out of the group a desire to act positively on the group's decision, then it is imperative that everyone accept, both consciously and unconsciously, the decisions reached in the group.

Often, it is true, we must fall short of ideal decision-making procedures. Deadlines and other immediate pressures force us to make majority or individual-leader decisions. But this will occur less often when we have built an atmosphere that makes consensus easier. Open two-way communication,

clarification of people's feelings, freedom to object—these
contribute to the ease with which consensus can be
approached. Sometimes even the most efficient group will run
into a decision for which consensus seems impossible to
achieve. Someone just cannot or will not agree with the position being taken. Here again, however, even if total
agreement cannot be reached on the problem, agreement can
often be reached about the need for some kind of decision.
Then, at least, the minority has expressed its position, has announced that it is not ready to change that position, has had a
chance to express its own feelings about its position, and has
agreed that some decision short of unanimity is necessary.

Leadership in groups

A leader obviously is a person in a role. Leadership is a form
of relationship between persons and, usually, with a task or a
goal. The organization can appoint or elect leaders, but it
can't appoint or elect leadership. Leadership is a set of functions, mostly of relational behaviors. The leader is a person
in the role called "leader."

For years researchers have sought to define the characteristics of effective leaders, that is, characteristics that are
related to performing effective leadership when such persons
are in leader roles. Not very many differentiating characteristics have been found. Sensitivity, personal security, and a
modicum of intelligence may be some. These characteristics
probably do help people somewhat to develop appropriate
relationships and perform appropriate leadership functions.
But the search for leader characteristics was bound to be of
limited value, because leadership is so clearly an interactive,
relational activity. That is, leadership depends at least as
much on those led as it does on the leader. If the leader is intelligent, sensitive, and secure, but a northern black, and the
rest of the group is rural southern white, the leader will have
problems in exercising leadership. And suppose that this
group whose leader is black and whose members are rural
southern whites happens to have as its assignment a problem
like designing a new educational system for the state of
Alabama; and suppose further that the black leader was just
another civil servant whose rank was no higher than any of
the other members. Do his (the leader's) personal characteristics matter much? Certainly they matter somewhat. He'll
have to drag out every bit of sensitivity and intelligence he's
got if he hopes to perform effective leadership functions in
that group, with that assignment, from that rank and role.

But isn't his leadership effectiveness more likely to be determined by such things as his blackness in comparison with the members' whiteness, his official power and authority relative to theirs, and the kind of task—programed or open-ended—that is at hand?

Leadership effectiveness, that is to say, has to be contingent upon many aspects of the relationship of leader and follower, and upon task.

But notice that this takes us to another related issue: leader flexibility. For having said that leadership effectiveness depends on conditions of task, power, and attitudes, we are still left with a range of autonomous behavior for the leader. If his power is small, if the job is broad and open-ended, if members don't trust him, what's the best way for him to behave? He may not have much choice, but perhaps some ways of behaving will increase his chances while others will decrease them.

Let's consider, then, what some alternative behaviors might be. Most researchers tend to range leadership styles from authoritarian to permissive or participative. But that one-dimensional scale is inadequate, isn't it? Another dimension is the old centralization-decentralization issue in another form. Some leaders, authoritarian or permissive, try to make like a leader by pulling all leadership functions in toward themselves. They set agendas; they navigate; they comfort people and finger people; they decide when and often how a decision is to be taken. In general, authoritarian leaders tend to behave in a more centralized way, but a self-conscious, permissive type also often inadvertently plays the same game.

On the authoritarian-permissive dimension, in any case, there is moderate evidence to suggest that being fairly tough and authoritarian is the leader's best bet when the problem is clear and solvable, and when he has legitimate power. At the other end, as in our black-and-white case, being fairly tough is again probably the leader's best bet, but not a very good one. It seems to be in the big middle range of messy problems and limited power that more permissive leader styles have the greatest hope. All of which is another way of saying what we have said and shall say often in this book: when we don't know exactly what we're doing, it's a good idea to loosen things up and let other people in on the act. Imaginative people working in an open environment are still a good tool for solving dirty problems.

If the task is large and messy, it makes sense to spread the leadership functions around, to get everybody in on the act. It makes even more sense to do this if the members themselves will have to implement the decisions taken in the group—that is, if member commitment is one of the leader's goals, as well as a satisfactory solution.

But everything we have said about leaders and leadership until now has implicitly assumed rather quiet problem-solving groups, committees in the company, or engineering task forces. In such groups the issue of personal charisma is not very central. Indeed, charismatic leaders in such roles in organizations often manage to get their strong and unusual personalities in the group's way. But there are conditions where personal charisma is worth its weight in gold—in crises, for example, or after a major defeat, when a group needs most of all someone to control it and lift it up off the ground. A personal sense of push and urgency, of enthusiasm, of confidence, of "soul," can become an invaluable leader-ship function.

But again notice the flexibility problem! Effective leader-ship style, we have now said, depends on group and task con-ditions. Being permissive is great under some conditions; being tough and decisive is great under others; being emo-tional, having a dream is just what's needed in others.

We leave it to the reader to answer the last question in this chapter: Even if you know what style is needed, can you do it? Can you change styles? Can you be tough if you're usually gentle and permissive? Can you exude enthusiasm and com-municate emotion if you're usually a pretty controlled, unemotional type? If not, maybe you need to share your lead-er jobs with others in order to guarantee effective leadership for your groups.

In summary

No matter what a group member's purposes may be, famil-iarity with the operating characteristics of groups can be useful.

Problems involving objectives are one major category. Ob-jectives often seem clearer than they are. These problems can be dealt with by building discussion of objectives into the agenda, by taking an early census of members' conceptions of the questions to be worked out, and by periodically reex-amining objectives.

Personnel problems are a second major category. These include problems of personalities, moods, individual needs, and the like. Again, open, permissive communication seems indicated to encourage consideration of these secondary but relevant questions.

Navigational problems also plague groups. Groups can get

so involved in content matters that they may lose direction. Periodic stops, to shift from content to process, can alleviate these difficulties.

Decision-making raises additional problems in groups. Unanimous consensus is an ideal goal if action and initiative outside the group are sought.

Group leadership is seen here as a relational job in a group, not as a set of personal attributes. Appropriate leader behavior is, therefore, contingent upon the relationship with followers and upon the nature of the job. And it therefore calls for flexibility in the behavior of people who occupy leader roles for extended periods.

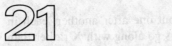

21

**Independence and conformity
The problem of truth
in the face of pressure**

Here is a problem:

You are a member of a committee. It doesn't matter what sort of a committee; you may be trying to select new products, or working out a strategy for up-coming negotiations with the union, or allocating space in the new laboratory, or deciding which of several men to promote to a new job. It is a committee made up mostly of people at about your level, chaired by a man who is intelligent and reasonable and rather well liked by all of you. He has circulated an agenda in advance of your next meeting, and you have thought a good deal about it and arrived at a position on the very first item—a position you feel rather strongly about.

When you arrive at the meeting room, a few of the eight members have not yet shown up, so you and four or five others chat about this and that until things get under way. After the late arrivals show up and you exchange a few pleasantries, the chairman gets things started and gradually one member after another begins to express his views about the first item on the agenda. By the time you get into the act, it has become pretty clear that most members seem to share one opinion—*an opinion very different from yours*. Most people seem to be nodding their heads and saying, "Yes, method X suggested by Joe Blow looks like a pretty good solution."

Then you come in rather strongly for method Y. Nobody seems very upset. Everybody listens politely. Some of the fellows ask you questions and make comments that are partially supportive and partially in disagreement. And the discussion goes on.

After a while the chairman says, "Well, we've been at this for awhile; let's see where we stand." And he tries to summarize the two positions that have been taken, essentially Joe Blow's position X and your position Y.

It's all done informally, but one after another, each in his own style, the members go along with X rather than Y. As one after another of the members goes this way, you begin to feel some discomfort. People seem to be turning toward you, psychologically if not physically; and the chairman casts an inquiring look your way. This is a committee that likes to operate informally, and you approve of this informality. You know that the chairman doesn't want to have to put this issue up to a formal vote and say, "We have decided seven to one in favor of X over Y." On the other hand, in your opinion, Y is right and X is wrong.

So the pressure begins to build and the spotlight begins to focus on you. The chairman says, "Well look, gentlemen, we've got a little time. Why don't we talk a little longer." And turning to you, he says, "Why don't you give us a rundown on the reasons for your position?" So you do. You lay it out in a way that sounds (to you) forceful and reasonable and correct.

The rest of the committee, which is now focusing rather intently on you, asks questions. It's as though you are the center of a star communication net. Everybody is turning toward you and talking to you. They are not shouting at you; they are not angry at you; they are simply asking you "rationally" to prove your position.

This goes on for a while and then people begin to get a little fidgety. Finally, one of the members turns to you and says, "Perhaps our differences aren't as big as they look. Perhaps it's all really just a matter of words. Sometimes differences that are really small begin to blow up to look like something bigger than they are." And the chairman adds, "Well, gentlemen, it is getting rather late and in the interests of getting this job done, I think we have to arrive at some kind of conclusion." Then somebody laughs, turns to you, and says, "Why don't you just come along for the ride, and then we can all go out and have a cup of coffee?"

You are no dope. You can really feel the pressure now. You know that what these people are really saying is, "You are one of us. We want to get going. Don't hold us up any longer."

But you're a tough and rugged individualist. You're a man of principle. Position Y is right, by golly, and you say so again rather forcefully. There is a long silence. Then one of the members says something forceful in reply: "Oh for Chrissakes! You've been riding that horse for about three-quarters of an hour now, and you haven't come up with a single new reason. Why the hell are you being so stubborn?" As though this first opening is a signal, others join in on the attack. People go at you from all sides. They point out that you've been wrong before when you've held out in situations like this. They attack your loyalty to the group. After all you know this group likes to operate by consensus, and that it is important to all the rest of them that you all agree. They hit you with everything they've got. Even the chairman seems to be joining in.

But still you hold out. You just can't bring yourself to accept position X when it is so patently clear to you that Y is the only reasonable answer. So there you sit thinking that this is a little like how it must feel to be interrogated by the Gestapo. Your mouth is dry and you seem to be all alone inside your own thin skin. But you've been raised right! You also think of individuality and honor. And so you grit your teeth and fight back. And the clock ticks along.

What comes next?

Pretty far down inside you, you know damn well what will come next. The floodlights will be turned off; but not to give you relief. Finally (and rather suddenly), one of the members turns to the chairman and says, "We've been at this for almost an hour and a half. We have other business at hand. I think we should adopt position X, and then go on about our business." And other people turn their chairs, facing one another and the chairman; and no longer facing you. They summarize the arguments for position X and someone says, "Okay, we've decided to do X; now let's go on with the next item."

You've been quiet for the last few minutes because people haven't been talking to you. You have listened to the summary of the reasons for accepting position X, and since one of them is clearly absurd, you open your mouth to say something about it. A couple of people in the group turn and look at you as you talk, but they don't say anything in return. The others don't even look, and the chairman finally says, "Let's get on to the next problem on the agenda." And the group goes ahead.

You know what's happened. You have been psychologically amputated. As far as the group is concerned, you are no longer there. When you say things, you are no longer heard. Your influence is now zero. This is the last stage in the process by which groups deal with deviating, nonconforming members. You have been sealed off.

The story we have just told is probably reasonably familiar to almost every adult. It is not limited to committees of executives in industry. We encountered the same pressures when we were kids in the family, in street corner gangs, and in school groups. We met it again as teenagers, when we were pressed to conform to group standards of dress and deportment—standards we often tried to resist. And we keep hitting it.

The stages of group pressure

But the fact that we have encountered it often doesn't make the pain and the pressure any less. In fact, our experience has taught this so well that we can foretell early in the process what we will be in for if we buck the group. We know they are likely to start out being reasonable and rational, discussing the pros and cons of the issue. But even at that stage, it is implicitly quite clear that the deviant, not the group, is expected to change.

We can sense what comes next, too. We know the seductive pat-on-the-back routine. We know that some members of the group will be friendly and smile and joke with us. They will, in effect, tell us how much they love us and remind us of how valuable the group is to us. They will behave like a woman who wants a mink coat from a man, chucking us under the chin and making up to us.

And we also know what is likely to happen if we don't come across.

Groups, like (some) women, are likely to get tired of playing games rather quickly. At some point, they will decide that they have wasted enough time on that tactic. Then the silken glove will come off to expose the iron fist. If reason won't work, and seduction won't work, then the group moves to stage 3, attack. Now they try to beat us into submission. They pull out all stops; the mask is off.

But even that isn't the last stage in the process of exerting pressure on the deviating individual. The last stage is amputation. It's as though the members of the group were saying, "Let's reason with him; if that doesn't work, let's try to tease him by emotional seduction; and if even that doesn't work, let's beat him over the head until he has to give up. Failing that, we'll excommunicate him; we'll amputate him from the group; we'll disown him."

This last and final stage is for most of us a very serious and frightening possibility; the more frightening, the more we value the group. The threat of isolation, physical or psychological, is a very grave threat indeed. We don't want to be abandoned by our families, nor by our friends, nor by our business associates.

Perhaps it is because we can foresee this ultimate stage that even mild and early pressures can often cause us to change positions or beliefs or attitudes. Most of us don't get all the way through meetings like the one we described at the beginning of this chapter. We are apt to give in a good deal earlier in the game. We "work things out" when we are still at the reasoning level or at the emotional seduction level. For the paradox in this process is that the greater the pressure the group exerts on the deviant through these steps, the more difficult it is for the deviant to give in. The stage at which we can give in most easily (and still save face) is the first stage; the reasonable, rational stage. If we say "yes" in response to the chucking under the chin and the love-making, we are apt to feel a little sheepish, but that isn't terribly embarrassing. To give in under a beating is a lot more painful, and a lot weaker and more shameful. And to give in after we have been amputated is darn near impossible because nobody is there to accept our surrender.

Is the group being cruel and capricious?

So far we have been viewing the group's pressures on the deviant from the deviant's perspective. For most of us the individual who holds out is the hero, whether he wins or loses. For we value individuality and nonconformity in our society, or at least we say we do. We identify with the underdog, with the deer attacked by wolves. But it is useful to view this same problem from the other perspective, that of the group. We may ask: Why are these people doing this? Why are they reasoning, seducing, attacking, amputating? Is it just a malicious, devilish kind of behavior to satisfy some sadistic needs of the group members? Not usually. If we think of the times we ourselves have been members of the majority, we can begin to see the other side of the picture.

Here is a group that is trying to get a job done. To get the job done well depends in large part on getting wholehearted agreement and cooperation from all members of the group. But there is a clock, and there are other constraints imposed by the world.

We go about the problem in good spirit, trying to cooperate, trying to understand, trying to work out a solution that we can all accept and to do it in a reasonable time. And we get very close to an answer. Everybody seems to be in perfect agreement except for that one character there.

Then what shall we do? As reasonable men, we do not steam-roller a person because he thinks differently from us. We listen to him and we ask him to listen to us. So we go through that ritual. We reason with him. But that doesn't work; he just doesn't seem to be able to see it our way. The clock is ticking away.

What next? Why then we try to appeal to him on emotional grounds, on grounds of loyalty or decency. We almost beg him to agree. This is a difficult thing for us to do, but we want to get the job done and we don't want to hurt him. We appeal to him to join up, to go along, to maintain a solid front. But he stubbornly refuses even to go with that one.

Now what? So now we hit him. Now we really are mad at him, so we let him have it. Maybe if we all jump up and down on him, he will have sense enough to come around. And the clock ticks on. But the stupid, stubborn s.o.b. still holds out.

What then? Well, then we must take a step that is as painful for us as it is for him. We must dismember our group. We must amputate one of our own members, leaving us less than whole, less than intact, but at least capable of coming to a conclusion. With this recalcitrant, stubborn, impossible member, this group cannot remain a group. To preserve it, we have no choice but to cut him out.

Viewed this way, the deviant individual is not such a hero. Much of the world's complex work is done by groups. When a group exerts pressure on an individual, it may thus not constitute an arbitrary imposition of power, but rather a set of increasingly desperate efforts to try to hold the group together in order to get the work done.

Does the deviant do anybody any good?

Besides the argument that it is good and wholesome and healthy for individuals to be independent thinkers—an argument that is not always as sensible as it sounds—is there any other good argument for encouraging individuals to take deviant positions if they believe in them, and for encouraging groups not to clobber people who deviate?

The answer, of course, is that there is at least one very good practical reason, in addition to all the moral reasons. It is the fact that deviants stimulate groups to think about what they are working on. Deviants, whether they are themselves creative or not, generate creativity in groups.

The process is simple enough and understandable enough. When like-minded people get together to talk over an issue, they are likely to come to agreement pretty quickly and then to pat one another on the back and go out and drink beer. When the same people get together in the presence of a person with quite different ideas, they are forced to reexamine their own beliefs, to go over them in detail, to consider sides and aspects of the problem which they never had to consider before. They must do this in order to argue effectively with the deviant, in order to attack him, in order to reason with him. As a consequence, they end up knowing more about their own problem than they would have if the deviant hadn't been there. It costs the group time and sweat. But what they earn is greater understanding, broader search, more knowledge of their own subject matter.

Can the deviant ever win?

We now come to the next question in this logical sequence: Suppose the deviant is right? Does he have a chance? Or will his presence simply cause the group that is already wrong to believe more strongly but more sophisticatedly in its wrong position?

The answer to this one is rather complicated. There is rather good research evidence that people can and will distinguish better answers from worse ones. And a deviant who comes up with a clearly better answer, even in the face of a large group that has agreed upon another answer, has a very good chance of getting his answer accepted. Such is the case at least for problems with a clear logical structure. If I can demonstrate to you a clearly easier way to add a column of figures than the way all of you are now adding them, it will not be hard for me to swing you over to my method. So the deviant who comes up with a new solution—one that other people had not even thought of, but clearly a good solution— is likely to have little trouble getting it through.

Unfortunately, many problems, probably *most* problems, tackled by groups aren't quite of that nature. They are fuzzily outlined judgmental problems, in which ordering the quality of solutions is not so easy. The "normal" problems are problems like selecting or promoting personnel, or allocating funds among several departments, or deciding on a promotion. On those kinds of issues the deviant doesn't have much of a chance in most groups.

And here we encounter another paradox. The guy with the different ideas, the deviant, is apt to have a better chance of getting his ideas accepted by a group that isn't very solid, isn't very cohesive, hasn't worked together very much, than by a group that is solid, whose members do know and like one another. So the executive may find himself faced with what looks like a strange dilemma. On the one hand he wants solidity, loyalty, high morale in his group. On the other hand, he may want the creativity he can get from the deviant. And yet it is precisely the high-morale, cohesive group that will go after the deviant hard and fast; that will clobber him even more quickly than the new group or the unsure group.

But the paradox may be more apparent than real. In a way all we are saying is that the guy with different ideas may be able to pull a snow job on a bunch of people who feel shy and uncertain with one another. He has a chance of influencing them, of getting his ideas through, more readily than he could in a solid group. But he is likely to get his ideas through, not because a pick-up group will examine and consider those ideas more rationally or more seriously than a solid group; but rather because they are constrained, uncertain, unwilling to open up themselves for fear of attack by others. So the aggressive deviant, the one who talks loud and fast, may be able to get to them.

On the other hand, when faced with a solid, self-assured group, the snow job is almost impossible. The deviant will have to prove his case and prove it rather thoroughly. But, of course, the probability of his being able to prove it to a group that is solid and self-assured is not very great. For they are not likely to break ranks unless the logic of the case is so clear, so rational, so obviously better than their own solution, that only a fool could reject it.

What kind of deviant can survive?

Interestingly enough, even powerful deviants don't seem to have much chance against a strong and solid group. As all of us know, a member of the group who is already peripheral and uninfluential—the new, young member of a street corner gang, for example—is in a poor position to try to push a new idea through. But we are apt to think that if a man is strong and central in the group—the leader of the street corner gang —then he should be omnipotent, and capable of getting the group to accept even extremely different ideas. The fact of the matter seems to be, however, that even strong men in groups, men with authority or with personal influence and power, have a very tough time pushing a group very far from its own standards. Even the kingpin has to move slowly, by bits and pieces, to get the gang to stop stealing apples and start playing basketball. If he doesn't move slowly, he will get the same treatment as any other deviant and eventually find himself amputated.

The same thing seems to be true in industry. Even the powerful boss will meet a good deal of trouble in pushing a very different idea through a solid group of subordinates. If he is a real Machiavellian manipulator, he will work first on individuals when he is trying to bring about a radical change, rather than on the face-to-face group.

The lonely executive

It may seem a shockingly soft thing to say, but one can interpret most of the research and common-sense analysis of conformity as essentially a problem of loneliness. Group pressures can be exerted on individuals—lone individuals—much more effectively than they can be exerted on pairs or subgroups. It is when the deviant finds himself alone, without a twig of support, without even another deviant (even one who deviates in quite different directions), that the pressures of the group are apt to become overpowering. It may be this fear of isolation, of singleness, that permits a group to press the individual to conform, even if that individual has authority or other kinds of power. Even the president seems to want and need some sources of support, some assurance of psychological backing from his people. He may need very little, but he needs not to be all alone. In fact, much of the effect of group pressure can be washed out in the sort of case we talked about at the start of this chapter, by the simple expedient of having just one other member of the group back up the deviant.

Thus again we encounter a paradox. For now we are saying that it is loneliness that will force a man to conform to the group. Which implies that he will feel less pressure to conform (and therefore feel more independent) if he is in the group—a member of it—and thus not at all lonely. So how now are we to answer the earlier question: Does the group force the individual to fit into its mold, thereby reducing his individuality, thereby brainwashing him? Or is it only when he is a psychologically secure member of the group that he can express his individuality without feeling pressure and restraint?

The answer begins to become a little clearer. It seems to

be true that people need psychological support, an environment free from the fear of loneliness. But if that support is bought at the price of constricting conformity, the individual loses his individuality no matter which way he goes. So the critical issue becomes the nature of the group. To what extent does it demand conformity, and on what dimensions of behavior? Does it demand, as the price of support, that he dress as they dress, that he believe as they believe? Or does it set more open standards, requiring conformity in fewer dimensions and perhaps less critical ones, requiring, perhaps, that everyone conform to certain time demands and certain demands of procedure, but consciously avoiding requirements of conformity in opinion or belief?

Since the individual needs the group, the group can exploit the individual, forcing him to bend to its demands. But individuals make groups, and it is possible to make groups that can work while exerting tolerable pressures on procedure without constraining beliefs and ideas.

In summary

Groups put pressure on members who deviate. Usually the pressure moves through several stages, from rational argument through emotional seduction to attack and finally to amputation of the deviant member. But the process is not usually capricious or sadistic. From the group's side, they exert pressure in an effort to survive intact and to get the job done.

Group pressures work mostly when the deviant feels all alone. Given any kind of minimal support, he can hold out much more effectively. And though a powerful deviant has a better chance than a weak one, no deviant can try to push a solid group very far very fast and expect to get away with it.

Clearly, deviants make groups think, even when they don't change the groups' mind. But we need to temper two prevalent notions about deviation: The first is the notion that nonconformity is somehow always better than conformity. We must remember that much of the world's work can only be done by conforming to agreed-upon standards. The second is the notion that groups kill individuality by exerting pressures to conform. We need to remember that most of us feel freer to be ourselves in groups where our position and membership are secure, than in settings in which we feel alone and unsupported.

22

Conflict and competition among groups My team can beat your team

Let's suppose that I am the manager of a large manufacturing and consumer marketing operation. I am democratic and progressive, though perhaps not very bright. I also want to get the best possible ideas out of my people. It is clear that we will need a new design for one of our key products to start the next season. So I ask the heads of each of three groups to submit proposals for the redesign. I ask each group head to get together with his people and develop what they think would be an optimal design.

But I don't want to get into the position of having to select the one design I think is best, especially since I am not a very competent designer myself. Moreover, I want to open up discussion and communication. So I inform them that after all three designs are in, I would like to have each group circulate its design to the members of the other two groups. Then when each group has had a chance to look over all three, I would like representatives of the three groups to meet together to decide which of the three designs is, in their joint opinion, the best one for the company to develop.

Thus, by keeping everyone informed of everything, by giving all groups a chance to look over three alternative designs, I figure that I should be able to get (1) the best of the three designs and (2) understanding and agreement among all three groups. Do you think this plan will work?

The experimental evidence says it won't work at all. This scheme of having several groups each work out a problem and then resolve differences among themselves is almost doomed to failure. And most of us know it, but we don't really believe it won't work even when we're right in the middle of it. Perhaps the best way to describe what does happen is to quote an insurance company executive who joined in an experimental version of the same kind of problem:

> We were divided at random into four teams. The instructor then asked us to draft a statement of policy for

our Company in answer to a certain hypothetical situation. Each group, working separately, was to draft its version. It took each group about two hours to hammer out its statement. Each group elected a representative to meet with one another to select one of the four statements. I was elected to represent my group. The members of my group, though naturally proud of their effort (they had reviewed the other three drafts in the interim), were confident that reaching agreement with the others would be easy.

The four representatives sat at a card table in the center of the room; behind each man, breathing down his neck, sat the group he represented. It soon developed that the over-all objectives of the four groups were quite close; it merely remained to choose one of the drafts. At the end of an hour we were further apart than ever. I asked my group for permission to vote for one of the other drafts. My request was indignantly turned down. Feelings had begun to run high. Logic had been tried; gamesmanship had been tried.

Notes were passed forward by each group to its representative. These notes were not helpful at all; they merely urged us to "get" the other man on some point or other. All had failed—the results were shattering.

Four judges, previously elected by their groups, were now called in. They had not participated in drafting the policy statements at all. During the time we had been working out our policy statement, they had drawn up criteria for evaluating the four drafts. The drafts were then submitted to them anonymously. In just one half hour and in a separate room in calm deliberation they had reached a unanimous decision. The experiment was over.

Most of the things that happened were highly predictable. They were predictable mostly because of the role of emotional and psychological elements, which we tend willingly to overlook when we concentrate on getting a job done. The uniform and predictable happenings include these:

1. As each group begins to develop its own solution it is more internally cohesive and solid. Morale within groups tends to go up, as their design takes shape. And when they have finally produced something together, they are apt to feel quite high on themselves. Sometimes, of course, a deviant or

two pops up; so the happy solidity is a little cracked and shaky.

2. When each group sees the comparable work of the other groups, the initial reaction is apt to be a slight letdown; followed by a quick recovery and continued increase in group morale. Usually, after the group members have seen the others' solutions someone will say, "I didn't feel very sure of our design until I saw these others. But if these are the only things these other groups have to offer it's pretty clear that ours is the only one worth a damn."

3. In each group this same solidifying, balancing process goes on; so that by the time the representatives come together each in effect is convinced that the design he is offering is the best of all the designs—"honestly" the best; and, moreover, he has now, he feels, been charged by his group to convince the other two that his design is the one they should all buy.

4. Initially, the representatives, when they meet together, are likely to behave like the majority dealing with the deviant in the preceding chapter. Each provides reasons to support his own group's design over the designs of the other two. But especially if this is a public meeting, this rational discussion soon turns into a duel. The representatives start to cut one another to pieces. They try to top one another in their cleverness and wit. The goal of finding a single best design soon fades out in favor of that of trying to be a hero to his own group. And if the representative cannot appear a hero, at least he must not be a traitor. He must not give in. So the representatives almost never become a functioning group. They become gladiators, battling for the approval of the audience, trying not to be publicly destroyed by the others.

5. The representatives then usually get gamy. They try to form coalitions, two or three against one; but they all know that these coalitions are opportunistic. They cannot count on their allies should they see some kind of opportunity for advancing their own causes. Sometimes, the representatives will thus come to some kind of a half-baked decision. Two of them will outvote a third, or one representative will be weak enough (or his group split open enough) so that he gives in. But most of the time they deadlock and finally give up in favor of an outside decision.

6. Suppose that at this point we argue that the difficulty is obvious; it is the social pressure of the groups on their members that is really preventing a decision. Somehow if we could get to the private opinions of the individual members —if we could get to the people, they, in their wisdom, would

recognize and admit to the design that is really the best one.

So now we take a secret ballot among all members of all groups. They have now had a chance to see all three designs, to study them, to discuss them, to debate about them, and they all have some expertise about design.

That doesn't work either. In almost every case the group members vote nearly 100 percent in favor of the design submitted by their own group. Even privately, one's own group's design looks best. Occasionally there will be a break in the pattern. One or two members of the team may admit that another design looks better. Usually these are peripheral or deviant members of their teams who were troublesome from the beginning.

7. So if the groups can't decide, and if the individual members can't decide, we can now throw the decision to authority—to the boss. Or if we wanted to, we could throw it to a board of arbitrators who would sit down impartially, and independently look at all three reports, perhaps without knowing which report was written by which group. In most cases, the boss or the arbitrators then have no trouble at all. They come to agreement quickly and quite easily.

8. Now we have a decision. We have taken it to the top and the top has decided. And isn't this the way we should have done it in the first place? Perhaps so, but what does "decision" mean? The design submitted by group X has now been chosen, group Y's is the the alternate; and group Z's is considered completely inadequate. Now what happens? In experimental runs of this sort, what happens is quite uniform. The winning group is elated. It feels good and thinks highly of the board of arbitrators that has chosen its design. The losing group feels hostile, aggressive, depressed. Privately, and sometimes publicly, they will insist that the arbitrators really didn't know what they were doing, and that any really imaginative expert in the field would recognize the superiority of their (the losing) design. So the fact of the decision from above does not completely solve the problem. It certainly has not solved it in the sense of developing loyalty and involvement of all groups.

9. We can follow this experimental design a step further, and put the groups to work again on some new problem. Then we encounter some interesting new results. The group that has just won is apt to be self-satisfied and comfortable and "frozen." Though its organization and social structure may be less than perfect, nobody dares to change it. The people who were powerful in the development of the first design

remain powerful on the next problem, whether they are qualified or not, because even though some members may want some changes, no one dares disturb the winning combination.

The third team, the losing one, may be in serious internal trouble. They may feel their representative has let them down. Individuals who took minority or deviant positions now come back in with I-told-you-so comments that engender further interpersonal bickering and stress. Usually such groups will recover from this internecine warfare; but sometimes they will collapse entirely. If winning groups freeze, the losing team melts. It so readily abandons its original organization that it has a great deal of trouble finding anything to hold it together.

The second team is a lot better off. They have lost but they have not been decimated. They are apt to be analytic and thoughtful in their reexamination of what happened in the first round. They are unfrozen in a sense, but they have not completely melted. Other things being equal they are a good team on which to place a bet for the future.

So psychologists have been conducting experiments of this kind that demonstrate issues that seem obvious and simple; that people develop great loyalty to what they produce themselves, and to one another when they produce something together; that this loyalty may be so overwhelming as to make it effectively impossible (at least within the structure set up in these experiments) for the groups to come to agreement.

Some morals

Let's turn now to the morals of this tale. In some ways these are negative experiments. They demonstrate how agreement cannot be reached, rather than how it can. They also show how easy it is to start a fight, even among grown-up and reasonable men. They reiterate the old truism that it is easy to build a solid group by providing them with an outside enemy. They tell us—as we all know—that representatives of groups are often much more concerned (and understandably so) about the groups at their backs than with the problem before them.

But they also offer some much larger, if tentative, morals. As we begin to realize the almost incredible ease with which conflict between groups can be created, two worrisome, related thoughts arise.

First, one begins to feel the wonder of the existence of large societies. The pressure toward fragmentation is so great and fragmentation itself so easy, that the survival of large groups such as tribes, nations, or even companies looks very impressive indeed. One wonders why we haven't broken up into little bits faster and faster.

Second, if social dikes are really as easily rupturable as it appears, perhaps it is time for more of us to get our fingers into them to try to hold things together.

A third generalization that is perhaps worth noting: Although most of us are properly proud of our uniqueness and individuality, we are to a great extent driven by the structures in which we find ourselves. Psychologists would be hard put to predict the behavior of any individual in the experiment we described earlier. But it's easy to predict the behavior of the groups. Once we have set up the structure, the overall human outcomes appear almost to be guaranteed. Autonomous and free though we may appear, we live in social structures, and our collective behavior is very much an outcome of those structural characteristics. If we had been raised in the USSR, we would not only speak Russian, we would think Russian, we would perceive Russian, we would fight Russian.

The positive side

But how about the positive side? If we want representatives to pay attention to the problem at hand we need either to reduce the pressure from their groups, or to make the representatives a sufficiently cohesive group so that membership in the *representative group* is something meaningful and important in its own right. By doing the latter we will put the squeeze on the representative, making his life miserable by requiring him to owe loyalty to two groups, even though those two groups are in partial conflict. But we will also increase the probability that he will indeed represent both points of view to both groups and thus increase the level of objectivity of the whole show.

There may be several other things we can do to increase the probability of an acceptable solution. We can search for "superordinate" goals; for objectives so large and important to every member that differences go by the board. These may be negatively induced goals—like Pearl Harbor—bringing subgroups together by threatening all of them; or better still —but harder—they may be positively induced, like the coalescence of all groups in a depressed community to lift the community out of the doldrums.

There is a third possibility—the method of education.

Perhaps if people are more aware of the traps around them they can avoid them more successfully.

Another note should be sounded here. Organizations can almost be said to have *styles* of conflict management. In some, for example, direct conflict is avoided at almost any cost. The culture demands that people be polite in meetings, that underlying differences not be discussed openly. In other organizations conflict tends to be confronted more directly. People express disagreement and argue for positions. It is easy for most of us to prefer the first to the second. It looks civilized, gentlemanly, courteous, and comfortable. But it may be wise at this point to take a better look at the second. For when the world is changing fast, it may behoove organizations to face internal conflicts openly, indeed to welcome argument and debate, as the catalyst for its own change.

Some varieties of conflict and accompanying tactics

We haven't said much yet about the several different kinds of conflict that can occur in organizations. In our example the conflict was among peer groups of about equal size, status, and power. But that isn't the way things always line up. Sometimes a small group finds itself up against a much larger group or coalition of groups. Sometimes power differences arise—workers versus management, for example. And sometimes a small and also subordinate group takes on a larger group with more power and authority, like a dissident subgroup in the larger church, or a small group of student radicals in a large, conservative university.

There are several, quite different means that groups can use to resolve conflicts.

The first is war—coercive power, as we called it earlier. If you're the big powerful group, you clobber the little group. You kill them, jail them, excommunicate them, banish them. You hang their heads on poles.

If you're the little group in a power war, you must count on other forms of power: hit-and-run tactics, guerrilla tactics, blackmail; and, of course, you seek alliances to increase your power. You curry public opinion. You try to prevail on other big groups to back you up.

Obviously these kinds of tactics are still with us, largely unchanged from the days of the caveman. But we have added a few new, hopefully somewhat more moderate and civilized tactics to the conflict scene, haven't we? Indeed, isn't the measure of civilization the degree to which conflicts, even between more and less powerful groups, can be solved by less coercive means? We have set up governments, organizations, and legal systems, all of which are intended to move the issue of conflict resolution away from raw power and toward—toward what? Toward reason? Perhaps it's still too early to expect much of that.

How about toward *bargaining* and *trading* situations? Nothing to be terribly proud of, perhaps, but nothing to denigrate too readily, either. From the bread and butter bargains made by congressmen who vote for one another's favorite bills, to the informal (and illegal) coalitions among business competitors to fix prices or agree upon territories, to union-management bargaining, society rides on bargains, trades, gamy compromises, and accommodations to conflicts. Most of them are legal; many aren't. Most don't truly resolve conflicts; they just keep them within bounds. But surely that's better than war.

Sometimes we inch a step beyond that, especially in the relations of large and powerful groups to small rebellious ones in their midst. Traditionally the resolution of these conflicts was simple: big steps on little. But sometimes because the big groups are unsure of themselves, or sometimes because the big ones are very sure of themselves, they have moved from direct coercive power toward *absorption* as a method for ending conflict with little groups.

All absorption means in this context is that large group A tries to deal with dissident little group B by behaving like a big pillow. University administration A, for example, says to its protesting students B, "O.K. We'll do some of the things you ask. But you must take a large part of the responsibility for doing them. You want to participate; we'll let you participate, part way. We'll put three students on the fifteen-man search committee for a new president," etc.

The big organization A bends, backs off, but in bits and pieces. The little one B gets some of what it wants, but at a price—the price of partial cooperation, of partial reentry into membership in the parent organization.

This process may at first seem indistinguishable from slaughter, at least to the dedicated and rebellious Bs, for its effect may well be the ultimate demise of B. Certainly it can be viewed as emasculation, for protesting Bs, founded on protest, cannot easily survive if they get most of what they want. But sometimes, depending on motives and intent, the process can represent a considerable degree of civilized effort by A to acknowledge the need for change and to bring it about at a price. For A pays a price in the absorption process, too. It remains the establishment, but a changed establishment, changed by the pressures from B.

Does it happen in business?

The reader may well point out that the kind of experiment we described at the beginning of this chapter seems more typical of situations that arise between governments or power groups in a community than between groups in an industrial setting. No intelligent manager, they might argue, would ever set up a situation like the one we described. He wouldn't put three groups to work doing the same thing, and even if he did he wouldn't let them decide among themselves which of the outcomes was best.

Let's grant that one. But even holding problems of union-management relations aside, aren't there other parallels in most large organizations? Can't we think of large organizations, at least in part, as sets of groups in power relationships with one another? The problem may not be a new product design. It may be the location and size of a new warehouse. And the groups may not be three parallel design groups, but a regional sales force that wants something very different from what a staff analysis group thinks would be optimal. Or the issue may be the allocation of slices of the capital budget. And the members of the capital budgeting committee may be, partially at least, representatives of one subgroup or another. Or sales groups vie for the same classes of accounts; or maintenance people want control of a process the technical people claim is theirs. And so on and on. These are less pure cases of identification of members of organizations with subgroups and special subgroup interests, but their essence is the same.

In summary

It is very easy to set up situations in which groups compete with one another. In such settings the solidity and morale of members within groups is apt to climb steadily as the competition progresses. But the feeling between groups is apt to degenerate into bickering and hostility. In such situations the naïve use of meetings of representatives may simply aggravate the problem. What starts out as an honest effort to reach a resolution can quickly become a public display of each representative's capacity to out-talk and outwit the others.

Members of groups identify so closely with their own product, and representatives identify so closely with their own groups, that the likelihood of resolution decreases as the morale of each group develops, rather than the other way around. On the other hand, outsiders, when not identified with the group, find it easy to reach agreement and to rate some group products as better than others. But if these outsiders then try to impose their choice upon the groups (even though the groups have invited it), the result is less than ideal. The group whose product is selected, of course, accepts the outsiders' decision. But the other groups will feel recalcitrant and generally dissatisfied. Nevertheless, while denying the validity of a decision that has gone against them, the losing group is apt also to lose its cohesiveness and to degenerate into internal warfare and bickering. The winning group, on the other hand, may sit on its hands, satisfied with itself and fearful of changing anything about its structure, lest it break up the winning combination.

This chapter offers no clear solutions to problems of intergroup struggle and competition. It suggests, however, that greater understanding of the extent to which one's behavior is dictated by group factors may contribute to more objectivity. It suggests that if we can tie representatives together so that they, too, develop loyalties to one another, they may operate more effectively, though suffering more personal stress. Finally, if we can somehow develop stronger identification with the total organization's goals, then, perhaps, the best of all possible worlds will result. We shall consider that problem in a little more detail in the next chapter, which is on management development.

Some tentative generalizations to broader problems of social and organizational conflict were included in this chapter, to try to show some varieties of conflict that can occur, the strategies that can be tried to cope with them, and their relevance to social and organizational survival and progress.

23

**Developing managers
Applied ideas about
influence, learning,
and groups**

A problem for the reader:

You are the training director of a large multiproduct
company. You are a lucky training director, because top
management is intensely aware of the need for training
at all levels. Top management also thinks well of you.

You are called to a meeting in the president's office
one day, where you find the president, the personnel
vice-president, and some of the senior line officers of the
company.

The president says: "Joe, we've decided to go all out
on intensive management development. We've spotted a
dozen younger men around the company, every one of
whom looks like at least vice-president timber. Right
now they're in third- or fourth-level jobs, as assistant
department heads or department heads in some of the
smaller departments. They're lightweights now, and we
want to make heavies out of them. And we have to
speed up the process. We're going to need several top-
level people in a year or two. We're willing to stand the
salaries of these men up to six months, even if they don't
do any productive work. You can have them. Do anything you have to do to make top-flight managers out of
them. You can keep them here or take them out into the
country somewhere. You can hire consultants and experts; you can send them off to a university if you think
that's best. Just turn them into men who can take over
in our top spots."

This is the assignment—a carte blanche. Now what would
you do?

A problem like this can be broken down into three or four
major subquestions. These seem to be the questions a
training director would, sooner or later, have to answer:

1. What is a top-flight manager?
2. Under what conditions can people learn to be more like top-flight managers?
3. What are the most useful methods for influencing people to think and act like top-flight managers?

The top-flight manager and the present generation of managers

The first question is probably the hardest one. What is a top-flight manager anyway? If the training director can answer that one, he can set the goals of his training program. But how does one find an answer to such a question?

Some people thought one answer lay in finding the common personality characteristics of successful business leaders. But as the conception of leadership became more sophisticated, most people abandoned that idea, having found as many different personal characteristics as they did leaders.

More recently, instead of working on specific traits or characteristics, researchers have devoted much effort to describing the social background and overall personalities of successful and unsuccessful executives. If clear-cut results emerged, a trainer might then try to use them as a model toward which to train his people. But the results have not been clear, nor would they be very useful for this purpose anyhow. Models of the personalities that can do a job are not, after all, models of a job. Besides, our engineering methods for achieving those models are pretty poor; so even if we could feel satisfied with building people who are like successful managers, we couldn't do it anyway.

Another direction in the search for answers is analysis of managerial jobs rather than of managers themselves. Once we have located and defined the significant aspects of managers' jobs, we can go on to imbue our acolytes with the knowledge and skills that are appropriate.

This search for adequate job descriptions has taken two major forms: job descriptions based on what present managers actually do and descriptions based on analysis of what they ought to do. The first has the advantage of practical empiricism. We can see what successful managers do. It has the disadvantage of limiting the goal of management development to the present limits of present management. We know the world is changing; we know that even the best-managed company will be faced with all sorts of new problems in the years to come. So why limit our goals to producing new managers who, ten years hence, will be able to do only what present managers do already?

The second alternative, to draw up an idealized version of what the good manager should be able to do in the world of 198?, is no mean task. It has no neat empirical basis. Different people project the future of our economy in different ways. It is somewhat, but not entirely, a shot in the dark.

It is not surprising that many present managers prefer the first choice while many educators prefer the second. For the present manager, what is a better standard for managerial behavior than his own behavior? For the academician, what is more appropriate than analysis and prediction?

The author of this book is an academician. So here is an attempt at a generalized but incomplete characterization of the manager's job in the present and near future. It is not entirely made up out of my own head; neither is it solidly based on experimentation. But my guess is that it will jibe fairly closely with the views of many present-day managers and many other academicians.

A characterization of the manager's job

We can partially differentiate managerial from other jobs by emphasizing the *change* quality of managerial problems as against the relatively static quality of tasks at lower levels. The manager deals largely with unknowns instead of knowns. He is a solver of *unprogramed* problems.

We can also differentiate the manager's job from the executive's job. For the word "executive" implies that the executing function is primary. The managerial job should be more than an executive one. It should also include information-gathering and problem-defining functions. Once programs have been worked out, the manager is likely either to "execute" them himself or to pass them on to other "executives."

The manager ought to do more than search for problems and alternative solutions to them. He must translate his understanding into decisions for action and thence into action itself. This part of the description is the Hollywood version of the manager—not an untrue version, but an incomplete one: the man of decision choosing instantly from among frying-pan and fire alternatives; the man of action implementing his choices in a continuous series of crises; never even given the scientist's freedom to experiment in a no-chips-down laboratory situation.

But the phases of problem and information-seeking,

searching for alternatives, decision-making, and action do not sufficiently differentiate the manager from the rest of us. According to chapter 6, all men seeking to satisfy their needs operate on more or less the same problem-solving basis, though their styles and skills may vary over a wide range. They gather information about a situation, search for satisfactory alternatives, act, and then, on the basis of information fed back to them about the effects of their acts, remodify their subsequent acts. "Success" for any man varies with his skill in developing broad and valid sources of information, with his skill in developing and choosing among alternatives, and with his skill in taking action in the chosen alternative.

The factor which differentiates the manager from the rest of us is the *organizational setting* in which he works. Unlike most men (including scientists), the manager operates from a *power position* within a pyramidal structure. He is blessed (or perhaps cursed) with the authority we discussed in chapter 13. Those below him in the pyramid usually see themselves as being more dependent on him than he is on them. And whether he likes the power position or not, he is in it, and many forces in his environment operate to keep him in it. But though he appears to have great and independent power, the actual balance of power in the industrial world seems to have shifted rapidly downward, making the manager's position somewhat awkward. The paralyzed brother has recovered the use of some of his muscles. Where once he knew every operation in his business better than anyone else, the manager cannot now come close to such sagacity. Where he once may have needed help only in the information-gathering and executing phases of his operation, he now often needs it even in the analytical phases. He operates, as we pointed out in chapter 10, in a position that is peculiarly dependent while seeming to be independent.

From that position he must somehow perform his functions through his influence on other people. For his task is not a one-shot task but must be performed in a way that will permit him always to return for more. Nor is the typical manager the top manager; he is dependent not only on subordinates but also on his peers and superiors. He expects, and is expected, to act as an extension of his superior's ego. He is expected to think creatively and originally but also to act as his boss would act in a similar situation. The young manager is perhaps even more an apprentice than apprentices at lower levels in the hierarchy. He learns from older managers in a close, personalized relationship. All these psychological factors complicate the problem-solving activities of the manager by requiring him always to deal with difficulties coming from his flanks as well as from the front.

Although the manager's personal ambitions are part of the man rather than the job, they cannot be ignored. For in the hierarchical setting, it does not always follow that the best problem-solver (that is, the best solver of industrial and business problems) becomes most successful most rapidly. Most industrial organizations have not been able to escape a kind of double standard for success. While good work does not go unnoticed, good work is not the only thing to be noticed. Executives are judged for their business performance but also for their methods and manners. And even managements that try hard not to judge on such bases seem unable to escape their subordinates' beliefs that such things count heavily. Young managers, anxious to move ahead, believe that the boss prefers certain styles of behavior to others, even if he does not.

This gross characterization of the manager's job suggests that a management-development program ought to be devoted to helping people learn to solve "typical" managerial problems in a "typical" managerial setting; to helping them develop skills in gathering information about diverse areas, skills in analyzing the information they gather, in searching for alternatives, in acting upon their choices. Further, since in large, technologically complicated organizations these skills most often involve many other people, the whole developmental process needs to be accompanied by training in getting the willing help of other people—if "getting willing help" is something learnable. Finally, since the manager's position is such an odd one, of both power and weakness, of independence and dependence, programs for the development of managers should include work in "how to maintain equilibrium and objectivity in the presence of temporal and psychological pressures."

How do people learn?

Our second question was, How do people learn to be top-flight managers? Chapter 6 was devoted to the learning process. In that chapter we tried to answer the question, "What are the minimum necessary conditions for 'higher' learning?" We said that a "learning machine" would probably need a memory mechanism—some device by which it could retain some traces of the information previously brought to it through its sense organs—and an output mechanism to allow it to act upon the world. It would probably have to be stingy, to try to reduce effort. It would need a choice mechanism and some decision rules. And, finally, it would need something like motivation—it would need some goals, some preferences (though they may be built in by the engineer) for certain things over others. In the absence of any one of these characteristics, the capacity to learn, the capacity to modify behavior "sensibly" after experience, apparently could not exist.

When we put these ideas together, we have a partial answer to the question, How do people learn? We can think of learning as a "reorganization" of perceptions. *When new or old things in the perceived world are related to one another in new ways, the person has learned.* When the aspiring manager stops seeing problems through a clerk's eyes and starts seeing them through a department head's eyes, then he has learned something about being a manager. For one difference between a developed manager and an underdeveloped one, we argued earlier, is that managers must tolerate and deal with unprogramed frontier problems. The change from lightweight to heavyweight in industry is largely a change in perceptual organization—in the angles and distances from which business problems are seen and in the definitions of problems.

This conception of how people learn has some useful implications for training people for the "ideal" manager's job. First, it emphasizes the relations of parts rather than the content. It says in effect that people can learn something new even when there is nothing new to be learned by putting old things together in new ways. The child learns something new when, without adding to his vocabulary, he patterns his words to form sentences.

In fact, skill in handling patterns of things helps people to solve new kinds of problems. When children understand the relationship between the height of a rectangle and its base, they can find the areas of many kinds of four-sided figures. When they have simply memorized a formula, their ability to generalize is more limited. The conception of learning as "perceptual reorganization," then, also implies that a trainer should emphasize *understanding* as distinct from *knowledge* in the learning process. It leads to an emphasis on simultaneous concern with all aspects of a problem rather than the building-up of individual elements; and by so doing it values mistakes, for mistakes provide insight into relationships.

Our question about how people learn is not yet fully answered. The factor of motivation needs to be brought in.

Aimless wandering by the trainee, with no destination in mind, is not likely to yield (from the trainer's point of view) very useful managerial learning. People seem to reorganize their perceptions best against the skeleton of a goal or objective. The mere fact of experience, without relevance to needs and motives, does not seem to yield much learning.

What we are saying now is something most of us implicitly believe anyway. *People learn when they have a problem to solve.* Knowledge and skill can be packed usefully into the human organism when some goals provide a sensible system for organizing them. In the absence of such goals, the human filing system has a hard time deciding where to categorize its experiences. Management training might therefore begin with practice on managerial problems.

Influencing people to think and act like managers

Learning to think like a manager, we just said, can probably be helped if people have unprogramed, managerial problems to solve. If our hypothetical training director accepts that idea, he has at least one anchor point from which to start developing a training program.

But granted that people learn by doing, seeing the effects, reorganizing, and doing again, how does a trainer influence them so that they will do, then observe and remember the effects, reorganize, and try again?

Our answer to that question should stem from part 2 on influence, especially from our consideration of the AA model. In that section and in chapter 8 we pointed out that changes in attitude seem to be brought about most readily in an atmosphere in which B sees a problem and takes much of the responsibility and A supports with knowledge and approval. Since what we want to do with fledgling managers is to make them see and work at problems from a new managerial viewpoint, the AA model should be applicable to our training director's problem.

If he uses the AA idea as well as the related learning-is-reorganization idea, he can begin to lay out the framework of a general training plan. First, his training program will focus on managerial problems. Second, the trainer's role will be much like that of the AA buddy's—not the boss's, but the coach's.

Where do groups come in?

These two ideas—the focus on unprogramed problems-to-be-solved and the trainer in an AA type of role—have of themselves little to do with groups. Yet this chapter appears in a section on group behavior.

Groups do come into the picture in trying to answer the very first question posed at the beginning of this chapter: What does a top-flight manager have to do? Part of our answer was that he has to solve managerial problems through groups. Size, technology, and lots of other factors have combined to make the manager more dependent on other people. He needs their help in defining problems, searching for alternatives, and acting out decisions. This is not to make the manager just a "coordinator" who needs only to "get along" with people. He has to be a thinker, too, but in an especially —whether he likes it or not—"groupy" environment—an environment of many, often competing, groups.

So now we can add to the framework for the training director's program. First, he focuses on managerial problems; second, he shares responsibility, à la AA; third, he sets up a program that requires trainees to work largely with, through, and between groups to solve problems adequately.

One more point is worth making here. Working with groups means influencing and being influenced by other people. In turn, we have already argued that "successful" influencers need to be aware of themselves, of their own motives, their own fears. So the training director might want to go back still another step in his program. He might want to include *opportunities for people to reexamine themselves* as individual human beings.

Alternative training techniques

With this sort of framework in mind, the trainer can begin to select some combination of methods and techniques to use as his training tools. Most training directors would doubtless, at this point, begin to reconsider the available alternatives currently in use in industry. They include job-rotation plans, classroom-education plans, apprenticeship plans, multiple and group plans, and problem-solving plans. They can be found in varying degrees and combinations because they are not entirely independent of one another. Some are techniques that can be used within others; some are primarily administrative devices that leave training itself largely to other people. Consequently, it is not proper to try to label any of these mechanisms as better or worse than any others. Any of them can be carried through naïvely and poorly, or well and with wisdom.

Probably the most widespread formal method of management development, even today, is job rotation. An executive-in-training is systematically or unsystematically rotated through many jobs at many levels of the organization. In some plans he simply observes the jobs; in others he may work actively in them for a period of several months or a year.

Underlying these plans is the belief that a variety of job experiences provides the trainee with an opportunity to learn "all about the business" and is therefore good preparation for managership. The advantage to a manager of knowing his own business is obvious. It is questionable, however, whether knowledge of the internal workings of his own organization is all he needs to know. It is even questionable whether independent experience in each of several jobs provides a man with knowledge of the relationships among the jobs, a kind of knowledge probably more useful to a manager than knowledge of any specific operation. Moreover, rotation plans may —although they do not necessarily—suffer from a kind of passivity and aimlessness resulting from the absence of a clear-cut central goal. Thus, for example, when a man works in a department for three months as part of a rotation scheme, he may learn quite different things from what he would learn either as a regular employee or as a manager who had to look into the department to solve some specific managerial problem. The rotated trainee is in danger of learning superficially, like a tourist in a foreign land. Organizations that use rotation systems often become aware of this difficulty. If they are wise they either lengthen the rotation schedule or set up special assignments which require trainees in rotation to be more concerned with the managerial aspects of the job than with its operational aspects.

It is sometimes claimed that a simple rotation plan is a good way of separating the men from the boys. Those trainees who are poor tourists, who learn only the minimum, can be differentiated readily from those who take initiative and find things to learn, even if those things have not been defined for them. It may well be true that a rotation plan is a useful selection method. The people who take initiative, who think up problems on their own, may stand out quickly. But that is selection, not training.

If there is a great strength in rotation schemes, it is an ambiguous one we have not yet mentioned—rotation can multiply and fragment the manager's loyalties so that he is part of all groups, not just one. And split loyalties will increase the probability of ulcers, and also of intergroup cooperation.

Classroom training, including lectures and discussions, is like rotation, both useful and incomplete. As the rotation system emphasizes experience, most classroom training emphasizes the provision of knowledge. Both knowledge and experience are relevant to the development of management. Both add to the trainee's breadth of perception of the world. But like rotation, classroom courses are likely to be psychologically sealed off from the solution of managerial problems. For in the classroom, learning is tied largely to the trainee's desire to be successful in the class. Only later, when he is faced with managerial problems in which classroom knowledge would have helped, is he likely to be fully aware of how many really useful things he could have learned if he had known then what he knows now. Three months of reading and lectures are likely to train inefficiently unless they accompany rather than precede the need tensions that come from having to solve a management problem. It is paradoxical that industry, which in the eyes of many educators presents an ideal training ground, should be turning to the classroom as an educational device while educators themselves are complaining that the classroom is an inadequate educational mechanism.

Again it is worth pointing out that the adequacy of the classroom must be judged not only against the content and method of classroom teaching but also against the motivation of the student. If a manager-in-training goes to a classroom in search of help with a problem he has already defined for himself, then the classroom, like the AA meeting, can be extremely helpful. But if the student is the passive party in the classroom relationship while the trainers try to pump him full of knowledge, it is likely to be an inefficient method. For learning cannot be exclusive of the needs of the learner. And what is learned best is what is relevant to the current needs of the learner, not what may be relevant to his future needs.

Apprenticeship systems, often combined with rotational systems, are another base for developing managers. Sometimes trainees are attached for extended periods to a particular executive, to serve as his assistant, to live in his office, and, insofar as possible, to do his work. Such systems may provide good opportunities for the trainee to practice working on managerial problems. They may also provide the motivation for acting like an executive. But the quality of the coaching is variable. Political and personality factors limit their usefulness, for the variety of executive problems the trainee is given is left largely up to the executive to whom he is attached. If the executive is either uninterested in the apprentice or feels threatened by him, that particular apprenticeship will provide few learning opportunities.

Still another effort to provide motivation and opportunities for practice in a group setting is the junior management "board." A group of lower-level people is elected or appointed to a kind of second board of directors which meets periodically to consider any business problems it chooses to consider, to gather information about those problems, to analyze them, to come to decisions, and to make recommendations to the senior board. While holding their lower-level jobs, young men thus get an opportunity both to tax their own brains on executive problems and to work at the peer level with a group of other "part-time" managers. This approach has the advantage of giving young men an opportunity to view the world as a manager, to be faced with and wade through problems of impending change, and to create changes of their own.

A problem-centered group training

Finally, and this is the model that best fits the requirements outlined earlier, a modification and expansion of the management-board method can be constructed by centering all training on unprogramed managerial problems, by requiring the trainee in a real situation to work back from a difficult problem to the kinds of skills and knowledge he needs to solve it. Thus, for example, our training director can ask the president to assign a group of trainees to work on precisely the kind of big and difficult problems that the officers themselves or consultants would ordinarily work on. The problem might be a reevaluation of the company's personnel program or a reexamination of the sales operation.

If such a project is assigned a group of young men who have never before been faced with a task of its scope and complexity, and if the young men are provided with AA-type resources in the form of company officers and technicians to whom they can go for help, then they will be faced with an almost ideal motivational situation for learning. For if the problem is broad enough, it will require of the trainees knowledge of the business, knowledge of the outside world, knowledge of the sources of information that are available within the company and without it, practice in gathering information from people in the company and perhaps from customers and competitors, practice in analyzing and organizing this information and in selecting among alternative choices, practice in communicating the information accumulated, practice in implementing their recommendations (if they can influence top management to accept them), and finally practice in organizing an unorganized group of young men in accordance with the interests and capacities of the men themselves.

With help, the presence of a large and difficult task and the requirement that these young men jointly carry it out can increase motivation to learn all these things. In fact, it is quite an easy step to work back to another level, to the level of the individual personality. Areas of weakness in individual trainees show up in such a program, so the individual trainee can see them. And if the training staff is wise and helpful, it can utilize this opportunity to encourage each man to reexamine himself and his relationships not only with peers but with superiors and subordinates. It can provide counseling and test data, if people want them. Certainly a large part of skill in working through others lies not only in the individual's understanding of himself but in his understanding of other people's perception of his behavior.

Notice too, that this model is hard to administer. It works backward. Time schedules cannot be pre-planned down to the hour. It is a plan-as-you-go operation. Time is devoted to areas of skill or knowledge when and to the degree that they become relevant to solving the problem. They cannot all be predetermined. So the trainer has to be on his toes to provide resources, like books and experts, as they become needed, and they are needed whenever the trainees hit a snag in trying to solve their problem.

Perhaps we have unintentionally underemphasized two important aspects of the management development issue. We have talked about the present more than the future, and we have emphasized training for work rather than self-analysis.

Neither of these should be given short shrift. A thirty-year-old going through a management training experience today probably won't be president for another fifteen years. By then the world will be different, so certainly our education programs need a strong future orientation.

But how is one to know the future? To some extent we can guess or extrapolate from present trends. The computer revolution was foreseeable in the early fifties, for example, though it didn't really hit until the late fifties. As of this writing it seems quite clear that problems of the environment will get bigger before they get smaller. Thus we can use our collective wisdom to select areas that we believe will grow in relevance, and include appropriate content about them in our programs.

But surely our greatest hope for educating for the future is to develop managers who will be self-educators, who will sense and reach out for understanding of all kinds of potentially relevant ideas throughout their lives. And that becomes a question of attitudes and values rather than of specific current content.

Note, too, that we have not placed very great emphasis on sensitivity or T-group training as such. Our intent is not, however, to minimize the value of such training in group process and self-insight for managers, but rather to recommend that such aspects of management development be carried on in the context of management rather than independently, that T-group-like activities be closely integrated into project and team-task activities and not isolated from managerial problem-solving tasks.

In summary

Anyone concerned with developing managers must deal with three key questions: How do people learn? How can a trainer train? And what is a manager?

Learning is defined here as a process of reorganizing perceptions so that new patterns of relationships are formed. Training, therefore, necessitates providing trainees with problems that require perceptual reorganization for their solutions and providing these problems in a situation in which relevant knowledge and experience are also available —including knowledge and experience about groups.

The "ideal" manager can be defined in many ways. The emphasis here has been on those phases of the manager's job involving the gathering and analyzing of information, decision-making, and action, with a recognition of the unprogramed nature of his problems, his continuous dependence on other people, and the pressures imposed upon him by his position in a hierarchy.

4

**People in hundreds
and thousands
Problems of
organizational
design**

Introductory note

This final section deals with some questions of organizational theory and some human problems that industrial organizations manufacture along with their other products. Of course, all the problems we have already talked about—problems of individuals, of relationships, and of small groups—also occur within large organizations. But the large organization superimposes some special difficulties on these others, difficulties that seem to be the product of the large industrial organization itself.

The first chapter in this section tries to provide an organizational road map; but it maps the organization as though it were a moving dynamic system, rather than a rigid static structure. In the next chapter we look at major ideas about key parts of the organizational system—parts like structure and technology and most of all, people. We consider where those ideas came from and when, and how they fit with one another. The succeeding chapters examine the present state of our knowledge about the four key variables that loom largest: (1) organizational tasks and decisions, (2) organizational structure, (3) the people in organizations, and (4) the technological side of the organization. In the last chapter we raise the issue of the organization's social life, its relationship with its environment. It's our guess that major new organizational problems of the seventies, which will be added to the major old problems, will lie on this boundary, this interface between the organization and the world in which it lives.

24

The volatile organization
Everything triggers
everything else

In this first chapter in part 4, we have just one purpose—to encourage the reader to think about organizations not just as simple, static charts or as milling collections of people or as smoothly oiled man-machine systems but as rich, volatile, complicated but understandable systems of *tasks, structures, tools,* and *people* in states of continuous change.

Toward that purpose, consider the following example:

If, as a manager, you have a rather complicated problem, you may want to call in a consultant for help. Suppose the problem is a typically hard one: One of your larger field units is turning in much poorer results than all your forecasts had predicted. It isn't performing the assigned tasks up to standard.

So you call in the partner in charge of the local office of one of the reputable older consulting firms—the largest in town. They contract to take on the problem and send some people out to the unit to collect information.

When they finally come in with a report, you scan it and then turn to the recommendations. They recommend the following: (1) You need tighter controls. (2) Job relationships need to be reorganized and redefined; job descriptions need to be rewritten with greater precision (to get rid of squabbles about overlapping authority). (3) The functional form of organization they now have down there ought to be switched over to a product form. (4) In fact, that unit has grown so big that it ought to go through a partial decentralization itself, with a lot more authority given to the product managers. (5) You need a thorough methods analysis. The number of reports that are being generated now is excessive. There is wasteful duplication of effort and communication. You ought to streamline the organization's procedures. (6) And you may have to move a few people out, too. There is too much fat in the organization, and so on.

If you are a manager with an experimental turn of mind and a pocket full of money, you will decide not to act on this consultant's report yet. You decide, instead, to knock on the door of another consultant and get a second independent assessment.

You had gotten to know the first firm by now. You had found that the people in it were active in the Society for the Advancement of Management, and highly experienced in business organization. You note, with some discomfort, that this second firm professes different allegiances and displays other pedigrees. This second group is active in the Operations Research Society, and the Institute for Management Sciences. Its experiences in industry really are not as extensive as those of number-one firm, but it has done a lot of recent military work, and its senior people all have Ph.D's. It looks like a group of whiz kids. But they have cut their hair and they sound reasonable, so you hire them to look into the same problems.

They send their people out to the unit, and they, too, come up with a report. But their conclusions are different. Instead of recommending modifications in the *structure* of the organization, they recommend modifications in the *technical* and *analytic* methods being used. They are technologists who think technological improvement is the means to the best of all possible worlds. They want to linear program the inventory control methods being used in that division, and to automate the purchasing operation. They want to modify the information flows, so that decisions can be made at different points in the organization, and faster. And instead of job descriptions and organization charts as their tools, their pockets are full of computers and long equations. You will have to hire some hot-shot college boys if you want to carry out their recommendations, because neither you nor any of your top people can fully understand them.

But if you are really an experimental manager, and if your pockets are really full of gold, and if you don't satisfy easily, you call in the only other consulting firm in town. Its members are Ph.D. types, too. Their offices aren't very elaborate, either. Their affiliations are different, again. They are members of the American Psychological Association, and/or members of the consultant network of the National Training Laboratories. They are clinical or social psychological types. And they view the world from the human side. They don't carry computers in their back pockets, or write job descriptions, or draw organization charts. Their favorite tools are the meeting, the discussion, the face-to-face group, and the open-ended interview.

So you hire them and let them take a look at your difficult unit. And they too come up with a report. But their report is different again. It argues that the solution to unit X's problem lies in changing the attitudes and interrelations of the people in that unit. Morale is low, they say. Apathy is high. People are constricted and anxious, afraid to speak up or take risks. What your organization needs is more openness, more participation, more involvement, more creativity.

So their recommendation is that you work on the people end of the problem. They want you to set up an organizational development program, in which you take groups of your people from division X out to a country club for a week at a time to talk things over, to open up valid communication among themselves, to express what they really feel, and to develop much more mutual trust and confidence. Then you go on to a continuous O.D. program of team-building and problem-solving back inside the organization.

Probably you could go on experimenting, but the board members are giving you strange looks by now, and the people in unit X are really up in the air. So you decide to stop there and take a look at what you have. Which of the three firms' recommendations should you follow up? Since you are the manager, we'll leave it to you to answer that question.

But though we can't answer it, let's not leave it quite there. As of right now we have a situation that looks like this:

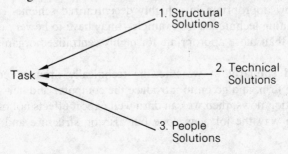

We have one group that wants to handle the task of unit X by working on structure, by changing the organization chart and the locations of authority and responsibility. We have another group that's going to solve the same problems technologically, by improving the analytic quality of decisions and applying new techniques for controlling and processing information. And we have a third group that's going to solve the very same problems humanly, by working on persons and interpersonal relations. But there is one more important point that needs to be made here, before you decide which one of these to use. They aren't mutually exclusive. The point is that the diagram above is incomplete. Because no one of these actions will affect the way the task of division X gets done without also involving each of the other points on that chart. Structure and technology and people are not separable phenomena in organizations. If we hire the structurally oriented firm, and if we decentralize the unit, or if we change the present allocation of responsibilities, it will not only affect the task but will also affect (perhaps adversely) people's attitudes and interpersonal relations. We will have to draw an arrow like this:

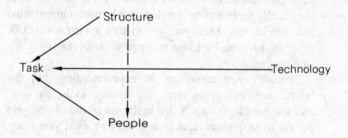

If you tighten controls, for example, some people may get angry or uncomfortable. If you switch from a functional to a product organization form, there will be new problems of interpersonal relations.

And if we play with the organization structure we will also get some effects on technology. The kinds of techniques that are now appropriate in a highly decentralized scheme—the accounting techniques for example—may have to be very different than those appropriate for highly centralized organizations.

And similarly, if we hire the technically oriented consulting firm, and go on to introduce the computer and new information flows, then we can darn well expect effects not only on the way the job gets done but also on structure and on people. If we can centralize information in locations where we couldn't centralize before, we will find decisions being made and responsibilities being taken in different places than they were being taken before. And while we may be talking about *de*centralization, that new information system may be pushing us toward centralization. We may also find that the kinds and numbers of people we need in our new, technically sophisticated organization may be quite different from the kind and number of members we needed before. Moreover some things that were done judgmentally and thoughtfully are now pretty well programed, so that essentially they can be done by the machine—with some consequent effects on the attitudes and feelings of persons.

Finally, if we move in on the people side, hiring the human relations firm, we will encourage people to be more open and more valid in their communication, encourage people to take more responsibility, and encourage people to interact more with other members of the organization. If we do these things, let us not for a moment think that we can do them without exerting great pressure on our existing organizational structure. The authority system will change and so will the status system. And we will exert pressure on technology too. The newly freed people may want new tools or the abolition of old ones that have been technically useful but are psychologically frustrating.

And so we move toward a diagram that looks like this:

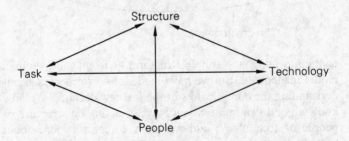

In this one everything feeds back on everything else, so that although we started out to worry only about the relationship between structure and task, or technology and task, or people and task, we must end up worrying about the effects of changes in any one on all of the others. Some of those changes may be very helpful, but some may be negative. And the manager has to somehow diagnose the secondary and tertiary effects of action in any one of these areas.

For organizations do not stand still. If we inject something into one part of the system, bells begin to ring and lights begin to go on all over the system, often in places we hadn't counted on and at times we hadn't expected.

We must take at least one more step before we rest. This model we have just drawn is still incomplete. It is a picture of an organization in an empty world. Certainly if there is anything U.S. organizations learned in the last half of the sixties, it is that their environments are anything but empty. The organization is very much shaped by its social life, by the pressures that are exerted on it by government, by consumers, by ethnic groups, and by hosts of other organizations. The modern organization is a city dweller. It lives in a pressing, crowded world. And it presses back. So let's enclose our model in a world.

This is not to say that the complexity of the organization is so great that we can never tell what will happen when we do something. It is only to say that an organization is complex

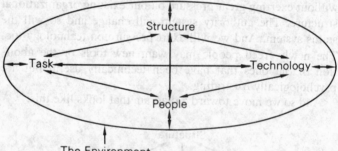

The Environment

enough to make any simple structural or technical or human model inadequate. But we have made a lot of progress in understanding the complexities in the last few decades. We now know a good deal more about ways of acting on structure or people or technology; and we know somewhat more about how they are wired to one another. There is real progress in the organizational world. The three classes of consulting firms in our example should not be taken as an indication that things have gone to pot. On the contrary they are an indication of how much we have learned about organizations. And about how much we now know of ways to change or modify them.

The practitioner in each of these three realms may be oversold on his own product. He may be overly enthusiastic about all that can be done by changing structure, or technology, or people. Each may be partially and understandably blind to the perspectives of the others. But the manager need not be blind. He has lots more to work from than he did in the days when we so naively believed that the simple line drawing on the organization chart actually did capture the essence of our vital, volatile organization.

In summary

Organizations can be thought of as lively sets of interrelated systems designed to perform complicated tasks. We can try to manipulate at least three dimensions of those systems in order to get the performance of tasks changed or improved. We can manipulate the organization structure—which means we can manipulate the communication system or the authority system or the system of work flows and processes. We can manipulate the tools and techniques used in the system— which means we can provide new and better hammers or new and better information-processing devices. And we can enter from the people side, to change bodies or attitudes or inter-personal relations—which means we can change the training and skills of our people or the numbers of people involved or the kinds of people we hire.

But we must never for a moment forget that when we tamper with any one of these three variables, structure or technology or people, we are likely to cause significant effects on the others, as well as on the task.

And we must never forget either that the organization operates in a world of other organizations and institutions, changing that world, but also being changed by it.

Structure, people, and technology Some key ideas and where they came from

In the last chapter we talked about several entry points into the organizational system: the structural, technical, and human entry points. We suggested that there have been theories and techniques developed around each of these points, all aimed at providing the manager or the observer with a handle for thinking about and working on organizations. But these theories and techniques have not always been with us. They have appeared on the organizational scene mostly over the last fifty years; they have traveled over fairly clear routes, and sometimes they have bumped into one another.

In this chapter we look back over those last fifty years and try to map out some of the key ideas, and how they got started. Such a map may be useful, for without one, many current ideas about organization and management can look like a disconnected hodgepodge of conflicting or unrelated positions. In this case a semihistorical map may be the most useful kind. For the key ideas about management seem to have entered American thinking in a fairly systematic set of successive stages.

Scientific management: Its key ideas

A first set of ideas came into managerial thinking in America back around 1911. It was primarily concerned with structure and technology—the definition, measurement, and planning of the work process. Among the key figures in that movement was Frederick W. Taylor, a name most readers probably remember from their college textbooks. He was by no means the only significant contributor, but his thinking and his methods seem to have had the greatest impact on organizations.

Taylor was an engineer; and, in the best sense of the word, he seemed also to have been a scientist, a questioning man, a fact-hunter.

If ever a movie is made about Taylor, the climactic scene

will take place in the yards of the Bethlehem Steel Works shortly after the turn of the century. It will involve two main characters: Taylor himself, and an immigrant laborer named Schmidt. In the scenario, Schmidt is seen going about his work of loading and unloading pigs of iron, moving them from position A to position B. Taylor, ever curious, ever imaginative, is watching Schmidt and conceiving a set of ideas that the world will later call *scientific management*.

As he observes Schmidt, he makes something like the following observations to himself: Schmidt is really doing two kinds of things: (1) He is using his arms and legs to move objects, but (2) he is also making decisions. The decisions are small ones but real ones nevertheless. Schmidt is deciding how to pile the pigs, whether to bend from the knee or the hip, and so on.

Taylor asks himself, "Is Schmidt doing this job in the best way that it can be done?" And he answers, "No."

Now he sets out to determine what the best way is. He searches for methods by which to measure work, and by which to compare alternative ways of doing the work. He argues that such search for the better way is a scientific job, a job that can be better done by people like himself than by people like Schmidt. So back to the laboratory he goes and there he devises the techniques of time-and-motion analysis, which he applies to Schmidt's job. From these, he and his colleagues go on to design an optimal plan for Schmidt's job. The plan specifies the nature of Schmidt's movements, the time that should be allocated to each distinct action.

Now Taylor returns to Schmidt with a message: "Let's stop doing it the way you are now doing it, and do it the way we have laid it out for you. Pick it up with your right hand, instead of your left; bend from the knee instead of from the waist, etc., etc., etc." He points out to Schmidt that what he (Taylor) has done is in Schmidt's and society's best interests for three reasons: First, more pig iron will be handled by the new methods, and that is certainly good for society. Second, Schmidt will end the day less fatigued than he was before, for Taylor will have taught him how to use his body intelligently. And third, Taylor, as an outsider, will urge the company to pay out to Schmidt some portion of the increase in profits accruing from this new method of work. For all these reasons it behooves Schmidt to carry out the work in the way that Taylor recommends. And it behooves the firm and society to adopt Taylor's methods, and to apply them to many other kinds of jobs.

For what Taylor is searching for is the best way to design and do work. He develops a technology for finding best ways, and in company with the industrial psychology of the time and the sophisticated managerial thinking about organizational structure, there emerges a whole conception of scientific management—carefully planned, allocated management. In its ideal form it would lead to a setting in which every man had his work fitted to him, so that he could do it the way best adapted to himself and most closely adjusted to the interests of the firm. The flow of work from position to position would be scientifically determined, the limits of responsibility of each man would be scientifically determined, and so on. From Taylor's rib was born the whole concept of industrial engineering and the "efficiency man." And coming as it did at a time when production and manufacturing processes were proliferating and modernizing, it was consistent with what was happening in the world around it. No wonder it caught on. So that within a very few years hardly a manufacturing firm in America was without industrial engineers and the paraphernalia of scientific management—the paraphernalia of job description, work standards, individual incentive schemes, organization charts, work-flow diagrams, and the other things that went with them.

For scientific management did indeed seem to pay off. Along with the parallel and consonant work of many other people in the structural areas, management became more formalized, jobs more specified, and mass-production technology, America's pride, came increasingly into being. The ideas that surrounded Taylorism became part of the standard vocabulary of almost every manager in the nation. The notion that management processes should be specified, that tasks should be measured and programed, that responsibilities should be "commensurate" with authority—all these were ideas that generated either out of Taylorism or from other parallel sources that were quite consonant with Taylorism.

The cost of scientific management

But the modern reader in reviewing these last few paragraphs has probably already made a mental note of one nagging difficulty in these developments. It was made challengingly manifest by Taylor himself, with comments that were guaranteed to generate trouble even in 1911. He wrote, for example:

Now one of the very first requirements for a man who is fit to handle pig iron . . . is that he shall be so stupid and so phlegmatic that he more nearly resembles . . . the ox than any other type . . . he must consequently be trained by a man more intelligent than himself. (F. W. Taylor, *Scientific Management* [New York: Harper, 1911], p. 59.)

The problem, of course, was the human problem. For what Taylor had done was to separate the planning, thinking, imagining parts of Schmidt from the moving, doing, acting-out parts. He argued partially on the grounds that the Schmidts were a dull group—a rather dull argument. But he also argued it on the same grounds so often used today. In effect, he was saying that specialized and highly trained industrial engineers, equipped with modern tools, could do a better job of specifying how the work ought to be done than the people doing it.

But the human problem is there, and it was to haunt Taylor and the industrial engineers for a good many years to come. Even in 1911 social reformers took up the cudgel against Taylorism, arguing that it was demeaning and degrading to reduce man to the level of the ox that Taylor judged him to be. For what distinguished man from the ox any more than man's capacity to think and judge and make decisions? And if Taylor was removing those from a man's job, he was indeed dehumanizing the man. There followed a congressional inquiry into Taylor's activities, and there was much social uproar at the time. But the easily observable and obvious gains that Tayloristic methods generated seemed to overwhelm the social critics who could offer ideas, but without any really useful alternative techniques for getting work done better.

The unhappy industrial engineer

So the methods proliferated and expanded. And with that expansion came the second wave of attack; this time not from the social reformers who were interested in protecting Schmidt's welfare, but from the Schmidts themselves. And this time it came in a form that was more difficult to handle. It came in the form of slow-downs, sabotage, pegged production. It came in the form of socially organized resistance. And it led to the unhappy industrial engineer—"the efficiency man"—distrusted, often hated, by the people in the plant. When he showed up, work slowed down. When he set high standards, people professed they didn't know how to meet them. When he asked for suggestions, people hid the jigs they had rigged up to do the work faster.

In parallel, some of the unforeseen costs of other classical structural ideas began to show up. For in company with Taylorism, there had also emerged notions about span of control and authority equalling responsibility, and other ideas about the logical design of organizations.

While at lower levels human resistance seemed to be the major cost of Taylorism, the costs at higher levels were the costs of tight authoritarian structure. They came in the form of inextricably overlapping areas of authority, and overlapping responsibilities that resisted all efforts at separation, and in the form of "depersonalization" of relationships consequent to the formalization and restriction of communication in the organizations. These costs seemed to become especially great and noticeable as the decades passed, largely because the numbers and kinds of people in middle-management levels were growing so rapidly. White collars became more numerous, the complexities of staff relationships increased, the varieties of specialists grew; and the problem of coordinating their activities became a much more difficult problem than it had been before.

The emergence of participative management

Into this great breach then stepped the people-people. Under the influence of Taylorism organizations had indeed grown and prospered, but the human costs were becoming increasingly apparent. Human resistance became a major problem.

Let's now write a second script for a second movie to dramatize a second large phase in American managerial thinking—the people phase. To do so, we must turn to another setting and another time. This time the most appropriate setting is the Hawthorne Works of the Western Electric Company, in Cicero, Illinois. The time is the late 1920s. The major characters are a group of researchers from the Harvard Business School on the one hand, and a group of workers from Western Electric on the other. The researchers are present to study several problems, among them some that are strongly Tayloristic in their implications. They are there, among other things, to study the effects of lighting on the productivity of hourly workers performing fine assembly tasks. They go about their business by selecting a group of workers, placing them in a special workroom and maintaining productivity records, under various conditions of light, over an extended period. In our movie there is shot after shot of production charts, showing a sure enough climb in productivity with increasing foot-candles of light.

But with dramatic license, we now sneak a hero into the scene, some unknown (and imaginary) junior assistant. In the interests of science and truth, he argues that these findings will not be truly scientific unless a control is instituted. So he quietly begins to reduce the foot-candles of light (without saying anything to anyone). And now productivity should decline, but it does not. As the lighting goes down, the productivity continues to go up; and that of course, is the moment of truth. For now the increases in productivity which had appeared to be caused by the lighting turn out to be independent of the lighting. It doesn't seem to matter whether the lights are bright or dim. These people continue to produce at an increasing rate.

And it is at this point that a new search begins. Now the findings must be accounted for. If it is not the lighting, what is it? And the search leads inexorably to the point that Taylor and his colleagues had been unable to handle. It leads to the social and psychological needs of the workers. It turns out that the increased productivity was caused not by lighting, but by attention. These workers were now in a small separate room. The environment was less formal. And a lot of other social and psychological factors were now operating that were much more difficult to measure and grasp than lighting. But ephemeral and intangible or not, they seemed to be closely and causally related to production.

Incidentally, it is worth pointing out that Taylor and his colleagues were not unaware of such human needs. They simply had no very good tools for dealing with them. But the Western Electric researchers stimulated a large new search for means and techniques for understanding and harnessing the social and psychological variables in the work-place.

From the late 1920s to the present, the people point of view has grown and prospered. The initial idea was simply that people would get things done better in organizations if they were willingly and enthusiastically involved in their jobs.

Thereupon we started to search for ways of getting such involvement. And gradually, through a series of steps and missteps, two key ideas emerged: First, that one powerful weapon for getting involvement and enthusiasm was the group—almost as a substitute for authority. People would be loyal to one another in groups, they would feel committed to groups that they had worked with. The second key idea was the idea of participation—and essentially the idea that people support what they help to create.

The war against Taylorism

Together these two led easily to the idea that people ought to be involved in planning and decision-making. But, this idea, the idea that people will work more effectively if they participate in decision-making is 180° away from Tayloristic solutions to the same problem. Taylor had argued that planning and decision-making should be taken away from Schmidts and given to specialized planners and decision-makers. Now comes the new people-oriented group, recommending that Schmidt's head be put back on his shoulders. It is no wonder then that clashes and small wars began to break out between these two conceptions.

At first the new participative people proceeded with considerable caution. They accepted existing organizational structures and worked with them. At Western Electric for example, they developed a program of counseling that lasted for a good many years. This early program was added to but outside of regular organizational structure. Counselors could listen to employees; workers could spout their concerns and worries and complaints. But the counselors were to stay outside of the operational scheme of things. They were not to feed back information to top management. They were not, themselves, to induce any organizational changes. They listened. And when people, having thus expectorated their concerns, felt a little better, they were sent back into the same setting that had been there before. So the relief was likely to be temporary. And the treatments had to be continued as new problems built up.

On the other hand, relatively speaking, this kind of an external arrangement did not disturb the organization very much. It worked only on people without reference to structure. But radical and revolutionary as it was at the time, in retrospect it seems a weak and compromising solution. More daring experiments were yet to come.

These new experiments, usually spoken of now as experiments in "overcoming resistance to change," used some of the same ideas, and some different ones too. They used group methods especially, since they conceived of resistance to change as a function of (1) individual frustration and (2) strong group-generated forces. If one can therefore provide opportunities for need satisfaction and if one can also corner the group forces and direct them toward the desired behavior, then the best of all possible worlds will result.

Hence we began to get experiments that took the following typical and challenging (to Taylorism) form:

An hourly job that had been very carefully industrially engineered would be used as a target. For example, a group of girls is producing product X. The girls have been classified into three jobs: Job A, feeder girls, feed raw materials into a machine that turns out finished products. Job B, inspector girls, sit along both sides of a continuing belt visually inspecting the finished products. Job C, packing girls, pack the finished product into boxes on pallets which are then taken away for shipment. The job has been studied and engineered in the best Tayloristic tradition. The speed of each machine has been set at an "optimal" level. The belt moves at a rate determined by the engineers and controlled by the foreman. The girls have even been selected by industrial psychologists so that the ones with high visual acuity are inspecting and the ones with high finger dexterity are packing, and so on.

And now onto this scene move the social scientists. They move into the home domain of the industrial engineer, to show him that he is all wet. They force a direct confrontation. They argue that by throwing all the industrial engineering standards out, replacing them with their new and better techniques—mainly the technique of the group meeting—they can get more productivity, less turnover, and more willing work than the engineers had ever achieved.

Now they sharpen up their major tool: the group meeting. They sit down with the girls to "talk things over." They listen to the girls' gripes, to the things that the girls don't like about the way the work is done in their own jobs. Then they get down to some group decisions. One may be that the girls decide they want to swap off jobs, to overcome monotony. The inspectors will pack every once in a while, and the packers will run the machines. They also decide that the rheostat controlling the speed of the belt should be controlled by the girls rather than the supervisor. The girls argue that sometimes they like to work faster than the belt is going, and sometimes they like to work much slower. And so on. The girls are thus now making a whole series of decisions usually made by management; decisions about the speed of the line, the jobs they will do, and when they will do them, much as Schmidt did before Taylor reached him. But these girls are acting in a group setting, following a group discussion. The outcome is a wiggly, uneven productivity curve, but with averages a good deal higher than under the previous engineered design, and with lowered turnover and higher morale as free riders.

Where has participative management found its home?

In the 1940s several such demonstrations occurred, showing that this much more human, much more participative approach could clearly increase productivity among hourly workers. Yet this approach has not swept American industry nearly as rapidly as Taylorism had swept it in the decades earlier. The preceding statement is a judgment, of course. Perhaps more girls are controlling more rheostats than this author is aware of. But in general it seems fair to say that the industrial engineer is by no means a gone goose. And work standards, job specifications, lines controlled by rheostats controlled by foremen, all of these are still a very large factor in American industry despite this apparently contrary evidence. In this viewer's opinion, these small wars between scientific managers and participative managers have not been clearly won by the participative managers—not at the hourly level.

One of the reasons may be that top managers felt anxious and uncomfortable about the apparent loss of control implied by these participative changes. Girls controlling rheostats might not be willing to give them up at some future date. There were fears, too, about the coordination problems that might be generated by lots of small groups operating more or less autonomously. Some things in the environment, like the development of national labor unions and legal controls over wages and hours required uniformity throughout the firm, and uniformity would be harder to achieve (or at least it so appeared), under participative management plans.

Whatever the reasons, it is probably fair to say that participative management has had its greatest impact at the managerial rather than the hourly levels, though it got its start at hourly levels. It was in middle and higher management that one found ever-increasing concern with participative notions during the sixties. Words like *communication* and *participation* have indeed become buzz words in management circles. The idea that staff people should interact and talk things over is now a commonplace. The idea that management people should lunch together and not worry too much about whether or not they return exactly at one o'clock is accepted practice. The idea of group discussions and conferences and meetings, despite their frustrations, has become a commonplace, too. The ideas of human-relations training and management development programs and lowering of decision points and encouraging team spirit have all shown up much more within management than they have at hourly levels. Not by any means because its originators wished it so, participative management has entered industry through the white-collar gate.

One of the results has been, in this observer's opinion, the development of a rather sharp and impenetrable line between hourly workers and managers. That wall has been created by many things in addition to the split between scientific and participative management. But it is now generally true in American management that one does not move easily from an apprenticeship in the machine shop to the presidency of a large company, even if one is bright. Movement to the top is easier if one starts out above the hourly worker line, as a sales or supervisory trainee. Hourly workers tend to stay hourly workers; in part, because they are trained differently, organized differently, controlled differently than managers and supervisors tend to be.

By the beginning of the seventies, however, there were signs that the whole hourly worker question was being reopened, as a consequence largely of environmental pressures. Job enrichment programs have been started and there is even talk about alternatives to the assembly line. It is as though the costs of Taylorism are becoming larger relative to their payoff, in part because the expectations and motives of the worker pool are changing, and changing ever in a direction that tends to reject the Tayloristic life.

The brave new world of information technology

But our series of organizational movies is not yet complete. Let's move to a third one. Again we must change dates and costumes—to the 1950s and the gray flannel suit. And we change cast to a great extent. Our heroes now are mathematicians, engineers, and such. While Taylor and his boys were armed with stop watches, and the participative people carried group meeting techniques in their back pockets, this new population rides on stage astride a man-eating computer. They carry tools that did not exist for Taylor or the participative people, tools for measuring and analyzing, not what men do with their arms and legs, but what men do with their heads.

Like many movies, this one is largely a variation on an old theme—the Taylor-Schmidt theme, but in modern dress. In lieu of Taylor, operations researchers and simulators are our stars, on one hand, and the middle manager stands in for Schmidt on the other. While Schmidt presumably achieved some fulfilment by being able to make minor decisions about how to handle pig iron, our new middle manager finds his fulfilment in making large and complicated judgmental decisions about how to estimate inventory or design products or allocate funds among a variety of alternatives.

And the computer people, sitting outside and observing these executives, can say in effect what Taylor must have said of Schmidt. Here are people who are doing things primitively, by the seat of their pants, by "knowhow," and by "judgment," and by "experience." Surely there must be a better, a more scientific, a more systematic, a more logical way, an optimal way.

And with the help of new tools, they now search for that way and very often find it. They find that they can solve complex multivariate problems that until now could be solved only by the good common sense and sound judgment of an experienced executive. They also find that they can sometimes make complex decisions faster than they were made before, by getting information into key spots more quickly and more fully than they could before. The climax of this movie, then, is not the tragic race between John Henry and the steam drill, but rather the race between the media executive in the ad agency and the computer. It appears that the computer must inevitably win, but that its winning need not be tragic.

But at this point in history this third wave is making its impact felt at several levels of the organization. Its effect on the Taylorized hourly worker is partially to eliminate the routine and monotonous from the human realm altogether, turning it over to the machine. Its effect on some participative middle managers may be to program them. This may be tantamount to doing what Taylor did to Schmidt. But looked at another way it simply means that we have once again found new and hopefully cheaper and easier ways of doing jobs.

The manager's problem is somehow to cope with these overlapping waves of progress. For indeed they can be called progress. Taylor offered a careful analysis to an area which had not been very well analyzed. The ideas of participative management have represented real progress both as mechanisms for improving the productivity of American industry and for improving the personal satisfaction of the people who work in it. The information technologist, a third wave, has added new kinds of analytic methods that impinge on areas never before subjected to analysis.

It is understandable that each of the three should feel he has the world by the tail, and that the best of all possible organizations will result from the complete application of his methods. But it is understandable too that in complex systems like modern organizations, none of these methods can be applied without impinging on the others.

Nor can any of them be applied without generating some costs not initially foreseen by their inventors. Taylorism generated resistance and sabotage. Participation generated new problems of control and coordination. Information technology promises to generate new social problems. It may also generate psychological problems among people in middle and higher levels of employment.

If this historical rundown of overlapping waves of ideas seems only to complicate life for the manager, it should. For the manager of this and coming generations will have to cope with problems of interrelating and estimating the relative impacts of all three of these kinds of approaches and any new ones that may yet arise. He has to decide where in the organization they can best be applied, and if applied, what kinds of costs he can expect to show up elsewhere in his company.

In summary

Taylorism separated planning from doing, created the industrial engineering specialist, and generated unforeseen problems of human resistance. It has found its more lasting application (at least in its original form) at hourly levels.

Participative management recommended planning and doing, but in groups. But though demonstrably applicable to hourly workers, it has had its great impact on managerial levels; thus inadvertently contributing to an enlarged barrier to movement from worker to manager.

Information technology has reseparated planning from doing in think-type jobs. It will affect all levels, and come into at least partial conflict with participative ideas as a partially alternative method for managing both managers and hourly jobs.

These three are not discrete and irreconcilable. One need not choose one or another. Each is a step forward in organizational problem-solving, if not in contributing to the fulfilment of the organization's members. And common sense tells us that these three do not represent the end of it. There will be fourth, fifth, and sixth major inventions out ahead.

Organizational decision-making Goals, problems, tasks

A couple of chapters ago we diagramed an organization as a system composed of structural, technological, human, and task elements in a world. This chapter is about the task part of that diagram. It is about problem-solving and decision-making by organizations in their environments. We have already talked a good deal about individual and group decision-making and problem-solving in earlier chapters. The questions to be asked this time are about the aspects of decision-making and problem-solving that are unique to large organizations. We shall try to spotlight those special aspects by talking about six questions:

1. How, in fact, do organizations seem to go about making decisions?

2. What are the major kinds of decisions that organizations work on? Can we classify and categorize those problems?

3. How and where do organizations find the problems they work on? Or are they just there?

4. How do organizations know whether or not they have in fact made reasonable decisions? How can they tell when a problem has been solved?

5. How does the last outcome affect the next problem? How do organizations handle successful and unsuccessful problem-solving?

6. And finally, what are the "real" problems? What are the goals and the tasks that members of the organization take seriously? And which ones are only for manuals and lip service?

How do organizations solve problems?

Most of the answer to this question has already come up in our discussions of individual and group problem-solving. Organizations behave much like individuals. They seem to go through processes of search among alternatives, but limited search. They behave rationally, but only within limits. And they satisfice. If we step back and watch the way an organization tackles a problem of diversification, for example, what we are likely to see is some reasonable amount of search for alternatives. Usually this search will be in the immediate neighborhood of the firm's own activities. It's cheaper and easier for a company that makes automobile bumpers to search initially at least for diversification into other automobile accessories, or into other allied products than it is to look into the manufacture of cigarettes or books.

But the bumper manufacturer will not search all possibilities. He would be foolish if he did. He pulls together a string of alternatives and then selects among them. And usually, with considerable rationality, he selects mostly on the basis of the ease of transfer of equipment from one product to another, similarity of markets, and so on.

So far the firm is behaving like an individual. But it is just at this point that the organization begins to show some differences. For the bumper manufacturing organization is itself composed of many groups and individuals. And any decision that is taken will be more consonant with the wishes and goals of some of these groups and individuals than with others. So the decision is apt to be mediated not only by the logic of the situation and by the available alternatives and the costs of those alternatives, but also by some issues of power and some ideas about justice. Choice A may result in expansion of department X and contraction of department Y. Choice B, which has been pushed by executive Jones, may be utterly abhorrent to executive Smith. And so the organization, faced not only with the problem of diversifying but also with the problem of keeping itself together, is likely to take its decision in the light of the internal facts as well as the external ones. These internal facts may or may not get formal, conscious consideration. But they will get consideration. Some "equitable" solution will be sought; a solution which can be seen as reasonably just; and one that will not severely threaten the existing power structure.

The evidence is pretty good that such "internal" factors really do significantly affect the kinds of decisions that organizations make, contrary to the older conception of the firm as though it were a single entrepreneur operating rationally in a perfect market place. The organization rather is a complex body, full of internal stresses and strains. And these internal problems affect the external ones. Certainly when we think of government organizations this kind of idea comes as no surprise. When our State Department makes a decision in international relations, it had darn well better take domestic public reaction into account. And it had darn well better take account of the groups in our society who will support or fight it.

Since organizations make decision after decision and face problem after problem, it is not surprising that they begin to develop some standard machinery. We begin to get something roughly equivalent to a body of laws in a system of courts. We try to satisfy the many groups within the organization by developing rules that make the organization's decisions seem internally just and impersonal. The capital budgeting committee, for example, sets up criteria to specify the kinds of budget requests that it will or will not approve. And executives, or committees of executives, are assigned as arbitrators and adjudicators of disputes.

The next step in the process is fairly clear. Suppose several parts of our organization recommend several kinds of diversification. We set up a group to make a decision. But the decision will make some groups happy and others unhappy, and the organization will have to live with those groups after the decision is made. So the decision-makers, reasonably enough, look for some ways to minimize the negative aftereffects. Nobody wants anybody to be angry after the decision is taken.

In general, organizations seem to work out two kinds of methods for solving this dilemma. One is the method of measurement. If we can put numbers on things, then we can come to impersonal solutions that nobody can argue with. If we can set the problem up as a straight problem in arithmetic, then nobody can claim that 2 and 2 do not equal 4.

But of course, lots of problems don't fall into that neat form. So organizations have a propensity to force them into that form, or to place those elements of the problem which are measurable up at the top of the list. Perhaps one of the reasons that human problems are so often overlooked in organizations is because it is hard to attach numerical costs to reduced human satisfaction.

The second organizational solution to the problem of internal justice is the lots-of-talk solution. No single individual or body need be identified as *the* decision-maker. The problem is kicked around, talked about, written about in a great many quarters over an extended period of time. Finally the decision "emerges." Nobody has ever said precisely that we will do this or that. Finally it is clear that the new build-

ing will be built or that the old product will be modified, but
nobody can ever put his finger on the individual or body who
made the decision, or the precise alternatives that were considered.

At first glance, this second mechanism seems sloppy and
wasteful. It may not be. Decisions are slowed by such
processes. But the negative costs of internal friction are apt
to be reduced. On the other hand, this is by no means a recommendation about organizational decision-making. It is
simply to say that organizations seem to behave in these two
ways, and that sometimes their behavior is not as foolish as it
may at first appear. For when time is not of the essence, and
cohesiveness is, then the long informal talking through may
be a reasonable way to behave. And vice versa.

What kinds of problems do organizations solve?

It may be worth looking at the kinds of tasks that exist in organizations. For it is becoming increasingly clear that what
organizations do influences to a great extent what organizations are. One dimension of tasks that is especially worth
looking at is the extent to which they can be programed.
There are some problems in the world that are easy to define
and clarify, and that have known tools that will help with
their solution. Mowing the lawn is an example. It is fairly
clear to most of us *when* the lawn needs mowing, about *how
long* it will take us to do it, at about what personal *cost* to us,
and with what *tools*. We also know that the tools may change
over time, to make the work easier and better but, perhaps,
also more costly. We can clearly define the lawn problem,
and we know many different ways of solving it. We can as-
sociate some kinds of costs with each of them. And we can
tell when the problem has been solved by looking at the
lawn. It is a repetitive task, too. One with which we become
familiar after a while.

There are lots of tasks like that in organizations. We have
called them programed tasks. They are easy to specify. Costs
are fairly easy to allocate. Methods can also be specified and
outcomes are easy to measure.

Some tasks are so highly programed that they are
"public" tasks; they can be transferred from one person to
another with relative ease. Some are a little less publicly
programable. I could come in and mow your lawn, for example, and I would know roughly what to do, and roughly
how to use your tools. But there would be some unprogramed
elements. Some particular characteristics of your lawn—its

topography, the trees on it—which would be hard for you to describe to me, and which I would have to learn about mostly by experiencing the problem once or twice.

But there are other problems and tasks which are a lot less clear than that. Problems like: Shall I install a fence? What kind? Where? Shall we diversify our product line? Where shall we locate a new plant? How much time, energy, and money shall we put into the recruitment of new personnel? How shall we develop young managers?

In complex organizations it is generally true—though not always—that new problems are initially unstructured and unprogramed. As we face them again and again we develop programs for them. There is generally a flow from unstructuredness to structuredness. One of the reasons is probably the nature of the human beast. He has a strong tendency to dislike ambiguous and unclear situations, so he tries to order them. Another reason is that as things get more structured it appears that justice is easier to mete out and so are rewards and so is control. If we can specify our task and how to do it, then we can make decisions about what to pay people to do it, and how they are to work on it. Programing problems, in other words, tends to reduce uncertainty and increase control, at least initially.

As technology changes, so does the task picture. For new and better tools can make possible today the programing of tasks that couldn't be programed yesterday. If we want programed rather than unprogramed problems, some part of our energy in organizations is likely to be devoted to a search for new tools that will allow us to program things that have been previously unprogramable. Much of what we usually call staff work is search-for-new-tools work.

What this adds up to then is a general movement of problems from a state of unprogramedness to a state of greater programedness. But in general *that flow is also associated with movement from higher levels in the organization to lower levels*. In most large organizations different people deal with different kinds of problems. Some people pick up mostly unprogramed new problems (staff groups are one example), work on them, eventually get them into a programed state, and then pass them on to some lower level.

Hence, we are likely to get movement toward differentiated organizations, in which different parts of the system work on different types of problems. It follows that if the kinds of people and methods that can handle unprogramed problems best are different from the kinds of people and methods that can handle programed problems best, our organization is apt to begin to split into suborganizations. These in turn can be very different from one another in their structure, their tools, and their people, as well as in their tasks.

How and where do organizations find their problems?

If you ask any executive where he finds his problems his reaction is apt to be laughter. He doesn't have to find them; they find him. His desk is loaded with them every morning. And so on.

It's true, of course, that this is the way the world seems to work; and it's probably also true, as some researchers in this field have pointed out, that a kind of Gresham's law prevails. That is that people respond to the programed tasks facing them before responding to the unprogramed ones. If there are specific problems with specific deadlines on my desk, those are the things I work on, not the unprogramed things I might work on if there were no immediate and local pressures.

But this is precisely, of course, where one of the major difficulties of organizations arises. Because programed, specified, deadlined tasks seem to grow and proliferate in organizations, and because most of us respond to these tasks before responding to the more vague unprogramed ones, some important things are apt to be neglected.

How then, do organizations get beyond this kind of "local" state, in which they deal first with programed pressing problems, responding always to the vagaries of their environments, but never acting upon those environments to change them?

There are several ways out of the box. One of them is the maverick executive. In some organizations one can find particular persons who by training or education or personality insist on breaking Gresham's law. They work on the unprogramed, the new, the novel, the unstructured, though their desks pile higher and higher.

Another way out is loosening up the whole organization; cutting down the number of structured and programed tasks. Job-enlargement programs fit into that category. So do many of the other participative activities designed to increase creativity among the organization's members. They can be thought of as ways of encouraging people actively to look for problems rather than to wait for them.

A third way is to develop specialized sense organs. Basic research represents such a development. It is a searching mechanism, although what it is searching for is not entirely known. But precisely because its task is to search for the unknown, top managements are apt to feel uncomfortable about it. How does one control such unprogramed activities? And how much of the resources of the organization should reasonably be poured into a well that seems bottomless? On the other hand, if we control basic research we destroy it. For then research would not be searching for new problems, but dealing with problems fed into it. How much does an organization need, somewhere in its structure, some open-ended, groping, searching bodies that don't know quite where they are going or quite what they'll find? Surely they will need more such scanning of the environment than ever before.

It is here, too, that we get back to the old problem of what we lose by programing other more mundane jobs in our organization even though we know how to program them. While we worry about the basic research group spending its time doing things that may be useless, we need to worry, too, about a routine production group spending all its time doing highly programed relevant things that are useful but unchanging, for the nascent creative idea may be completely blocked in that controlled setting.

How do organizations know when they have solved a problem?

This seems a beguilingly easy issue in organizational problem solving. But people who have been around organizations know that it is not. Finding out how well it worked is especially difficult for those interesting unprogramed problems in which no one knows quite what all the alternatives might be; and in which the delays between actions and effects are long ones. When delays between cause and effect are long, it is hard to isolate cause. Some primitive societies, for example, don't seem to make any logical connection between intercourse and childbirth nine months later. Too many other things happen over nine months that can account for the appearance of the infant. Too many other things often happen in our primitive organizational decision-making, too. It's apt to be a long time, for example, between the introduction of an idea and the marketing of a product that it generated. Sometimes we can't remember the original idea. Sometimes the product flops—but is it because the market changed? Or because the idea was no good? These kinds of questions make it truly difficult to determine whether or not a decision was a reasonable decision.

Second, we live in a satisficing world. So all we are apt to know, if we know anything, is whether or not the decision we chose got us generally in the direction we wanted to go. We seldom know in organizations whether an alternative decision would have worked better than the one we chose.

Third, we have a kind of cognitive balance problem again. Once we have committed ourselves to an organizational decision, once we have built a plant or decided to manufacture widgets, there are lots of psychological forces to keep us from rejecting that decision. The failure of a decision has to be very dramatic indeed for it to be accepted as such. And even then, organizations have a strong propensity to develop silver linings for their failures.

But the thing that is clear is that feedback about the effects of behavior is just as necessary for organizational learning as it is for individual learning. Getting quick and accurate feedback on organizational problems, however, is probably even harder than it is for individuals. Not only are the problems likely to be bigger and more complex, and the results apt to be delayed, but there are. also problems of blocks and biases in internal communication. How quickly and accurately shall we report negative outcomes of something we have been responsible for? Do we dare tell the boss that his plan has flopped? Won't he feel that we just haven't done a very good job of implementing it?

Technology seems to be helping a good deal in speeding up the feedback process both within and without the organization. Telephones are faster than letters. Quick samplings of sales, statistically controlled, may tell us whether or not the style change is having the impact we want. Simulation devices allow us to pretest and get certain kinds of feedback before we have committed ourselves to the decision.

But though technology has speeded up feedback rates, it has helped only a little in the decisions regarding what we need to know about the world out there. Some of what an organization needs has been obvious for a long time—like consumer reaction to styles. But other sources of useful intelligence about the environment are harder to specify. What does the company need to know about the community in which it lives? About race relations? Drug abuse? Crime? The activities of college students? It's easy and safe to say that the company needs to know more than it ever did before. But exactly *what* and *how* are more difficult and not yet fully answered questions.

Yet we are probably making progress by turning our modern information technology toward the problem, by trying to model the important parameters of the environment so that the manager can better assess the likely effects of environmental changes on the organization, and the likely effects of changes by his organization on the environment. The techniques are progressing rapidly; the more human question of inputs—of what parts of the environment we really need to look at—is a little harder to handle.

Feedback mechanisms within the organization are perhaps more important than ever, too. Although most managers are ready and willing to grab new tools that will help them assess their impact on the market, they are less enthusiastic about new devices for sensing the internal problems of their organization. And it is on the internal side that one of the major people problems of organizations exists. But more of that in a following chapter.

Still another source of bias in developing accurate and speedy feedback in organizations is the tendency of most of us to keep our pockets full of many different yardsticks. If our profits decline, can't we take solace in the fact that our share of the market went up? This tendency to select only the good yardsticks is one large part of the human balancing act. It is also a source of distortion in large organizations.

In the same vein, one of the key problems in getting accurate and quick feedback in organizations is the organization's own history. Suppose we have a great idea. It has worked by all of our yardsticks. The effect on our success is often to cause us to lower our guard. We check less carefully, pay less attention to small cues, especially internal cues, when we are riding high on a previous series of successes. On the other hand, if organizations have met miserable failures, even greater distortions in feedback are likely to occur. For now the atmosphere is apt to be hostile and recriminative, and in that environment truth is hard to come by.

What problems are the real problems to
members of an organization?

For a long time economists have liked to treat organizations as though they had single goals. Businessmen have often echoed this notion too, although they probably don't really believe it. The goal of the business, one often hears, is to maximize profits. And that is probably a reasonable statement in many businesses. But if one pushes it, one is likely to notice one important thing: Many people and groups within the firm seem to place *maximized* profit quite far down the

list. They like to *improve* their profit positions. They feel
good if they have done better than they did last year or if
they have hit some target they set out to hit. And more important, there are many people and groups in organizations
who place the whole profit issue fairly low on the list of operational goals. They will talk about improving quality, or getting a larger budget next year, or getting management to accept an organizational change.

This is only to say that in most organizations there is not
one goal but a diversity of goals. Different individuals, different units, different groups are striving for different kinds
of things. We solve a large part of this problem of different
goals in the same firm by setting up formal roles and duties
and expecting people to operate within them. We say to a
man, "When you come to work for us this is the job we want
you to do." And most of us accept that role and spend a good
part of our lives trying to achieve the goal associated with
that role. But that isn't the only goal we strive for. We also
try to enhance the role itself. Sometimes, even in trying to
fulfil that role, we run into clear conflict with our own personal goals. That is the subject of the next chapter. But even
if we operate within our roles, even if we do what we ought
to be trying to do, even if our own personal motives are kept
out of it, the goals of different parts of the organization are
apt to be diverse and sometimes in conflict.

One important fact is that the meaningful, operational
goals that people really work at tend to be local goals. Sol-
diers don't generally really fight for their country so much as
they fight for their local units and their buddies. The district
manager, although he is a good company man, may see himself as working mostly for his district.

No matter how much the planners try, they are not in most
organizations able to set up a system of roles in such a way
that all goals are consonant with all others. So that even if
people do their jobs, conflicts of interest will arise. The organization, in fact, is not an orderly hierarchy of subgroups,
each of which is striving toward some subgoal such that,
together, they will maximize the company's total goals. That
just isn't the way it works. The way it really works is much
more like a political system. Group A wants a larger share of
the budget. So does group B. There are active conflicts and
competition to get their shares. Group C has to mediate between the two contestants, and it must worry about the negative effects on one if it finds for the other.

And so we come back around, in closing this chapter, to

the notion that we raised in opening it. Organizations are complex arrangements that deal with many problems. The nature of the problems is critical. But so is the nature of the organization's own internal structure. In deciding whether or not to enter the race a man must make estimates about the strength of his legs. In deciding whether or not to enter the market with a new product an organization must make relevant estimates about the strength of its people and its internal structure.

In summary

Organizations, like individuals, search and satisfice in their efforts to solve problems. But unlike individuals, issues of group power and justice contribute to the choices the organization makes. For the organization is a system of subsystems, with partially conflicting goals and interests. Therefore, in dealing with the world, task decisions must also be such that the internal coalition of forces will not be split asunder.

The subgroupings in organizations are determined partially by the degree to which different tasks are programed. The people, tools, and structure appropriate to some unprogramed tasks can be very different from those appropriate to others. Hence wide diversities may develop among different groups and levels.

Since programed tasks tend to drive out unprogramed ones, organizations need mechanisms for making sure the unprogramed ones get worked on. Deviants are one mechanism; specialized staff groups are another; participation is a third.

Organizations also often fall down in assessing the outcomes of their decisions. One major effect of new organizational technology is to make faster and more accurate feedback feasible and thereby to make assessment of outcome much easier.

Organizations and individuals
The people part of the system

This chapter focuses on the people part of the organizational system, especially on the relationship between people and structure. We shall talk about people and technology in the next two chapters.

The particular people problems we shall look at here are the problems generated in individuals by living in organizations. We shall then consider one of several methods for trying to rebuild the organizational house so that, as long as it has people in it, those people can live in it productively and healthily.

Much of life for people in organizations is not very different from life on the outside. Getting along with oneself and with other people is no more or less of a problem within organizations than without. But the organizational environment, especially the structural parts, exerts some pressures of its own, over and above these others. Organizations are a source of stimulation in their own right. Their effects are less easily discernible, perhaps, than the effects of particular people or particular things. Organizations are more like neighborhoods than specific neighbors. But like neighborhoods, they can significantly influence behavior.

Unlike the neighborhood, however, the industrial organization is a place to work, not a place to live. Many people in industry therefore claim that the effect of organizations on people's comfort is unimportant unless comfort is related to productivity. Often, for example, industrial managers committed to a *structural* view hold that the eight hours a day people spend in business organizations are not hours designed for need satisfaction to begin with. They are *working* hours. Americans distinguish work from play precisely because work is not intended to provide contemporaneous need satisfaction. When a man goes to work he should therefore feel that he is sacrificing his eight working hours in order to earn the wherewithal to obtain satisfactions *off* the job.

This clean-cut separation of work from play encounters two difficulties. First, it carries with it the unrealistic assumption, talked about in part 2, that people can actually make such a separation on some neat, rational basis. People cannot shed their personalities at eight o'clock or their personal, nonorganizational goals and interests. Even if they sign a frustration-in-exchange-for-pay contract, they are not likely to be able to fulfil their commitment. "Illogically" (but with the internal logic described in part 1) they go on using up organizational time trying to avoid personal frustration and to find positive satisfactions on the job.

Second, even if a manager could get his people to accept their jobs as necessary periods of frustration, he probably could not, if chapter 4 is right, get them to stop responding to frustration with aggression. Feelings of aggression are also outside the scope of the contract.

The questions raised in this chapter, therefore, remain appropriate: How is the organizational neighborhood likely to affect the residents' opportunities for need satisfaction? And is it likely to affect behavior? We already said, in talking about communication nets, that the answer to the second question is "yes" for small groups. But what about large ones?

To try to answer these two questions this chapter looks at several common organizational characteristics that exert direct pressure on people's behavior: First, the hierarchical, pyramidal shape of industrial organizations; second, the ideas of individual authority and responsibility that are an integral part of most industrial organizations; and, third, the sheer size of many modern American business enterprises, both in population and physical extent.

Pyramids and people

All American industrial organizations are shaped more or less like pyramids. At least they become narrow at higher levels. Coupled, intentionally, with this narrowing design is a more-or-less-conscious effort by people at higher levels to encourage people at lower levels to climb. This effort need not be great to be successful because early training and education have already encouraged climbing behavior. Industrial organizations simply continue the process by offering greater rewards at higher levels, rewards that are perceptually real for most of us. They also help the process along by selectively screening out those with less intensive climbing desires.

These two factors, narrowing toward the top and desire to

reach the top, combine to create *competition* for advancement. Such competition is likely to be less intense when the whole pyramid is rapidly growing and more intense as the growth rate decelerates. For when the whole pie is getting bigger, everyone can move with it. When the pie's growth ceases, but the diners' appetites do not, competition for a piece of it is likely to be more intense. Fortunately, however, the world is bigger than the company; so even when an organization has stopped growing, its members may continue to climb by leaving the organization—a characteristic and accepted phenomenon in some industries (merchandising is probably the outstanding example) but one fought by management in others.

Still another escape, in static or slow-growth periods, can be found through personnel selection. It is possible to find competent people who do not like to climb or whose levels of aspiration will tolerate a more moderate rate of climb. Some American unions have found a need to remake or replace some of their people at the point at which the battle to organize gave way to the problem of consolidating the union and establishing more "gentlemanly" relations with managements. The old-time battler, useful and effective in winning the war for organization, became a difficult problem when war gave way to diplomacy.

It should not be necessary to add, after the section on influence, that "remaking" people is not always a hopeless process. Experienced industrial counselors will probably agree that helping people to lower their levels of aspiration is one of their most common tasks. Counselors must deal with the young man who did not become superintendent after one year and the older man who did not become president—but whose best friend did. People can, in a great many instances, successfully learn to accept something short of supremacy.

If individual competition results from the combination of the pyramid and egoistic climbing needs, how does such competition affect the productivity of the whole organization? It does not seem safe simply to generalize the advantages of interorganizational competition and apply them to interpersonal competition. A football team may compete successfully with other teams, but it does not follow that it will compete best if its members are in competition with one another.

Interpersonal competition also hits another complication that interorganizational competition manages to avoid: the problem of personal conflict between egoistic and social needs discussed in chapter 5. While parents and education have encouraged us to compete, our dependency has also encouraged our social needs. Climbing at the expense of others is unchristian and unsportsmanlike. So required interpersonal competition may disturb people and evoke feelings of guilt, feelings that are not usually present in competition between firms or other large organizations. Again, though, if the criterion is the total productivity of the organization, internal conflicts are relevant only if they hurt productivity.

Still another complication deriving from interpersonal competition is that people at higher levels in companies are the umpires and judges. In competition between organizations no such complication exists. The impersonal "market" is the judge of success. But within organizations the climbing game is played differently. The climber is largely dependent on the personal evaluation made of him by people at higher levels.

This personal element in the climbing process is much like what dependent children encounter. How "good" the job of mowing the lawn is depends largely on parents' reactions. It is a good job if they say so and a bad one if they say so. The youngster may learn that "good" depends as much on parental moods or on his ability to ingratiate as it does on the neatness of the lawn.

Considering all these complications, under what general conditions can increasing interpersonal competition be expected to increase organizational productivity? At least three conditions come to mind: If the jobs of the competitors are *independent*, not interdependent; if *objective*, not subjective, *standards* for advancement can be established; and if *success* for one *can be separated from failure* for others; then interpersonal competition should result in a net increase in productivity.

Suppose, for example, that a sales manager decides to select an assistant from among ten salesmen. The salesmen know that one of them will get the job, but they do not know which one. Competition for the assistant's job would probably increase total productivity if:

1. The salesmen operated in independent, non-overlapping territories.

2. The manager could devise and communicate an objective standard for selection. For example, he might select the man with the greatest sales increase in the next six months over his past three-year sales average. An objective standard is not easy to achieve. It requires a method for equating territories; it must avoid the pitfall of encouraging salesmen to

overload some customers and ignore others for the short-term prize, and so on. And it must mean what it says: the subjective judgment of the manager must not count.

3. The salesmen see the objective standards as reasonable and fair; the salesmen prefer the assistant's job to the satisfactions derived from being out in the territory; and the salesmen do not feel that they are hurting one another in the process of striving for the promotion.

Such conditions are difficult to meet, and to the extent that they are not met, the productive advantages of interpersonal competition would be decreased.

In general, these conditions are probably easier to approximate at lower than at higher levels. Jobs are often more independent of one another at lower levels; measures of performance are easier, too. But even at those levels, questions of job separation and individual incentives create difficult, perhaps impossible, problems. At higher levels, where interdependent decision-making plays a larger role, a design for ideal competitive conditions is even less likely to be successful.

For at higher levels, as we suggested in the last chapter, jobs are unique rather than standardized. They change, too; new problems show up. The right decisions, even after they have been made, are often hard to judge objectively. And probabilities play a larger part, so that a series of successful decisions, or of unsuccessful ones, may occur by chance. All these things force managers to evaluate high-level subordinates more personally, more subjectively.

Further, the same characteristics of pyramids and people create difficulties for superiors as well as for subordinates. One of the rewards for the superior's own successful climb is the right to rule the roost, the right to the attention and respect of subordinates. That reward must be partly given up when the manager is asked to set up impersonal, objective standards for his subordinates.

Managerial resistance to setting up objective standards, even where they are possible, is understandable. The best man objectively may not be the best team member (for we want cooperation, too) or the easiest to work with. A successful pattern of people in a group, even if each is not perfect, may be more productive than a group of "perfect" but poorly related individuals.

Even where competition is an effective stimulus, the reward of promotion up the administrative ladder may not be a reward for some useful people. Research people and other professionals often fall into this group. The goals of many of them lie in their professions, not in the administrative hierarchy. But the organizational pyramid builds in the assumption that higher levels in the organization are more important levels, more deserving of higher income and higher status. It becomes awkward for the pyramidal organization, therefore, to have a man at a lower level regularly contributing more than men several levels above him in the structure.

This picture of the costs of interpersonal competition can be easily overdrawn if one does not take into account the many other purposes the pyramid serves. It is a shape that simplifies many problems of communication and control. It is, on the face of it, a logical structure for handling the many levels of decision-making that must go on in an organization. So, despite all the difficulties that are consequent to the competition created by the pyramid, there is not sufficient reason for abandoning it, especially since no good substitute is available. A more likely outcome will be a differentiating and separating of different parts of the pyramid, with the parts in less close contact with one another.

But if the emphasis on competition often causes trouble, the simultaneous emphasis on cooperation causes more. For like inconsistent parents, managers talk out of both sides of their mouths. While they want "aggressive," "competitive" young men, they also want people who "get along," who can "play on the team." The worst part of these clichés is the conflict they produce for the young man who wants to get ahead. Shall he be competitive or cooperative? Does the manager himself know what he wants, or ought he to spend some time, like our good influencer, reexamining his own motives and objectives?

Authority and dependency

A second characteristic of industrial organizations is the hierarchical, unequal distribution of power among the members. Roughly, power follows the pyramid: higher levels have more of it; lower levels, less. An earlier chapter pointed out that this distribution is brought about primarily through the delegation of authority. Through authority (in addition to personal power) given people at higher levels, power is generally distributed through the organization so that more stays at the top than sifts to the bottom.

The other side of this coin is the psychological one. This distribution of power through authority means that people lower in the organization probably feel more dependent on higher levels than the other way around. So the hierarchical system of authority, in serving other organizational purposes, also causes feelings of dependency.

One important outgrowth of dependency, we have said, is ambivalence: the tendency simultaneously to like and dislike being dependent. That most of us like dependency is apparent when we lose it—when the lonely, independent assignment (like the presidency of the company) ultimately comes our way. That most of us also dislike dependency is shown by our efforts to attain the presidency.

Dependency, by splitting people down the middle, can affect organizational behavior in important ways. It can cause tensions in relationships between subordinate and superior, limiting freedom to communicate and increasing concern about the meanings of the superior's behavior. The signs of these difficulties show up everywhere in industry. At the office party the boss drops in and the atmosphere changes; some people drift away; others talk a little louder or a little faster. Idiosyncracies in the behavior of peers are passed over quickly, but the boss's oddities become legendary; his moods become prime subjects for gossip; his occasional off-hand comments are scrutinized microscopically for their hidden but significant implications.

These behaviors are clues to the subordinate's perspective on the same problem higher management usually defines in terms of merit rating or personnel evaluation. Both perspectives recognize the extent to which life in an industrial organization is life in a medium of dependency, of continuous evaluation—a partial replication of childhood when every act was judged to be good or bad by adults. Such a medium necessarily must draw some of the subordinate's attention away from job functions so that he can focus it on methods of improving his position with superiors. To a greater or lesser degree, any assigned job becomes, in this medium, two jobs: One job is to carry out the assignment, to get the job done; the other (but not always secondary) job is to please the superior. Maybe the two tasks can be melded into one, or maybe the second one can be minimized (some alternatives are considered in the next chapter), but basically dependency causes concern over being judged in any task undertaken within the industrial setting.

Dependency on other people for the satisfaction of one's needs is not unique to industry. It is characteristic of many other phases of American life. Nor is it a new phenomenon. Nevertheless, this problem may be more important today than it was a few generations ago. The veteran businessman's claim that today's young people are too "security conscious" may be valid. Certainly some sociologists agree that Americans today are more "other-directed"—more concerned with other people's judgments and with meeting other people's standards—than they used to be. This concern about approval, about security, about conforming to the "right" kind of behavior intensifies dependency. While such attitudes may simplify the superior's task of controlling behavior, they may complicate the task of bringing about creative, independent behavior.

Another factor bears on this question. Partly to protect their relationships with their own superiors and partly on rational grounds, superiors tend to demand that subordinates objectively justify their actions, often in advance of the actions themselves. The superior expects his subordinates to be "businesslike" in their methods as well as their results. This requirement may force people's dependency underground, so they act more and more independently, though they really would like a shoulder to weep on. The results of chronically unexpressible feelings of dependency can be serious, sometimes physically harmful, for the individual.

The same conditions can be organizationally harmful, too. Most executives are probably familiar with the problem of reporting back to top management some unhappy discovery about the adverse effects of one of top management's pet ideas. Often it is personally dangerous to communicate such information, despite behests by superiors to report the facts "objectively." Even the good subordinate may end up with a watered down, selective report of what he observed, though he cloaks it in the paraphernalia of facts and figures. And if the findings reflect on the subordinate himself, rather than the superior, objectivity becomes even more unlikely.

One result of this "evaluation fear" may be the loss of a most useful organizational tool—the sensitive, intuitive judgment of experienced people. Pressure on the superior to evaluate and on the subordinate to get a positive evaluation can team up to destroy unverbalizable judgment in favor of rational, objective justification.

For instance, the fact seems to be that we do not know very much about how advertising works. But to be businesslike, advertising people often have to act as if they do. There would be nothing inherently dangerous in such play-acting if the actors knew they were acting and if they knew they were really using their uncommunicable knowledge and experience. Instead, they often behave as though they could write down and communicate all the relevant facts. The result, for the present, is that many business decisions have more the appearance of rationality than the actuality.

The jigsaw puzzle of responsibility

A third related characteristic of industrial organizations is that they live by the principle of individual responsibility. This is the belief that a task can be subdivided into person-sized pieces, each piece independent of every other and each piece just the right size for an individual. Some doubt exists about whether such an atomistic breakdown is possible in complex modern organizations, and some doubt also exists about whether organizational charts which purport to demonstrate such a breakdown are reality or mirage.

The idea of individual responsibility probably grows out of the fact that industrial organizations are built from the top down, with a continuing need for control from the top. But as the size and complexity of organizations grow, control from the top becomes more difficult—at least the complete, unequivocal control that includes exclusive ownership of all significant decision-making rights.

With growth, management must ask: Now that we are so big that we must allow lower levels to make some decisions, how can we do so without giving up our independent sovereignty? The idea of responsibility to correspond with authority seems to be the best answer that has been found. Top levels give subordinates some of their decision-making prerogatives, but they hold on to control over the relationship itself. Delegation of authority and responsibility are not irrevocable. They do not include a tenure clause. Thus, the dependency of the subordinate on the superior can remain almost intact. Moreover, by delegating specific, carefully defined areas of responsibility to individuals in individual-sized pieces, control from the top can be maximized. With one individual responsible for each separable phase of activity, difficulties can be spotted quickly and correctives can be applied to a manageable unit—an individual.

This is practical reasoning. In a structure controlled from the top, it makes sense to subdivide the total job into parts, to hold one individual responsible for each part, and at the same time to maintain control over means to the individual's key need satisfactions.

But these same ideas have some secondary effects. The principle of individual responsibility assumes that all decisions can be made by individuals. It assumes also that the whole of an enterprise equals the sum of its separable areas of individual responsibility. These two assumptions lead the traditional concept of responsibility into difficulty in modern big business.

One difficulty arises when the assumption that the whole equals the sum of its individual-sized parts meets the factor of technical specialization. At that point the individual-sized parts stop being entirely independent of one another and become interdependent. The subparts and the sub-subparts begin inextricably to intertwine, and so, too, do individual areas of responsibility.

Consider, for example, an organization that is subdivided primarily along functional lines. It is made up of three major functions: procurement, manufacturing, and selling. Vice-presidents are in charge of these functions. Over time the company's products begin to grow in numbers, so additional people are assigned responsibility for supervising particular classes of products—"product supervisors." Still all products derive from the same raw materials; many are manufactured on the same production lines; and all are sold by the same sales force. Who is now responsible for the manufacture of product X—the manufacturing people or the product supervisors? Who is responsible for deciding how much raw material to procure for product X, especially if procurement of raw material for X automatically requires procurement of raw material for Y and Z? If the product supervisor is held responsible for the overall success of his product, but not for procurement, isn't he in the position of having responsibility without equal authority? Moreover, if the manufacturing vice-president is responsible for manufacturing, then what is the product supervisor's relation to him?

Overlapping circles of responsibility seem to show up more and more as organizations increase in size and complexity. Individual jobs become more and more dependent on other, previously unrelated jobs. Staff and service activities come into being, and defining their authority and responsibility becomes a nightmare.

Within the general medium of continual personal evaluation, subordinates must come more and more to demand wider and wider realms of authority in order to fulfil their responsibility. Private little kingdoms thus begin to emerge. Department heads get protective about their prerogatives and about other people moving in on their territory.

These complications are to be expected if a man knows he

is being watched and judged continually and also knows that his job is defined in such a way that he cannot hope to do it adequately through his own efforts. He is dependent on his superiors for promotion and advancement and dependent on his peers for help in getting his job done; but he is evaluated by his superiors as though he were not dependent on either. So the plant superintendent is in continual conflict with the industrial-relations manager, because the superintendent's performance is partly dependent on his relations with his union. The industrial-relations manager, on the other hand, to do his job adequately, cannot permit plant-to-plant variations in labor contracts, even though a particular plant could profit from a special contract. The product manager is in continual conflict with the general sales manager because his products are not getting the sales attention he thinks they deserve. But the sales manager feels that he cannot do an adequate job unless he controls the way his salesmen subdivide their time and effort among products.

Size

Still another set of human problems derives from the large numbers of people whose activities must be coordinated in modern industrial organizations. Large groups are harder to systematize and control than small groups. Large groups can, in fact, be different in kind as well as degree from small ones. We pointed out earlier that some communication nets, for example, are unique to small groups. They are not applicable to a ten-man group, let alone to a hundred men. For a group of five people, ten channels of communication are possible; but when the number of people increases to ten, forty-five channels open up, and when the number is one hundred, 4,950 communication channels are possible.

The point is that big groups are different from small ones. As organizations grow, some of the principles by which they are organized no longer apply. One writer has drawn some analogies from biology. He points out that Jack the Giant Killer's giant is sixty feet tall and well proportioned. He is ten times as tall as Jack, ten times as broad, ten times as thick through. His volume and mass are a thousand times those of Jack. But being built like Jack, his leg bones are probably ten times as wide and ten times as thick, or a hundred times as big as Jack's in cross-section. So now the giant has to carry a thousand times Jack's weight on supports only a hundred times as big. He probably cannot stand up. Simple proportionate increases in the size of each point do not necessarily make the system grow successfully. The same writer goes on to suggest that as industrial organizations grow, ideas such as span of control, the suggestion box, etc., which may have been useful at one point in an organization's size, lose their usefulness and require complete redesign.

Size, then, goes on to generate many varieties of individual human problems. Increased size increases every man's distance from people who influence his organizational fate. Although immediate superiors have a lot to do with determining where he goes, decisions beyond the immediate superior or even beyond the immediate superior's superior set limits on the speed and direction of his movements. Direct communication with those distant decision-makers is almost impossible. The subordinate's anonymity increases, and so does his uncertainty about what will become of him. Each man knows that he is being evaluated and also that he can have little effect on the information his evaluators use or on their interpretation of that information. So size adds to the tensions already instigated by the atmosphere of evaluation.

Size also separates people at the same level from one another. Because free and open communication among all persons becomes more complicated with growth, any man at any level becomes more isolated from others involved in other activities at the same level. So people's opportunities for a "general" business education, for varieties of experience, are fewer. Opportunities for an overview of the whole operation become more difficult. A modern foreman, for example, can easily live his life in a present-day organization and never meet a man who sells the product he is manufacturing. When related people and their related activities are mutually unknown, their perceptions of one another may become dangerously distorted.

Size, by increasing the complexity of communication, increases the probability of misinformation as well as the probability of decreased total information flow. As the number of people between a decision-maker and his source of information increases, the probability of error and mistiming increases—a phenomenon that is most important because of its multiplying effects on attitudes as well as on the quality of business decisions. People, an earlier chapter showed, get frustrated and angry at one another when they have difficulty in sending or receiving information. Field people come to feel that the home office is made up of dunderheads, and the home office reciprocates the feelings. Managers recognizing these difficulties may try to compensate by forcing more information through the channels. They may require more periodic reports, set up forms, and themselves make it a point to disperse more information to more people. But though this counteraction may alleviate the problem, it may create additional difficulties—an oversupply of material that the recipient finds difficult to evaluate or even to read. As long as the structure itself makes for long and difficult communication lines, changes in the structure itself would seem to be the only cure.

Changing organizations by changing people

If the problems just cited are some of the major people problems that cause a drag on both organizational effectivenesss and human growth, what's to be done about them?

In the early days, as we have pointed out, one answer was to use punishment and threat; next, individual incentives were tried. Then we tried to keep people in line by manipulative means—by "making them think it's their idea." In all those cases we were looking at people after setting up a structure, which meant that structure took first place. The problem was to get people to work within it.

Since then another different kind of idea has moved in over a wide front. It is the idea that structure, in large part, ought to follow people. This is the idea behind the third consulting firm in chapter 24. If we can first develop a solid, loyal, hardworking group, with valid communication within it, then appropriate structure will follow.

O.D.: Organizational development

A great deal of recent research and application has centered around the people-first approach, and over the last twenty-five years one broad set of techniques has evolved for changing organizations by changing people. The whole set has come to be called O.D., for organizational development, but operationally it refers to a particular scheme of organizational development emerging from the sensitivity training described earlier.

In the late forties, when such groups got started, they were pick-up groups, made up of people from many different organizations—people unlikely to see much of one another after their group meetings were over. Usually, if a person liked what he had found and tried to carry it home to his own organization, he fell flat on his face. Other people saw him as a guy who had gone through some sort of mystical experience that he couldn't describe but thought everyone else should have, too.

The next step was to carry the T-group into the organization, so that many members could develop together. And the step after that—one only now getting serious attention—was to follow sensitivity training up, so that many organizational problems were worked on by continuing teams, trained and developed by T-group methods. With this move, too, has come a greater emphasis on realism, a lesser emphasis on happiness.

Thus the O.D. approach makes the open group—now freed in its interpersonal relations, and more understanding of its intergroup problems—a central tool for organizational change, invading and supplanting much of the traditional structure.

Many other tools have been tried on the people side—selection devices, training programs, evaluaton schemes, group incentives or company-wide ones. I emphasize O.D. for two reasons: first, because at this point in time it has become a common denominator among most of the competent people-people, the human-relations researchers and practitioners interested in bringing about organizational change; second, because O.D., with its emphasis on power *equalization* rather than power *differentiation*, represents a clear confrontation with the traditional structural approaches, which are so deeply based in a differentiated hierarchy of authority.

In summary

Some characteristics of present-day industrial organizations necessarily affect people. Some of these effects are bad, either because they damage people or because they interfere with the problem-solving activities of organizations. Perhaps none of the bad effects is so bad that it outweighs the advantages of control and economic integration that the same characteristics also provide.

The characteristics discussed are the pyramidal shape of organizations, with its tendency to increase interpersonal competitiveness; the hierarchical distribution of authority, with its tendency to increase dependency and "evaluation fear"; the idea of individual responsibility, with its assumption that a large and complicated task can be cut down into non-overlapping, individual-sized pieces; and the sheer size of modern organizations, with consequent difficulties of communication.

In general, each of these characteristics carries a potential for intensifying conflict and frustration in individuals and for increasing psychological pressures on the manager.

On the practical side, a variety of devices has appeared for dealing with such problems. One broad approach that is gaining widespread use is an outgrowth of sensitivity training. It is called organizational development. While changing interpersonal relations and providing opportunities for reducing conflict and frustration, O.D. programs also try to change the organization's structure and the way jobs get done.

28

Organizational structure
The fall guy

For most of us the phrase "organizational structure" means the organization chart. And the organization chart, for most of us, means trouble. It specifies constraints on our behavior and our relationships with other people in an organization; and it usually specifies them in ways that do not conform to the "real" organization.

It is the purpose of this chapter (1) to point to some other dimensions of organizational structure than those usually associated with organization charts, (2) to reiterate the importance of structure for problem-solving in human behavior, and (3) to point up some general changes that have been occurring in the structure of American firms.

This will be a short chapter because we know so little about what is important about organizational structure. That last statement may seem strange because organizational structure has been a favorite of classical organization theorists for a long time. But I think it is an appropriate statement because, although we have a surfeit of logical-deductive notions about what a good organizational structure ought to be, we know very little about the actual effects of different kinds of structures on the behavior and actual performance of organizations.

Some dimensions of organizational structure

Most organization charts confound three important dimensions of organizational structure, trying to describe all three with one set of lines and boxes. They describe something about *authority structure*, usually by locating particular boxes at higher or lower positions on the chart. They describe something about *communication structure* by drawing lines between boxes. But these lines connecting boxes on organization charts usually mean both that these are the people that other people can talk to, and also that these are the people that other people have authority over (or under). It is assumed that one does not communicate with people with whom one has no authority relationship. Third, the organization chart usually specifies, in a very shorthand kind of way, the *roles* of persons in the organization. There are titles in the boxes that presumably specify something about what the people in those boxes do. Implicitly, incidentally, organization charts always assume that people and only people belong in boxes, packaged one person to a box. One does not draw the positions of typewriters, steam shovels, or computers on most organization charts, even though they may be important elements in the organizational structure. Perhaps in the future, other actors than human beings will be boxed. And perhaps, too, boxes will be big enough for more than one person.

One important dimension of structure that organization charts almost never show is the nature of work flows; because work usually flows over a set of channels different from the authority set. Work, that is, is apt to flow horizontally, without regard for the number of stripes on the shoulders of the people it touches. Very often, in fact, one of the problems of organizational design is the problem of somehow making authority and communication structures consonant with work flows.

The declining place of authority

But to return to the general interest of managers in organizational structure, it seems fair to say that the issue of authority has been an overweening issue. Ever since the early classical theorists, Western designers of organizations have laid a heavy emphasis on the importance of factors like command, discipline, and authority in organizational design. Many of the early structuralists, indeed, frankly drew their ideas from military organizations, so that this quasi-military flavor still shows through in many large American organizations.

Recently the role of authority has been diminishing noticeably. The idea of decentralization has contributed to its decline. For what does one decentralize? One decentralizes authority for decision-making. One may decentralize for any of several reasons; sometimes for humanistic reasons, more often for motivational or control reasons, especially as firms grow larger. But whatever the reasons for decentralization, the general effect has been to reduce the amount of authoritative control in organizations and increase the amount of local autonomy.

The emphasis on authority has diminished for other greater reasons, too. Professionalization has challenged it. As we have hired executives who identify themselves more as professionals in some specialized fields and less as "locals," organizational authority has been a less effective tool. The human-relations movement has also contributed to the decline of concern about who has authority over whom in organizations. It has demonstrated that control can often be maintained with much less authority than we used to think.

But let us not confuse the decline in authority with a decline in the role of organizational hierarchy in general. The hierarchy of roles in organizations serves purposes of coordination and integration that are becoming increasingly vital to organizational life. What is declining is not the hierarchy but the tool of authority—just one dimension of hierarchical design.

The rising place of communication and role structure

In contrast, American organizations have lately shown much more interest in problems of communication and coordination, and much more concern about redefining appropriate work flows. We have gotten more interested in who can talk to whom in organizations because as organizations have grown larger the losses from communication failures have become increasingly apparent. This new emphasis on communication has also contributed to the decline of authority. Opening up communication is often dissonant with the notion of highly authoritarian structure. Authoritarian organizations constrain and specify who can communicate with whom, and therefore tend to reduce the amount of communication. More recent structural approaches have tried to open up communications and have thereby come into conflict with notions of authority. Certainly both the communication-network experiments and the intergroup-conflict studies described earlier have demonstrated that the communication structure of an organization can influence the output and attitudes of its members, even with authority held out of the picture.

The great early emphasis of structural people on authority led us for a while toward rejecting the whole structural approach. We tended, as we so often do, to want to throw out the baby with the bath water. Recently, however, we have begun to come back to structural questions from very different angles. We have come back to structure largely because we have been forced to—because it has become so patently obvious that structure is an organizational dimension (1) that we can manipulate, and (2) that has direct effects on problem-solving. If we decentralize, things happen.

Maybe not all the things that we wanted to have happen, but things happen. If we change the definitions of roles of members of our organization, things happen. If we change communication lines by removing telephones, or separating people, or making some people inaccessible to others, things happen.

All of those kinds of changes are fairly easy for managers to carry out. So structural dimensions become doubly important—important because they constrain and thereby influence behavior, and important because they are readily manipulatable. Yet there is an important limiting factor in the structural approaches. The structure of an organization makes some things possible, but it does not guarantee that they will happen. When we open up communication, as in the circle network, the structure will permit people to do things they could not do in the star. It does not guarantee that they will do them.

Something else is beginning to push students of management to take a second look at structural problems. And that is new knowledge and new ideas about structure. There has been a good deal of work, for example, in exploring the problems of roles in organizations, and conflicts between roles. We have begun to get some handles on more sophisticated ways of specifying roles than the old job description. And we have begun to understand the conditions under which particular roles, even conflicting ones, can be important and useful. Thus, for example, the idea of the "linking pin" role has been proposed by one author. It is a liaison role between groups in organizations, a notion that has been useful to many managers. For it does not try to describe a job in such a way that it will in no way overlap any other job—as the old job descriptions tried to do—but rather to recognize the interdependency of many jobs with others, and to include these overlaps, rather than to exclude them.

We have begun, too, to find out some things about the relationship between work flows and the people part of the organization. We are beginning to realize that if work steps are contiguous with one another in certain ways, the people who perform those steps are apt to establish relationships with one another and form groupings that they would not otherwise form. Earlier studies on housing developments have demonstrated the same point. The location of the garbage cans in an apartment building has a good deal to do with the kinds of friendships and relationships that develop within it.

The importance of organizational design

Most of these works, from the communication nets to the work on role conflict to the work on the relationship between work flows and interpersonal factors, are surface-scratching operations that are only beginning to reopen an old but terribly important issue—the issue of the design of organizational structures.

From another side technology is reopening the same issue, for with computers and new analytic methods we have to make room (even in old-fashioned organizational structures) for new kinds of equipment, new kinds of people, new kinds of relationships. These two developments, rather than killing off the idea of organizational structure, are putting it back in the spotlight, making us ask ourselves again, "What is the ideal structural design for an organization?"

One answer to that question is now clear. There is no ideal structural design. Appropriate design is contingent upon task, environment, people, and the state of technology. The ideal is adaptability and self-modification much more than it is a fixed structure.

Grossly, we can go a bit further than that. For unprogramed tasks, structures with less restricted communication and a looser authority hierarchy generally look better. But check your environment's traditions and standards before you move that way. And check the history and expectations of your people before you radically alter the structure they have always worked in. And check your current technology, lest you discover that you could, with modern tools, program the previously unprogramable task.

There is another aspect of contingent structural design, too. Organizations aren't made of just one kind of stuff. They don't do just one kind of job. Increasingly it makes sense to think of large organizations as differentiated components of many smaller organizations, each performing its own set of tasks, in its own world, and structured accordingly. The large organization is thus a set of interconnected structures, rather than *a* structure. And more and more, designers must worry about the articulation problem, about sewing these structures together into an integral functioning whole. The new big problem of organizational design is not setting up the factory or the research department; it is relating the factory to the research department with a minimum of destructive conflict and a maximum of mutual contribution.

In summary

Organizational structure should mean more than the organization chart. The organization chart depicts authority structure, communication structure, and role structure, as though they were entirely consonant with one another, and as though authority were the senior and by far the most important of the three. But organizational growth, professionalization, and new knowledge have all tended to reduce the significance of authority in our thinking about structure and to increase the weight of other variables like communication and role structure.

But we are really just beginning to reattack the structural problem after leaving it alone for many years. It is an important issue to attack, both because it is clear that the structure we work in has a great deal to do with how we behave, and also because structure is susceptible to relatively easy manipulation and change.

In the last few years emphasis in thinking about design has shifted toward a contingent and a differentiated view. Design for what, where, and with whom? How many different organizational structures should there be inside the total system? And how should they be integrated and related to one another?

Technology and organization Brave new organizational world

In the diamond-shaped diagram at the beginning of this section we listed technology as one of the factors that can have a real impact on structure and on people as well as on problems.

The technology we were referring to was internal technology—tools for management—rather than tools for making products. Many such managerial tools (like Taylor's work measurement, or the more recent development group of the participative manager, or the selection test of the personnel man), have been around for some time. Each one of them has had considerable effect on the way organizations have come to operate. We seem now to be in the midst of a revolution in such tools, with the introduction of new ones that may be much more powerful than any of the old ones. Most of these new tools derive from developments in information processing, mostly from the computer and the methods that accompany the computer.

Any active manager will attest that they are new (since 1954 or thereabouts) and that they are important in his own organization. But he may not be sure how important they are. For computers, like human beings, are general, multipurpose tools. They may therefore turn up doing new and unexpected things tomorrow. They have taken, so far, the forms of control devices—as small machines for steering big ones; as oversized and very fast adding machines, replacing the team of the clerk and the hand calculator; and as decision-making devices, permitting operations research techniques to be applied toward decisions in complex problems. And if we look into the laboratories around the country we can see still another use that will be felt much more strongly in the near future; the use of such tools for learning, that is, as mechanisms that can make decisions today, and also learn to make better ones tomorrow.

It is worth re-emphasizing that organizational change is

most apt to ride on the shoulders of new tools. Only when ideas have been converted to tools do things begin to change. When the ideas of information theory have been converted into computers and programing methods, then they begin to influence organizations. Such conversion is taking place very rapidly, and the organizational impacts are increasingly apparent.

Since this book is largely about human problems, let's limit our discussion to the effects of such technology on people in organizations. To do this we can probably best start by looking at the organizational entry points of these tools, considering the problems generated at each entry point. Then we can go back and look at the organization as a whole.

Automation

The first entry level, and the one with which we are all now familiar, is automatic control over heavy machinery. Out of information-processing technology have developed low-energy machines that serve, as it were, as the brains of high-energy machines. The revolution in automation lies not so much in the development of large devices that can do more work faster as in the development of controls that can steer and command and adjust the work of machines that have already been around for a long time. It is the automatic part of the automatic lathe that is having its present-day impact on the machine shop. The rest of the lathe is familiar enough, and we have long since adjusted to it.

Human problems are generated by the automatic lathe, and by automatic controls in general, only insofar as they move in on territory previously reserved to human beings. The adjustments that used to be made by people, skilled people, are now being made by automatic equipment. So the human being seems to be pushed back a step in his struggle for control of the world.

The initial reaction therefore is likely to be scary. Any time work done by people can be done by machines, the people being displaced by machines have plenty to worry about. And now, when machines begin to do work that has always been done by people's heads rather than by their arms and legs, the effect is likely to be doubly disturbing.

Our society is still in the process of trying to assess the effect of automation on the general problem of displacement and downgrading of human workers. Depending on where you sit, the problem may look large or small. For unions and for skilled workers it seems very large indeed, because some people are finding themselves without work. Some economists, on the other hand, thinking about the problem from the national and long-term point of view, argue that human displacement is temporary; and that mechanisms exist in the economic market for absorbing displaced workers, no matter how elaborate our technology becomes. In fact, things may go the other way. The impact of automation may be to expand the economy so much as to cause a shortage of people, rather than a surplus.

The social problem closest at hand lies in the gap between present displacement and future absorption. It is occurring at two polar points in our society. Increased automation tends, on the one hand, to increase the need for specialized and highly trained people and to decrease the need for the unskilled. Hence it is one contributor to the increasingly serious problem of finding jobs for poorly trained, unspecialized young people. On the other hand, automatic technology tends also to knock out certain classes of highly skilled but specialized jobs, usually held by older people, less able to move readily back into the labor market. Thus the job of roller, highly paid, often salaried, in the old steelrolling mill, no longer exists in the computer-controlled mill. But neither do jobs for ghetto youngsters.

It used to be that company presidents could feel comfortable, even saintly, in the knowledge that they provided good termination pay and re-employment counselling for their laid-off workers. That was enough. In the social environment of the seventies, it seems clear that that is not enough, that the company must reach out to and connect with society in much more active ways. But more of that in the next chapter.

Some internal effects

Let us turn now to some of the internal effects of automatic controls on people. If there will be fewer members doing a particular job, how about those who are left? In one sense automation enlarges people's jobs, adding to the responsibilities of the individuals working with the automatic equipment. Often the variety of activities that a man carries out will increase. For automation often means that simple, routine, repetitive tasks need no longer be done by human beings. And every man becomes, as it were, a supervisor of many, often high-cost, activities carried out by machines.

Now "job expansion" is seen by most of us as a good thing, rewarding and satisfying for the people involved. In this case, though, another important factor begins to loom large. Although variety and responsibility have increased, the control of automated jobs may shift from the man to the machine. In effect, the man must respond to decisions or demands set up by the machine. So the increase in variety and responsibility need not be accompanied by any kind of increase in autonomy or control. If anything, people doing these jobs are apt to feel somewhat more tied down than they were before; therefore, instead of greater feelings of security and fulfilment, we may get anxiety and dependency.

On the structural side, it is worth pointing out that the automation of tasks often reduces the need for supervision of persons. It may, therefore, have some important effects on structure. In a sense some of the supervision passes to the machine in automated situations, and the need for a human supervisor's motivating and training activities is much reduced. Consequently, even at the bottom end of the organization, we may see fairly radical changes in our ideas about the place of authority and human-relations skills. The emphasis may shift to technical know-how, capacity to handle emergencies, and such issues; and away from doling out discipline and keeping the boys at their benches.

The level of electronic data processing

Let us shift now to the more central concern of this book, managerial problems, the ones that are likely to be generated by information-processing technology. The same kind of technology that is used to control machines can be used in another way for processing large amounts of data. Most computers have come into industrial organizations for that purpose—as data-processing devices. In that capacity they are usually seen mostly as gigantic, rapid calculators—things that can do arithmetic a lot faster than people.

Again, as in the automation of manufacturing machinery, the initial impact is likely to be the displacement of persons from particular roles by the machine (if costs favor the machine). Again, too, the jobs that are displaced are likely to be those using human beings at far less than full human capacity; that is, the more monotonous and routine clerical jobs.

At this level our values can lead us to boo or to cheer. While we may be concerned about clerks losing their jobs because billing is turned over to computers, we can also cheer the news that such drab unfulfilling tasks need no longer be done by psychologically imprisoned humans in green eyeshades slavishly plugging away at their adding machines. Is it not, after all, one of the great sources of American pride that we have eliminated so many routine and monotonous jobs? While in underdeveloped countries people must break rocks by hand to build an airstrip, America has bulldozers. In our up-to-now underdeveloped America people have shuffled papers for most of their lives; now they are liberated by the computer, science's great new contribution to the advance of civilization.

Beyond that, perhaps the human problems generated by EDP are much like those generated by automation—the social problem (real or imagined) of the displaced clerk; the question of the role of the firm vis-à-vis that problem; the issue of expansion of remaining jobs, but with more control on the machine's side; and the problem of secondary effects on supervision and training.

But in both of the cases we have discussed so far, the case of automation, and the case of EDP, we are really just talking about new versions of an old problem: the introduction of faster and more powerful machine substitutes for tedious human effort.

Technology and the managers

Let us move up to another level of jobs now, to jobs in which the tasks are not very well structured and in which decisions are complex. These are the jobs that typify middle and higher levels of management: jobs like production scheduling, inventory controlling, merchandising, or research administrating; or jobs like media selection in advertising agencies, or investment counseling in banks, or buying and pricing in department stores. In all these cases, until recently, a good man for the job was necessarily one with brains, experience, judgment, energy, ability to get along with people, and more. If you want to train a new man for one of these jobs you do it essentially by apprenticeship. He has got to work at it for a long time, coming up through the relevant ranks. He has got to be broadly educated and understand his organization's operation inside out.

Until recently it would have been sheer nonsense to think about machines doing any significant part of these jobs, and in some of these jobs, it still is sheer nonsense. But the same information-processing theory, carried on the technology of the computer, is moving in at this level, too. And the move is a fascinating one to watch. Sometimes it is an algorithmic move, of the sort we talked about in an earlier chapter. Sometimes, that is to say, we search, technically, for a way to get a complex problem specified down to the large number of variables that enter into it. Once specified, we try to find a combination that provides a better solution than we've had from the judgment of experienced people. Scheduling a particular quantity of a particular set of products for production, for example, has usually been done judgmentally until now, not because it was an infinitely complicated problem, but because it was just too big for a man's head to handle feasibly within the time available. Now with new methods of analysis and new tools, many such too-complicated problems are no longer too complicated. And they may be handled by people who know a good deal about programing, and darn little about the company and its production problems.

Sometimes attacks on these complex decision problems are made heuristically. Some of the problems we are facing are so complex that it is still effectively impossible to deal with all the factors, even given the modern computer. There are just too many moves that are possible in a chess game, for example, to have even a good computer figure out all of them and decide which one is best. But it can be done heuristically. That is, the computer can be programed to simulate the behavior of a human being, and to act as though it has the kind of judgment that the person has. And human beings, even good chess-playing ones, apparently only look ahead a couple of moves. Their skill is in their heuristics. Such heuristic approaches have now been carried out with investment officers at a bank, for example. And the same approach is underway in many other problem areas within organizations. And again the kind of expertise that is relevant here is not so much twenty years of experience in investing, but some equivalent experience and know-how in simulating. And so on down the line.

And so we may end up with a scope of change that is quite different from earlier industrial revolutions. For until now it has been clear and true and right to all of us, Taylorists and participative managers alike, that only people could think and use judgment. And now we come along with machine programs that look, by any reasonable standards, like they can use judgment too.

As these methods develop, will we then, like Taylor, be removing the thinking part of men's jobs in a new way? Are we therefore in danger of demeaning man, taking from him the essence of his humanity? It may be. But maybe, too, all we are doing is advancing the state of human knowledge, and making it possible for humans to accomplish a great deal more in the world.

But let's come back a little bit to what seem to be the practical organizational effects of the introduction of informational techniques to the solution of complex decision problems. Let's consider some of the effects that information-processing technology appears to cause inside the organization when we begin to apply it to complex decision tasks.

It seems unlikely that we will simply get rid of many middle managers and replace them with decision-making devices, at least in the short run. What seems to be happening is the shifting around of activities, reallocating responsibilities among old men, machines, and new men who are at home with machines.

But since we can often handle more information, and faster than we used to, another trend is that many decisions are being shifted not only from man to machine but from one level of men to another. Some decentralized decisions can now be handled efficiently at higher levels in the organization. One of the reasons, after all—though not the only one —that presidents have been willing to decentralize, has been because they have not been able to centralize large and complicated organizations successfully. If they insisted on making all the decisions, too many were made too late; and too many were made without sufficient information. Now, however, we can get more information, get it faster and better digested, and get decisions out faster. Now perhaps, we can make more reasonable decisions higher up. Then decisions can be better integrated with one another, so that there will be fewer conflicting decisions made.

Or perhaps all that will tighten up at the top will be control rather than actual decision-making. I asked the president of a large company recently whether computers had increased or decreased the centralization of his company. "Oh, we're much more decentralized now," he said. "We can let people make their own decisions because within twenty-four hours our information system can give us a pretty good idea about whether or not they made the right one." Is it decentralization or centralization? Or is it like arguing that that lion in the zoo is perfectly free? He can do as he pleases, as long as he stays in his cage.

Another outcome of advance in informational techniques is that a new class of managers has opened up. This is the class of "information technologists" or "systems analysts" or "management scientists," planning and control specialists in some ways equivalent to the industrial engineer born earlier out of Taylor's rib. They are likely to be staff people at first, but since the distinction between staff and line is getting fuzzy anyway, they often end up as something in between.

Another possible trend is that mobility may be reduced within the management ranks of organizations. A few decades ago people moved relatively freely from an apprentice job in the machine shop to the top of a large organization. But partially as a consequence of Taylorism, and partially as a consequence of other social forces, a rather thick wall has been built between the hourly worker and the manager, a wall that reduced the ease of movement from one group to the other. Hourly workers tend now to stay hourly workers throughout their working lives, in part because many hourly jobs do not provide very good training, practice, or motivation for management. We tend to draw our managers from above that line. If we want our sons to be president, we send them into the firm after college, not before, as executive trainees rather than office boys. We do this because we know that the route from apprentice upward is likely to be blocked rather impenetrably at the level of first-line supervision.

Now, with the addition of new information technology, another wall seems to be abuilding; a wall between newly programed middle-level jobs and the more wide-open and creative jobs that go on upstairs. As middle-level jobs are programed and specified, they become less appropriate training grounds for unprogramed higher-level jobs than they were before.

We may begin to get much more professionalization of management than we have had in the past. Until now we have mouthed a lot about the "professional manager," by which we have usually meant a man with much experience in the field. We have not meant a man with any particular specialized education. With information-processing tools added to the kit along with the tools of Taylorism and participation, the professional schooling of the manager looks like a much more important reality than it did in the past. Doctors used to learn their trade by apprenticeship, and lawyers read the law under the guidance of other senior lawyers. They both moved out of that stage a good while ago. Management may also be leaving it. Should that kind of professionalization occur, one can expect changes, in turn, in the manager's attitudes—in his notions about loyalty to the firm, about his career span in one firm, and about other common present-day standards. These may go by the boards as surely as the standard of working one's way up from apprentice to president.

To continue the speculation—which, I hope, the reader will permit in these last few pages—these same developments suggest a bigger role for the egghead in management. Managing, that is to say, will probably be a much more analytic job than it has been in the past, much more a scientific operation than a seat-of-the-pants one. It is not just a question of the manager knowing more mathematics. The manager will have to know and use several kinds of analytic tools for solving problems, both human problems and nonhuman ones. This idea of movement from a highly personal, almost artistic model to a colder, more impersonal scientific one is apt to seem an unpleasant idea to many of us. For when we think of science, we think, among other things, of long and difficult technical training. When we think of management, we like to think of personal, idiosyncratic behavior for which we have natural abilities that have nothing to do with education. In our managerial mythology, at least, most of us probably picture the "great" manager as unique and individualistic and "natural." That day may be coming to a close.

We don't want to emphasize the increasingly analytic nature of management, however, without at least a warning about a countertrend. Again, we suggest that there ain't no free lunch in management. While the manager needs more analytic skills, he also needs more human ones. To his steel-trap, highly trained analytic mind, he had better add, in the societal seventies, a good sprinkling both of human understanding and of soul.

Still another challenge is arising out of the rapidly progressing state of technology: Until now, with management based largely on apprenticeship, we have expected a competent manager to be worth his salt for thirty or forty years; in fact, we expect he will be worth more salt every year. But if new knowledge generates at the rate it has been coming along lately, the good manager may easily become obsolescent within his own career span.

This problem of obsolescence has always been with us to some extent. Us oldsters have always looked at the young men and seen in them (unhappily perhaps) some strengths and capacities that we did not have. But those strengths and capacities have always been more than overbalanced by our experience and know-how—our veteran status. But the relative value of experience to the value of new knowledge seems to be changing. A little new knowledge may be worth a lot more experience than it used to be.

There are, of course, ways to handle such obsolescence if it arises. We can do the obvious and foolish, like kicking the older men out, or we can tackle the problem of education in a different way than we have ever done in the past. If our managers tend to become obsolescent after ten years instead of after thirty, we can control the problem by spending a lot more energy on re-education. And we may not be talking about another six-week executive training course; but about something more like the investment of one year in every five or six.

Technology and the structure of the organization

Let's shift our field of speculation a little bit from the manager to the structure of the organization and the effects of technology thereon.

We talked about the possibility of centralization of decisions more than in the past, and about the expansion of a technological group that may be more line than staff. Another corollary of such events could be greater separation of planning-activities from doing-activities in the firm, one aspect of the differentiation we discussed in the chapter on structure. By this picture, our new wall will house mostly planners and deciders on one side of it, and doers on the other.

And if that does happen, then some new problems will be generated: problems of the transmission of plans and ideas from above to below, or from the center to the sides. And other problems will emerge as a consequence of such differentiation of organizations. For certainly one implication of such a picture is increasing differentiation of the organization into different kinds of suborganizational structures.

In Taylor's day we might have argued that the whole organization should look like a star communication net, with everybody's job specified, programed, and controlled by the level above him. Under the scheme of participative management, we have been ready to do an about-face; opening up the organization into a set of overlapping circles, with fuller communication and more interaction between levels as well as within levels. But if (1) our capacity to program some jobs increases very radically, and (2) our capacity to program others (like research, for example) does not open up, then the result can be that the unprogramed will take different organizational forms from the programed parts. We may run production organizations like stars all right, but within the same parent-company, research may operate in wide-open circles. This suggests a world in which people are not treated equally but quite differently, depending on the tasks their parts of the organization work on. And as that happens (as it is happening every day), then the problem of communication between the differentiated parts will get to be much more important in the scheme of things.

In summary

In this chapter the issue has been information technology and its effects on people at several levels of the organization. We have suggested that information-processing techniques are having a very large impact on all levels of the organization, but in rather different ways at different levels.

As pessimists, we can worry about the general impact of the displacement of men by machines. This time the displacement is not of arms and legs but the displacement of judgments and decisions. If we are optimists, we see the same kind of technology opening new opportunities for problem-solving, permitting solutions we have never been able to tackle before, allowing quicker and righter decisions than we could get before.

The consequences of information technology are likely to bump into some of the notions of participative management described earlier. For participative management has its greatest personal and organizational payoff in settings in which the task is ill-programed and novel, and in which, therefore, creativity and originality are much needed. The programing of some tasks previously of that class may leave some new dissonance between the path toward human fulfilment and the path toward efficiency.

The growth of information technology opens up the real possibility of professionalization of management, in which case the education of managers will become not only more important, but longer and more arduous. The standards for entry into the profession in 1980 may be a lot harder to meet than present standards.

These ideas and their accompanying tools signal us in business and business education that it is time to revise our organizational notions. Sometimes we become understandably defensive about the beliefs we have invested in. We are apt to take pleasure, as we did with the early industrial engineer, in the failure of newfangled experimental decision rules

—pleased because the operations researchers who built them were so blind to human issues, crying out that the steam drill will never replace John Henry. Or we may be defensive in the other direction, complaining that sensitivity training is a lot of dangerous nonsense that should be ruled out of existence.

Perhaps what we are really doing is just what research and thoughtfulness are supposed to do: add to the fullness of our understanding of the complex and intricate problem of organizing human (and nonhuman) effort. The prospective manager of an enterprise would do far better to try fully to understand all offerings than to pooh-pooh any of them.

30

Organizations and their environments From back then to out there

Organizations, like persons, are shaped by their times, and shape their times, too. If we look back over the last few decades, it seems quite easy to see how our business organizations have reflected our societies, and if we look ahead a decade or two, perhaps we can make some reasonable guesses about the relationships in the future. That's what we shall try to do in this last chapter: to look at the way organizations relate to society. And we shall do it by first reviewing much of what we have said earlier in this book, but with a broad base and a panoramic view. Then we'll go forward. Let's get a running start on the future by first backing up into the past.

Organization for productivity

Consider the American environment around 1900, an environment ripe for organizations designed for one great purpose: productivity. It was a relatively sparse world we lived in then—sparse of people and of other organizations. Government was supportive. Vigorous entrepreneurs were heroes. The market begged for material goods. Our immigrant labor force was big and badly educated, but it was dedicated to finding a better world for its children. It was a period of personal immobility, too: people didn't usually move from one city to another. The family was big and important, in the European tradition. And it was a colonialistic period: the notion of the white man's burden, of an ignorant and somewhat irrational laboring class, was widespread, and with it the notion that the planning and thinking had to be done by the superior people, even over the objections of the ignorant childlike worker—for his own good.

Into this ripe setting—and no wonder—marched the organizational structuralists and technocrats, the classical organization theorists touting the gods of order and control, and the pragmatic technicians like F. W. Taylor and Henry Ford. Taylor, we said earlier, provided the techniques to back up classical organization theory, techniques which separated planning from doing, so that large populations of non-craftsmen could be organized to produce large quantities of highly crafted products. Taylor moved the craft from the individual man to the organization, and he got what he was after: productivity.

Now shift forward a few decades into the thirties and forties. In the United States, unions become strong, partially as a reaction to Tayloristic rigidities. Mr. Roosevelt's New Deal, with its new social orientation, moves into the United States. At the same time, technology has begun to explode, and the explosion is magnified tremendously by World War II. Colonialism comes to an end. In the States, immigration slows to a trickle. Our people become much more mobile with improved communications and transportation. The early image of the glorious, heroic entrepreneur gives way to the caricature of the ruthless robber baron. He is watched more closely now and reacted to more strongly by a society that is somewhat more sensitive to the negative effects of unfettered profit-seeking.

Under such conditions, what shape shall business organizations take? Or shall they, like turtles, develop shells that help keep them impervious to societal change?

As is so often the case, several, not necessarily consistent, things happen. Some firms change, but their first changes are ameliorative. They find Band-Aids to cover the minor wounds inflicted by the changing world. They become concerned about morale and human relations. They begin to worry about how to keep people happy while doing miserable jobs. They devise new incentive plans and suggestion systems. But they don't abandon the basic old Tayloristic structure. That is both productive and sacrosanct, and besides, they're getting locked into it by their investment in physical plants consistent with Taylorism. They continue to design the organization holes first and only then to search for the human pegs to fit them. The participative management movement begins to take shape in this period, and attacks Taylorism on Taylor's own playing field. These new social science types championing participative management try to show that participation and industrial democracy are better routes to the old nirvana of productivity than hard-nosed Taylorism itself. But in so doing they actually help to patch up Taylorism, to make it more endurable, more human, because *productivity* continues as the primary organizational goal and participation is touted only as a means to greater productivity. If we can make employees think it's their idea, the old argument runs, they will produce.

Organization for marketing and product innovation

But the emphasis on productivity began to show signs of cracking in those years, perhaps because of its own past success. Once we had produced a large number of refrigerators, the issue began to shift from producing more to marketing them better or to developing new products. Everybody could produce. Who could market? Who could innovate? These emerging questions led to a new emphasis, not on the management of production workers, but on the management of management itself. In this newly emerging executive world of marketers and technicians, the old Taylorism was just about useless. Time clocks in the research department just didn't make sense, nor did stopwatches in the president's office.

A different kind of managerial organization was needed. And gradually we backed into it. We began to worry about improving communication, about coordination, about setting up a climate for creativity. But we began to worry about these issues chiefly within the ranks of management itself, leaving the production worker pretty much in the hands of old Mr. Taylor.

Notice, however, that the new organization form that emerged was a more complex form than its predecessor. The new one was, in effect, divided into two layers—not only two classes of men but also two structures within which the two classes were expected to work. Participative organizational structures began to be used widely, but almost exclusively within management working toward the goals of growth and innovation, while well-structured Taylorism remained the rule for the organization of clerical and blue-collar production workers.

Within management, the theory of participation became almost an analog to the theory of the husbandry of plants. Neither social scientists nor anyone else really understood much about the *nature* of innovation and complex problem-solving, but everybody needed them. The agronomists didn't understand how plants grew either, but they did the next best thing. They asked, "What are the conditions under which greatest growth occurs?" And the answers were that plants needed sunlight and moisture and appropriate soil chemistry. Under those conditions, but still mysteriously, plants grew. Participative theory and behavioral theory occupied about the same position with management. We didn't understand the processes, but we knew a lot about the conditions under which they flowered. We learned that autocracy tended to kill those attributes. So we marched in with human-relations training and brainstorming programs and sensitivity groups and attitude surveys and a whole variety of paraphernalia intended to release managerial effectiveness within the diverse ranks of management. *Innovation* became a new organizational goal.

But as we all know, the new doesn't replace the old, it's just added on. So the goal of innovation was superimposed upon the old goal of productivity. Developing managerial potential became a major new means added to the old. Also superimposed on the old means was the tight and controlled blue-collar organization.

Then the informational organization

But once again our world insisted on changing. Enter the real technological explosion of the mid-fifties. Enter the computer and information technology and management science. Now for the first time we could seriously reexamine the catalyst theories of participative management. Now we could ask, "What is the true nature of problem-solving? Of creativity? Of innovation?" Part of the answer was clear: Since by now we had an excellent theory of information-processing, perhaps we could even build artificial problem-solving devices to substitute for, or at least to supplement, human abilities.

Perhaps it was not accidental that this whole new analytic-informational package came to be called management science, for it was very much the same as Taylor's old scientific management, but it rode a computer instead of a stopwatch. It was Taylor's scientific management in that it separated the planning of decisions from the decision-making itself, just as Taylor had separated the planning of physical work from doing it.

Now what kind of organizational changes could be expected to accompany this brand new capacity to program the hitherto unprogramable, this new ability to replace at least some classes of human judgments with systematic procedures?

One major change was the emergence of a new quality of dynamism in the organizational world, a new quick feedback cycle that permitted the organization to know the effects of what it had just done and therefore to become a much more self-modifying system. (In the past we hadn't always been sure of the effects of what we had done, of what had caused what.) Hence also a new temporary quality in organizational life. This temporariness was mirrored in the nature of the information technology itself, which even now continues to grow at an exponential rate. And it was reflected in the attitudes of the new population of professionals who rode upon this technology, a highly mobile group, with the typical attitudes of professionals everywhere: high professional loyalty, low organizational loyalty.

Another and opposing change was the extension of humanistic, participative management even further upward into the still unprogramed, open-ended areas at the top of the organizational hierarchy, while simultaneously tightening up controls over other parts of the organization, particularly sectors of lower middle management. As a result the organization became even more differentiated, with even more different parts operating within different organizational forms, forms that ranged from open, loosely controlled structures to the most minutely controlled structures imaginable. For the people behind management science, for the whiz kids, the planners, and for top management itself, the new technology made for a less programed world, more ambiguous, more challenging, more judgmental, more open-ended. As for the guy on the line, he continued to be told what to do, how to do it, and which finger to do it with.

By the sixties, the old Tayloristic organization, steered by its traditional tasks and its traditional structure, found itself either supplanted or dominated by this new form, steered by its new technology and by its highly trained professional planners. Viewed as a whole, the organization became not one structure but many structures, not an undifferentiated mass but a highly differentiated set of subsystems capable not of a single task but of a wide range of tasks, from routine to creative. And the new challenge was the one we mentioned in chapter 28, the articulation of the parts with one another, more than the operation of any particular part.

It was with this problem, articulation, that the new organization of the sixties began to struggle. The new central issues were not just production, or even just imaginative marketing, but rather problems like these: How do we get the subparts of this system to coordinate with one another so we can solve that huge problem out there? How do we reduce conflict and competition among these parts? How do we deal with our new prima donnas who are forever at each other's throats?

The Socio-political organization

Another way of saying all this is to say that the newly added organizational problems became increasingly like political problems of whole societies, because the new large organization had become like a society, a complex set of interacting power groups with different backgrounds, different objectives, different mores, different beliefs.

Now what about the seventies? What's happening to the organizational environment in this decade? And how are organizations likely to respond?

This author's clouded crystal ball shows some big things happening out there, and several of those things are the unforseen harvest of the organizational past we have just been discussing. For not only do social changes cause changes in organizations, but the organizations in a society cause social changes.

Values, we all know, are changing, and so are attitudes toward industry. Two years ago if a company had wanted to build a new plant in my town, it would have been welcomed as a supplier of new jobs and a contributor to the local economy. Not so as I write this, at least not for a significant portion of the population. A new plant now means new jobs all right, but new jobs mean new people, new people means overcrowding, overcrowding means less open space and more destruction of the physical environment.

Perhaps such apparent value changes, especially among the young, are transient. But if the reader will return his thoughts to part 1, he will remember that attitudes once formed are not readily reversed.

Another real change we are undergoing is an organizational population explosion. The population of organizations, in the United States at least, is climbing at a much more rapid rate than the population of men. Nonprofit organizations particularly seem to be growing at about ten times the rate of population.

For almost any given organization this growth will surely mean an environment very different from what it was. The organization, whether it likes it or not, will find itself an urban apartment-dweller rather than a country boy in an isolated cabin. No longer can it wander at will across virgin terrain firing its shotgun at anything that moves. What moves may be another organization. The neighbors claim our organization is too noisy; the government claims it is unlawful; the competitors complain that it is unfair; youth claims that it is immoral; the local society for the protection of the green hills claims that it befouls the atmosphere; and the world union people claim that its activity is an insult to our Canadian neighbors. The empty world is gone. Privacy—organizational privacy—is gone. And the exploitive, devil-may-care, roughhouse, produce-it-and-peddle-it organization of the early days is going, too. Organizations are caught in a large, permanent traffic jam.

Moreover, the people inside organizations are members of the outside society. So their values are changing. Pressures for change are thus building from within. Employees, too, are seeking a new, but not yet well-defined, quality of life.

Couple these changes with the continuing expansion of those that lay just behind them: The continuing growth of technology, the still shrinking world, the even higher levels of education, the high degree of professionalism, and the massive size and complexity of new organizational tasks. Let's wrap that bundle up and ask how organizations will reshape themselves in the decade ahead.

Part of the answer looks reasonably clear. Upon the Taylorized blue-collar organization of the early 1900s, we superimposed the participative white-collar organization of the forties and early fifties; and then upon that we began to superimpose the information-processing organization of the late fifties and sixties. My guess is that the new superimposition, the new layer, will be the social-political organization of the seventies. The problems of the seventies will lie not so much within the organization as between it and society. We shall have to look much more to the social and family life of organization. We shall begin to know organizations by the company they keep. The future will be social, political, interorganizational.

Way back at the beginning, before Taylor, in the virgin world, organizations were nomadic. They were wandering, entrepreneurial bands of men. They were companies in the original sense of that word: companies of men. With Taylorism and Henry Ford, that nomadic form gave way to a more static life style. Organizations became like tough, independent farmers, staking their claims, carving out their plots of land, and exploiting their soil—routinely, but also autonomously. Then the knowledge explosion provided a kind of rebirth of nomadism. Organizations no longer had to be anchored to their traditional tasks and to their traditional structures. The new, highly flexible technology and the new, high-powered technologists could provide a different sort of anchor. The organization could become mobile again, searching for tasks unlike anything it had undertaken before. It could become nomadic again not in a geographic sense, but creatively, searching for new applications for its new, expensive, and perpetually hungry technology.

But the nomadic organizations of the seventies will be nomads in a crowded and interdependent world. Now the environment is more differentiated, more populous. It provides more opportunities, but it also makes for harder going. In the new environment, the traditional free-moving, autonomous business organization will surely have to give way. So will the tough-thinking, rapid-fire, decision-making, crisis-eating company president. So too will the kindly morale builder. The appropriate new company president begins to look much more like (heaven help us!) a politician who must juggle both the conflicting forces rising from within his organization, and those pressing in from outside groups. He will need wit and sensitivity as well as analytic skills. And he will need what the black brothers call "soul."

Such an image of a company president may seem almost 180 degrees from the current beliefs of many businessmen. Many of them feel, for example, that current business types, tough and decisive, should be running universities. Then student disturbances would cease forthwith. But the converse may be the more likely future: not that businessmen will run universities like businesses, but that university-type men (the ones who survive) will be running businesses like universities.

For the university may present an interesting parallel to the business organization of the future. Internally it is made up of many diverse groups over whom the administration can exert little direct authority. The faculty is a collection of prima donnas who may have some departmental loyalty, but mostly are loyal only to their professions. The students are a kind of transient body, vocally self-interested, but neither clearly consumers nor employees, neither well organized nor rational. And then there are the board of trustees and the community groups and all the other factions of society who feel it appropriate to exert pressure on the university—factions ranging from local industry, which wants more engineers and business students, to the black community, which wants black studies and more black students, to the alumni, who want a better football team.

In that kind of setting the university president does not sit at his command post, punching out action decisions and ordering people about. On the contrary, he arbitrates, he confronts, he debates, he negotiates. And out of the negotiation process he tries to build not only viability and innovativeness, but adaptiveness.

Many company presidents of the seventies will have to do just such political and diplomatic juggling, inside the organization and outside.

All this projects an organizational world which is very different and yet in many ways very much the same. It is not, we must repeat, a question of the new replacing the old, but of the new added on to the old. Certain tasks, for example, and certain kinds of industries are likely to remain highly routinized. The changes they will be experiencing are perhaps of only two kinds: they will be automating, and they will be involved in a new blue-collar participative revolution because economics and sociology will force them to make the life of the production worker a more challenging one.

At the middle levels of line management, which had been going slowly participative in the fifties, the two quite polar trends should continue and remain somewhat in conflict. In partial opposition to the participative trend is an accelerating trend toward greater programing and control, emerging from management science. We are already seeing some of the oddities generated by those counterforces; for example, greater centralized control over greater decentralization.

But upward and outward in the organization, among the planners, the staff people, and top management itself, there perhaps we should expect a desperate race for the better utilization of human resources. It is with our staff people and our higher levels of executives, with our technologists and professionals and researchers that we shall continue to search for the conditions that catalyze creativity and imagination.

If, finally, we take the total situation we are facing—the shrinking world, the explosion of knowledge, the organizational population explosion, our massive social and economic tasks, emerging new value systems—at least one thing seems clear: Rigid old authoritarian mechanisms will slowly fall to lower and lower positions, for they were designed for an orderly, slowly changing, almost static world. Organizational ambiguity, uncertainty, and irregularity have already become the normal state. We shall have to build new tools and new organizational structures to deal with that sort of continuously exploding world. Another thing is also certain: management will never be simple again.

In summary

Since this is our last chapter, we have taken the liberty of painting with a very broad brush. Our thesis is interactional —that organizations respond to their times, and the times to their organizations. Grossly we seem to have moved from productivity-oriented organizations to marketing-oriented organizations to informational organizations, and perhaps we are now moving to social-political organizations. Each stage is reflective of the pressures of the times, some of which are reactive to earlier pressures by organizations on the times.

But these stages have been more additive than serial, building one upon the other rather than succeeding one another. The outcome is therefore greater diversity and pluralism among organizations, and greater complexity within.

Questions

1. If people behave to satisfy needs, why will some people starve to death before they give away a secret? Are they satisfying needs?

2. We said in this chapter that "people are alike" in their efforts to satisfy needs. Do you think that Eskimos are like us in their efforts? How about the inmates of mental hospitals? Do they all abide by the same rules? Or do the rules apply only to normal people?

3. If all our behavior is "caused" because things in the world stimulate our needs, how can people be held responsible for anything they do? Aren't they just pawns, pushed about by the environment? So why punish the murderer? Why not punish the world that "caused" his murdering behavior?

4. What is a "habit"? Is it behavior that is an exception to the rule that "people behave to satisfy needs"? What needs can the "habit" of biting one's nails satisfy?

5. Is there any such thing as a really free choice? If behavior is caused, isn't the choice always predetermined by the cause?

6. Think of whatever it is you want most. Suppose you got it. Would you then sit on your tail, fat and happy? Do "satisfied" people really stop searching and trying? Do we have to keep people dissatisfied to keep them working?

Chapter 2

1. Most of us would like our children to be independent and ambitious but not hostile or suspicious of the world. How can we get the former qualities without the latter?

2. Suppose I gave you a newborn infant and the following assignment: "Train this child so that at age five he is badly spoiled." What behavior might I mean by "spoiled" behavior? How would you carry out the assignment?

3. Now consider the exactly opposite treatment. Are you sure that it would not spoil the child equally well?

4. Suppose I gave you a new employee and the same assignment. How would you spoil him?

5. Look back fifteen or twenty years. Do you think your personality has changed as much as your body? Or would your mother still recognize your personality even if she couldn't recognize your face or voice? Just how have you changed? New needs? New ways of satisfying needs?

6. We often say that children are dependent on their parents. Are parents independent of their children? Are managers less dependent on employees than vice versa?

7. We keep on comparing parents with bosses. Is the comparison fair? How is a boss different from a parent? How is a good boss different from a good parent?

8. Which levels of needs in the hierarchy operate for you? In the classroom? On the job?

Chapter 3

1. If it is true that each of us sees the world through the rose-colored glasses of his own needs, is it ever possible for people to be objective? How about scientists? Are they objective? What if we get the perceptions of several people instead of one? Does the pooling of perceptions make for greater objectivity?

2. Suppose you were an advertiser of automobiles. Suppose you know some people want power more than safety and some want safety and are a little afraid of power. Do you think you could advertise both without scaring off all your customers?

3. Suppose you hold an opinion about something. You find that your boss and all your peers hold the opposite opinion. You don't know why they do, just that they do. Do you think your opinion would be changed? Do you think anybody else's would? Why?

4. We sometimes say that businessmen perceive the whole

world in terms of their business. If there's a flood they only think about how it will help or hurt their business, and so on. If that is true, do you think businessmen's perceptions should be "broadened" so that they would perceive the world as public-spirited citizens instead of just as businessmen? Why or why not?

5. Do you and your wife see children, politics, and friends the same way? Do you perceive some things differently? Is it necessary that two people see the world from the same angle in order to get along together? If not, why not?

6. Do you have an "act"? Does it work?

7. Consider the first born in your family. Is he or she more affiliative or more responsive to social pressures than the others? Why? Or why not?

Chapter 4

1. Suppose you wanted to raise your child to act like the "third man," to treat most adverse experience as a deprivation instead of as a frustration. What kind of experiences would you want to put him through?

2. If you set high standards for junior executives, some of them will experience failure. Does that mean you should not set high standards?

3. Subordinates often frustrate their supervisors by acting stupidly or by making mistakes. A competent supervisor, when frustrated, will want to blow off his aggression at the subordinate. Should he? What does it teach the subordinate? If he doesn't blow off, what should he do with his feelings?

4. Suppose you have an ambitious subordinate. He's pretty good but not so good as somebody else. You appoint the somebody else to a new job. How do you tell the ambitious subordinate that he didn't make it?

5. Suppose you have a man who you feel sure will never go much further than he is now. But he wants to. Would you tell him he isn't going to get far in your organization? Would you tell him to keep trying? What would you do?

Chapter 5

1. If I put two quarters on a table and tell you you may have one, will you be in conflict over the choice? What if you know one of the quarters is burning hot, but you

don't know which one? Conflict? What's the difference between the two cases?

2. Is it "right" for parents to try to build conscience into their children? Wouldn't we be mentally healthier if we didn't feel guilty over things? What would life be like in a conscience-less society?

3. Does repression serve any purpose? Suppose we didn't deny to ourselves the existence of some of our own needs. Could we get along any better in the real world?

4. Is it possible for people to recognize their own needs and still ignore them? Can someone who knows he's jealous of another person get along with him? Could he get along better if he was not conscious of being jealous?

5. Many people get anxious or even freeze up altogether when they have to make a speech or presentation. Why do you think that happens? What kinds of people would it not happen to? How do people learn to feel scared of an audience? Or is it "just natural"?

6. Suppose one of your children (whom you love) suddenly married a strong advocate of a political position you hate. How would you feel at first? A couple of years later? What would you do?

Chapter 6

1. We use dollar bills frequently. Do you know how many times the figure "1" appears on one? Can you draw a good facsimile? If you can't, why can't you? Haven't you had a lot of "experience" with dollars? You've also had a lot of experience with the alphabet. Can you say it backward as fast as you can say it forward? Why not?

2. Do you think machines can be designed to replace middle managers? Or is there some quality about human problem-solving that will always make it superior to machine problem-solving?

3. Do people learn better and better under more and more pressure? Do you? Do people learn better when there is no pressure?

4. Suppose your company were trying to decide how much to invest in research. Is there a single best answer to that question? What steps would you go through to find a satisfactory answer?

5. Suppose I give you a crossword puzzle to do and you do

it. Does that teach you anything about doing other crossword puzzles faster? Does it teach you anything about
wanting to do other crossword puzzles faster? Suppose I
put a very tight deadline on the first one. Would that
help you do later ones better than a loose deadline on the
first one?

Chapter 7

1. Categorize yourself. Are you, in your own opinion, an
   iconic-intuitive type? Or a symbolic-analytic type? Have
   you always been? Will you always be? How do you
   know? Can you cite examples?

2. Do you think think there is any relationship between
   cognitive style and student "radicalism" or "conserva-
   tism"? How and why? Or why not?

3. Are we an enactively and iconically "mute" society?
   Have we become symbolically skilled at the expense of
   those other modes of understanding?

4. If intuitive-iconic types ran the world, what sort of world
   would it be?

5. Consider some person(s) with whom you find it hard to
   communicate. Is cognitive style a factor in the problem?
   If so, can you translate your communications into his
   style?

Chapter 8

1. When students and other critics of the "establishment"
   attack it as hypocritical, they seem to mean that it holds
   to logically inconsistent attitudes and values. For example, it is against pot but for bourbon. It is against violence but for capital punishment. Do such "inconsistencies" serve any social purpose at all?

2. Following up on question 1 above, are there any political organizations, right or left, that are perfectly consistent in their positions?

3. If logical argument is such a poor means for bringing
   about attitudinal change, why do we put so much emphasis, in schools and in the political process, on debate and
   argument?

4. What about the ethics of attitude change, especially by
   nonrational, affective means? Should advertisers use sex
   or masculinity or fear of social isolation in their
   approaches? If they shouldn't, should political or social

groups who want to effect change? Should you, if you want to get your girl to stop smoking?

5. Do you think it's true that "you believe what you do" and that "you do what you believe"? Is one of those "truths" truer than the other?

6. Consider the following common view, among older people: "Once these crazy kids get out of school and have to make a living, they'll settle down and vote Republican, too." Is the statement psychologically sound? How about this one from the other side? "Don't let them get you into the Establishment. Once you're in, you'll be brainwashed." Also true?

Chapter 9

1. After reading this chapter, how would you handle the job of selecting a new research director?

2. Suppose a test salesman came to your door. Suppose he claimed he could evaluate your executives, showing you their strengths and weaknesses. How would you decide whether or not to buy?

3. Do you think top management should pick people for promotion who can get along with top management? Or should their ability to get along with present management be irrelevant?

4. Suppose your company were using tests for promotional purposes. Do you think you should know your own results? Should you know other people's results? Do you think the use of tests for this purpose would make you like your company better? Would it make you work harder?

5. What about the ethics of assessment centers? Should executives (or anybody else) be required to go through several days of personal evaluation? And should the findings then be made available to the executives' superiors in the hierarchy? To all of them? All of the findings? Should subordinates also be informed of their boss's purported strengths and weaknesses?

Part 2

Chapter 10

1. Is it ethical to try to influence your peers? Your subordinates? Your boss? Is advertising ethical? Is it ethical to try to get people to want things they didn't want before?

Is it ethical to act as though you like people in order to get along with them, even though you really dislike them?

2. In a research operation, a scientist way down the ladder may know more about an important piece of research than the department head. Is the scientist still the subordinate in the relationship?

3. If there are lots of other jobs around, is a superior in a worse position to influence his subordinates than he is in a tight labor market? Isn't the authority written into his job description unchanged? Then why should the labor market have anything to do with it?

4. Suppose you wanted to get your wife to stop serving a dish you didn't like. How would you do it? Why would you do it that way? Do you think that your actions would have any side effects on your relationship with your wife?

5. Is it always easier to influence unorganized employees than organized ones? Why or why not?

Chapter 11

1. How would you decide whether communication in your organization is "good" or "bad"? What would you look at? How could you test it?

2. Is it possible for people to respect a superior even if they know he makes many mistakes? Does a superior need the respect of his subordinates to function?

3. In general, is two-way communication easier between peers than between superior and subordinate? Why or why not?

4. How is the communication between boy and girl before they are married different from after they are married? When is it more valid? Why?

5. Why are receivers often frustrated by one-way communication? Why do they get emotional about it, even in a game situation like the experiment described here? Why don't they just feel deprived and treat it lightly? What needs are involved?

6. What about communication between blacks and whites in the United States these days? Do the same rules apply as between any two peers? What are the special problems involved in trying to achieve valid interracial communication?

Chapter 12

1. Sometimes a superior will say: "Go down to the Oshkosh plant and bring their quality control into line, but don't upset people down there." Is it possible to change organizations without upsetting people?

2. When you feel anxious or uncertain about your ability to do a job, can you admit it to your boss? To your wife? Would it help if you could? Why or why not?

3. Have you ever begun to like someone you disliked at first? Why did it happen? Did you ever dislike him more as you got to know him better? Why?

4. The supermarket, people say, has depersonalized the old personal relationship between housewife and grocer. Is that, in your opinion, bad or good? Hasn't the large company depersonalized relationships among its members? Is that bad or good?

5. In some companies the threat of firing is kept ever present. In others everybody knows that nobody ever gets fired. What are the pros and cons from the management point of view?

Chapter 13

1. Sometimes we say that children want someone to exert authority over them, to require them to do certain things. They cannot decide everything for themselves. Does the same hold true for people in industry? Should a superior use his authority if his subordinates seem to want him to? Would you then say he was using his authority "restrictively" or "rewardingly"?

2. Sometimes a supervisor has to use his authority to enforce a rule he himself does not believe in. Should he claim he believes it? Should he pass the buck by telling his people that he is only doing what top management is forcing him to do?

3. Should top management use its authority to make middle management act as though it believed in all company policies? Or should it allow middle people to tell their subordinates they disagree with a policy?

4. Sometimes bosses worry about using their authority, even when they feel they should. They don't like to fire a man or bawl people out. Why do they feel this way? Is it only because they don't like to hurt other people?

5. Even if we don't want to use our authority to restrict

people, don't we have to? Aren't people restricted just by their awareness of our authority? Can we abdicate our authority?

6. Are you obedient to authority because it is authority? Or don't you pay any attention to the position of the person asking you to do something? Or are you responsive only to the message itself? Are you sure of your answers?

7. Should you be obedient to people in authority? Always? Never? What would society be like if no one paid attention to rank?

Chapter 14

1. Do teachers traditionally use coercive power in dealing with students? Can you cite examples from your own educational life? If so, were other means of influence available to the teacher?

2. Is anyone ever really powerless in a relationship with another person? A prisoner? A slave? A student? A worker?

3. In this chapter it was stated, "American business organizations are now among the most civilized institutions in American society." Do you agree or disagree? Why? Are universities more "civilized?" Is the medical profession? The military? Government agencies? The church?

4. Are you a coercer of others? Do you control anybody's behavior by exploiting fear? By using reductive techniques? Do any organizations to which you belong employ such techniques?

5. How does one draw the line between ethically "legitimate" and "illegitimate" pressures? Is it legitimate for me to demand that my employees work actively for the Republican party? That they cut their hair? Is it legitimate for me to "let it be known" that employees who work for the Republican party are looked upon with favor? Ditto for short hair?

Chapter 15

1. Consider the notion of "making them think it's their idea." Does it work? Is it right? What needs in A might be operating if he chooses to approach B this way?

2. In selling situations, under what conditions need a salesman's motives be kept to himself? How about non-selling situations?

3. Do you know anyone who tries to use his relationship with you as a means of influencing you? How do you respond?

4. Is "participation" ever "manipulative"? When?

5. How can you determine whether or not a person is "sincere" in his opinions? Are you ever insincere? When?

Chapter 16

1. Is it ever possible for a subordinate to influence his superiors? How would you go about convincing your boss that your idea is better than his? Would you have to go over his head to higher authority? Any other alternatives?

2. Suppose you were starting on a new job as office manager of a small plant. On your very first day the manager says: "I know it takes time to change a department, but I want you to do something right away about the people in your group. They've been coming in at all hours of the morning. The old office manager was very lax about it. Do something about it fast, because it's hurting morale in other departments." What would you do? Suppose the people you were dealing with were all old-timers and you were young and new.

3. Suppose you were a market-research man reporting to the president. The sales manager thinks market research is nonsense, but to finance any studies you have to get sales department funds. How would you attack the problem?

4. Suppose a friend asks you for advice on a personal problem. You think you have just the right advice to offer. Would you give it? Do you think it would be accepted? Why or why not? What is advice, anyway?

5. A good department head under you comes to you very upset because he can't get his people to accept a methods change, even though other departments are succeeding. How would you handle him? Would you try to make him feel better? Or worse? Would you offer to help him? Or encourage him to go on alone?

Chapter 17

1. I once had a job in which the incentive rate was based on the productivity of a three-man work group. The foreman used to put one new or unskilled man with two experienced ones and then change the group every few

days, arguing that it kept the bonus down and motivated the two good men to train the third. What do you think of his arguments?

2. If you got a big raise in pay, would you work harder? If you were promised a big bonus for completing a particular assignment successfully, would you work harder at it?

3. With taxes what they are, do you think the promise of a money bonus would "motivate" the president of your company to work harder?

4. In some multiple incentive plans, employee committees have a right to full information about sales planning and progress. They also have a right to criticize the sales department and to suggest changes. If you were the sales manager, what would you think of such a policy?

5. If you ran a candy store, how would you keep your stock boy from eating up your profits? What incentives could you set up for him?

6. If I raised your pay 10%, would you work 10% harder? Why or why not?

Part 3

Chapter 18

1. Does your boss (or do you) say that his "door is always open"? Is it? Would it be a good idea if it were? Should the president of a company with ten thousand employees try to make himself accessible to any one of them who wants to see him?

2. What is the actual pattern of communication in your department? Does everyone communicate freely with everyone else? Would freer communication help? How would you go about encouraging it?

3. Suppose you are the personnel manager of a small company. The president says: "Our communication is lousy around here. People always claim they didn't get the word. I don't hear about problems till after someone has fouled them up. You're the personnel manager. Do something about it!" What would you do?

4. How would you go about cutting down the disorderliness and wastefulness of a two-way, equalitarian communication net without destroying its advantages?

5. If you look at your own department, is there only one net that works for all kinds of information, or different ones

for different information? Does gossip follow the formal network? Should it?

Chapter 19

1. Suppose you resolved to say exactly what you felt from this moment on. Do you think you could actually do it, even if you wanted to? How do you think the people around you would react to it? Would you make friends or lose them?

2. Have you ever felt one thing in a group meeting and said another? Why? Did this covering up help the group solve its problem? Would it have helped more or less if you had said what you felt?

3. Do most people in a work group or a classroom make the same judgments as you do about other members? Do they all think the way you do about the people who you think talk too much? How do you know whether your opinion is shared? If it is, what ought to happen? If it isn't, how ought you to behave?

4. If you were chairman of a committee and thought people were covering up their real feelings and taking the safe course, just yessing, what would you do about it? How would you do it?

5. Should the senior man on a committee serve as chairman? The junior man? Is seniority irrelevant?

Chapter 20

1. Sometimes we feel that particular people are "bad" committee members. Just what is a bad member? How does one say that a man has talked too much? Or not enough? Is it "bad" for a committee that one of its members is grumpy or disagreeable?

2. Suppose one member of your committee insists on putting his feet upon the table, or swearing, or doing something else others don't do. Should he be stopped? Why or why not?

3. Should a group chairman not express his own opinions for fear that group members will disagree with him? What if he has useful opinions? Does "permissiveness" exclude the leader?

4. Suppose a supervisor operates his department "democratically." At a meeting his people decide to do something he thinks is wrong. Should he shut up and go along? Should he veto?

5. Suppose the supervisor agrees with his people but knows that his boss would disapprove. Should he shut up? Should he say that he knows the people upstairs would disapprove? Should he veto without explanation?

6. Even if you wanted to, could you use different leadership styles on different occasions? If you can be tough, can you also, on other occasions, really behave in a way that your members will see as permissive? Or vice versa?

7. Are there people in the world who are leaders no matter where they are or what the situation? Do you know any? How did they get that way? And what have they got that makes them that way?

Chapter 21

1. Is the United States a "nation of sheep" ? More so than France? Or Japan?

2. In what kind of tasks would you want deviant thinking in your group? When wouldn't you want it?

3. Do you know any "chronic deviants" ? Why do they behave that way? Has their tendency to deviate affected their influence in the organization? Which ways?

4. Suppose your new secretary started right out calling you by your first name. Should you do anything about it? Would you do anything about it? Why?

5. Do you see any relationship between the studies described in this chapter and the tactics used by the Chinese Communists to try to brainwash our prisoners?

Chapter 22

1. When a group has won a competition, we said, its internal morale and solidity go way up. Then how come, after the Algerians "win" against the French, they get into internal conflict and rebellion within the Algerian group?

2. Is conflict between groups in a business organization ever useful? When?

3. In competitions like the ones we described, it is usually the lowest-level executives in a group who fight hardest for their team and against the enemy. Can you explain why that happens?

4. If an "enemy" group is supposed to cause our group to become more cohesive, what about Vietnam? Did Vietnam increase American cohesiveness? Why not?

5. Design a program whereby two groups could produce two independent products and then select one of them, with minimum conflict and maximum final acceptance of the one selected.

6. "Groups may get into squabbles about small issues, but when the chips are down—if the survival of both groups is at stake—people manage to work things out." Do you agree? Do you think British unions and managements will work things out to keep the British economy from going down?

7. Many of us tend to pooh-pooh compromises as ways out of conflict situations, denigrating them as violations of "principles" and "integrity." Do you think your organization could survive without compromise?

Chapter 23

1. Suppose you were given the carte blanche assignment described at the start of this chapter. What would you do?

2. Do you think it's possible for a college to teach people to be managers? Or is "experience" in nonmanagerial jobs necessary?

3. Does personal counseling have any proper place in management development? Or should a man's personal life be his own business? Should we involve his wife? What is a man's own business and not the company's? Where should the lines be drawn?

4. Do you think a manager trained in the airplane industry could move to the ladies underwear industry and still be successful? Is "managership" distinct from any *particular* company?

5. How about the transfer from managing a small company to managing a large one? Is that possible? Why or why not? How about the other way, from large industry to small?

6. Can you teach an old manager new tricks? How?

7. If you were running a business school, how would you prepare a man for management in the 1980s?

Part 4

Chapter 24

1. If I invented an inexpensive automatic typewriter that

could take dictation and convert it to type, would it affect the *structure* of an American business firm? Would it affect *people*? How?

2. Suppose I invented a fast, cheap, and easily accessible psychoanalysis, guaranteed to change any of us from neurotics into stable, secure, psychologically healthy types. Would organizational structures change? Would the tools of organizations change?

3. *Should* people be treated alike in organizations, no matter what their jobs or status? Why or why not?

4. *Are* people treated alike in the organizations you know? If not, what factors determine how they are treated?

5. "At any level in an organization we find people who are organizational superiors to other people who are organizational subordinates. This superior-subordinate relationship is basically the same whether it be between foreman and worker or between president and V.P." Do you agree or disagree? Why?

Chapter 25

1. Has your work ever been programed by someone else? What was the outcome?

2. Is Taylorism dead?

3. Do you treat your family "Tayloristically"? "Participatively"? How did your parents treat you?

4. From your observations, is the wall between middle and top management bigger or smaller than it was ten years ago? Guess about its size ten years hence.

5. Do you think you are better equipped to plan and schedule the housework of your wife (or mother, or somebody else) than she is? Why? Do you think you could get her to accept your plans? If she won't accept them, are the plans therefore worthless?

Chapter 26

1. Consider any organization you belong to: By what means did it reach the most recent major decision it took?

2. Does that same organization optimize or satisfice?

3. It is said that a group decision created the camel. Do you think group decisions should be avoided? When and why?

4. Again consider some organization you belong to: Does it

348   Questions

have any machinery for resolving internal conflicts?
What machinery? How did it develop?

5. Does your organization know when it has solved a large
problem? How?

6. How can any organization become "more sensitive" to
its environment?

Chapter 27

1. What are you trying to teach your children about cooperation and competition? Why?

2. Is "cooperation" the same as "conformity"? Can people
be independent and individualistic and yet cooperative?
Or does one negate the other?

3. A friend of mine is an executive in a small plant owned
by his family. He says that everybody has to know everything, everybody is the boss, everybody countermands
everybody else's orders. Though he admits they all say
what they think and the business is profitable, he wishes
it were "better organized" so that each man would stay
in his own area of responsibility. Do you think "better
organization" is called for? If so, what would it consist
of?

4. Do you think your specific job could be so defined that it
would be really independent of other jobs?

5. Would more valid communication help or hurt your organization? Why?

Chapter 28

1. Does the structure you work in affect your behavior?
How?

2. If a man two levels below you came to you directly with
a work problem, how would you react?

3. If a man one level below you went directly to your boss
with a work problem, how would you react?

4. Is there too much communication in your organization,
or too little? How much is too much? How much is too
little?

5. Can two people be given joint responsibility for a job?

6. Are all segments of any large organizations structured in
the same way? Should they be? If not, what are the costs
of having a system in which different parts of the whole
operate by different rules?

Chapter 29

1. Has technology affected the organization of your family?

2. Draw an organization chart for an organization you know. Draw a second one for the same organization twenty years from now.

3. Must industrial organizations always be human? Or can machines run them?

4. Advise a good young man just starting college on the education and kinds of jobs he should try to get to help him toward the presidency of a large company in 1984.

5. Consider the role of the businessman in American society. Do you think his role will change over the next couple of decades? How and why?

6. Will business organizations eventually be run by technocratic whiz kids? If not, why not? If so, what will be some secondary consequences for the rest of the system?

Chapter 30

1. Will the new attitudes and values of the young change future organizations? Or will the young be brainwashed before they achieve enough power in the organization to change it?

2. Lots of people want business organizations to behave with more "social responsibility." What is the social responsibility of the local car dealer?

3. If you felt your organization was out of touch with society, how would you get it in touch? Would you set up a department of social sensitivity? Why or why not?

4. If the organizational world does become stickier and more crowded, won't organizations be less free? And won't that make entrepreneurial activity more difficult? And won't that in turn limit individual freedom?

5. "Organizations will continue to move the world. If you want to change the world, change organizations." Do you agree?

6. One last question: Can life in a large organization be fulfilling, rewarding, etc., for you? Can life outside an organization be fulfilling, rewarding, etc.?

Notes and
suggested readings

Some references that I list are nontechnical, some quite technical. I have starred (*) the ones that should require no special background for industrial people, though they are not necessarily a lazy man's readings. Although some of the others are difficult, I have included them for readers interested enough in a special problem to want to track it down.

PART 1. PEOPLE ONE AT A TIME

The material in chapters 1 through 5 is based on many sources. The design and some of the specific examples came primarily from Douglas McGregor and Irving Knickerbocker. They had laid out this kind of material for an introductory course in psychology for engineering students at the Massachusetts Institute of Technology, and I taught it there for a couple of years a long time ago.

Chapters 1 and 2

In this edition I have added some material on "growth motivation," but without abandoning the equilibrium-deficiency idea. For a comprehensive view of growth motivation, see:

*Maslow, A. H. *Motivation and Personality*. New York: Harper and Row, 1970.

Other useful books covering the territory in these two chapters, and a good deal more, are:

Haber, R. *Current Research in Motivation*. New York: Holt, Rinehart and Winston, 1967.

Hall, C. S., and Lindzey, G., et al. *Theories of Personality*. New York: Wiley, 1970.

For the relationship of motivation to work, try:

*Ford, R. N. *Motivation through the Work Itself*. New York: American Management Association, 1969.

*Herzberg, F. *Work and the Nature of Man*. Cleveland: World, 1968.

*Vroom, Victor. *Work and Motivation.* New York: Wiley, 1964.

In chapter 2 there is a brief consideration of executive personality. For more, see:

Campbell, J. P., et al. *Managerial Performance, Behavior, and Effectiveness.* New York: McGraw-Hill, 1970.

*Dale, E. *The Great Organizers,* New York: McGraw-Hill, 1960.

*Dill, W. R., et al. *The New Managers.* Englewood Cliffs, N. J.: Prentice-Hall, 1962.

*Levinson, H. *The Exceptional Executive.* Cambridge, Mass.: Harvard University Press, 1968.

*McGregor, D. *The Professional Manager.* Edited by C. McGregor and W. G. Bennis. New York: McGraw-Hill, 1967.

For comparative work on managerial motives among executives from several nations, see:

*Haire, M., Ghiselli, E., and Porter, L. *Managerial Thinking: An International Study.* New York: Wiley, 1966.

And for the work on achievement motivation, see:

*McClelland, D. C. *The Achieving Society.* Princeton, N. J.: Van Nostrand, 1961.

*McClelland, D. C., and Winter, D. G. *Motivating Economic Achievement.* New York: Free Press, 1969.

Chapter 3

The reader may be interested in other perceptual illusions and ambiguities. Any introductory psychology text is likely to have half a dozen. The figure in this chapter is from a German psychology laboratory and was drawn before 1900. For some really impressive perceptual illusions, people willing to do a little carpentry will find the following useful:

Ittleson, W. H. *The Ames Demonstrations in Perception.* Princeton, N. J.: Princeton University Press, 1952.

For a fascinating consideration of the human "act," see:

*Goffman, E. *The Presentation of Self in Everyday Life.* Garden City, N. Y.: Doubleday, 1959.

For work on interpersonal perception, try:

*Hastorf, A. H., et al. *Person Perception.* Reading, Mass.: Addison-Wesley, 1970.

Tagiuri, R., and Petrullo, L., eds. *Person Perception and Interpersonal Behavior.* Stanford, Calif.: Stanford University Press, 1958.

Chapter 4

The reader may be interested in this classic:

*Lorenz, K. *On Agression*. New York: Harcourt, Brace and World, 1966.

Chapter 5

The original source on cognitive dissonance theory is:

Festinger, L. *A Theory of Cognitive Dissonance*. Evanston, Ill.: Row, Peterson, 1957.

For the end-of-the-world study see:

*Festinger, L.; Riecken, H. W.; and Schacter, S. *When Prophecy Fails*. Minneapolis: University of Minnesota Press, 1956.

See also:

Brehm, J. W., and Cohen, A. R. *Explorations in Cognitive Dissonance*. New York: Wiley, 1962.

Chapter 6

The reader will get a good picture of current learning theory from:

Hilgard, E. R., and Bower, G. *Theories of Learning*. New York: Appleton-Century-Crofts, 1967.

Some other important books on thinking and problem-solving are these:

Bruner, J. S.; Goodnow, J. J.; and Austin, G. A. *A Study of Thinking*. New York: Wiley, 1956.

Miller, G. A.; Galanter, E.; and Pribram, K. H. *Plans and the Structure of Behavior*. New York: Holt, Rinehart and Winston, 1960.

Wertheimer, Max *Productive Thinking*. New York: Harper, 1959.

For the work on higher-order problem-solving as studied by machine simulation:

Feigenbaum, E. A., and Feldman, J., eds. *Computers and Thought*. New York: McGraw-Hill, 1963.

Reitman, W. *Cognition and Thought*, New York: Wiley, 1965.

*Simon, H. A. *The New Science of Management Decision*. New York: Harper, 1960.

It is also from Professor Simon that I borrowed the analogy of the needle in the haystack.

Chapter 7

For cognitive development in the child, see:

Bruner, J. S., et al. *Studies in Cognitive Growth*. New York: Wiley, 1966.

*Bruner, J. S. *On Knowing: Essays for the Left Hand.* Atkinson, 1965.

For cognitive style differences among British school boys see:

*Hudson, L. *Contrary Imaginations.* London: Methuen Press, 1967.

And for some of the problems involved in communication between people with different styles, see:

Huysmans, J. *The Implementation of Operations Research.* New York: Wiley-Interscience, 1970.

A broader social view of some of the same problems appears in:

*Snow, C. P. *Two Cultures and a Second Look.* Cambridge: Cambridge University Press, 1969.

And for a good summary of what we know about the problem of creativity in organization, see:

*Steiner, G. A., ed. *The Creative Organization.* Chicago: University of Chicago Press, 1965.

Chapter 8

There is much good recent work on attitudes and attitude change. Two of the best and most readable are:

*Bem, D. J. *Beliefs, Attitudes and Human Affairs.* Belmont, Calif.: Brooks-Cole, 1970.

*Zimbardo, P. G., and Ebbeson, E. B. *Influencing Attitudes and Changing Behavior.* Reading, Mass.: Addison-Wesley, 1969.

Chapter 9

The section on informal assessment comes out of an effort made by the author with Paul Albrecht and David A. Rogers to train a group of executives in this area. I have purposely avoided citing the source of the excerpt from a test report.

For a good contemporary review of personality assessment, see:

Mischel, W. *Personality and Assessment.* New York: Wiley, 1968.

For nondirective interviewing, see:

Rogers, C., and Dymond, R. F., eds. *Psychotherapy and Personality Change.* Chicago: University of Chicago Press, 1957.

For a good review of experience with assessment centers in industry, read:

*Byham, W. C. "Assessment Centers for Spotting Future Managers." *Harvard Business Review*, July–August 1970.

PART 2. PEOPLE TWO AT A TIME

Chapter 10

Good background for this chapter and this whole part may be found in these two commentaries on American culture:

*Reich, C. A. *The Greening of America*. New York: Random House, 1970.

*Riesman, David, et al. *The Lonely Crowd*. New York: Yale University Press, 1950.

For more microanalytic examinations of interpersonal behavior, try:

Argyle, M. *The Psychology of Interpersonal Behavior*. London: Pelican-Penguin, 1967.

*Bennis, W. G., et al. *Interpersonal Dynamics*. Homewood, Ill.: Dorsey, 1968.

*Hall, E. T. *The Hidden Dimension*. Garden City, N. Y.: Anchor-Doubleday, 1969.

Chapter 11

More details on the feedback experiments described can be found in:

Leavitt, H. J., and Mueller, R. A. H. "Some Effects of Feedback on Communication." *Human Relations* 4 (1951): 401–10. Reprinted in A. Paul Hare, Edgar F. Borgatta, and Robert F. Bales, eds, *Small Groups* (New York: Knopf, 1955).

Chapter 12

For a thorough background on these approaches, see:

*Bennis, W. G.; Benne, K. D.; and Chin, R. *The Planning of Change*. New York: Holt, Rinehart and Winston, 1967.

Chapter 13

Our definition of authority is more psychological than many. Traditional organization theorists define it variously:

Brown, Alvin. *Organization of Industry*. New York: Prentice-Hall, 1947. Here it is called "the aspect of responsibility which represents its power of performance."

*Peterson, E., and Plowman, E. C. *Business Organization and Management*. Homewood, Ill.: Richard D. Irwin, 1946. Here it is called "the power to make and issue executive decisions."

For a more realistic definition and analysis see:

Simon, H. A. *Administrative Behavior*. New York: Macmillan, 1957. See especially chapter 7.

The original work on obedience may be found in:

*Milgram, S. "Some Conditions of Obedience and Disobedience to Authority." *Human Relations* 18, no. 1 (February 1965): 57–76.

Chapter 14

On "protest absorption" see:
Leeds, R. "The Absorption of Protest." In *New Perspectives in Organization Research*, edited by W. W. Cooper et al. New York: Wiley, 1964.
*Zaleznik, A. "Power and Politics in Organizational Life." *Harvard Business Review*, May–June 1970.
See also:
*Gamson, W. A. *Power and Discontent*. Homewood, Ill. Dorsey Press, 1968.
*Schelling, T. C. *The Strategy of Conflict*. Cambridge: Harvard University Press, 1960.

Chapter 15

Take a look sometime at good old:
*Carnegie, D. *How to Win Friends and Influence People*. New York: Pocket Books, 1958.
See also:
*Martin, N. H., and Sims, J. H. "Power Tactics." In *Industrial Man*, edited by W. L. Warner and N. H. Martin. New York: Harper, 1959. Also reprinted in H. J. Leavitt and L. Pondy, *Readings in Managerial Psychology* (Chicago: University of Chicago Press, 1964).
*Zimbardo, P. G., and Ebbeson, E. B. *Influencing Attitudes and Changing Behavior*. Reading, Mass.: Addison-Wesley, 1969.

Chapter 16

*Argyris, C. *Interpersonal Competence and Organizational Effectiveness*. Homewood, Ill.: Dorsey, 1962.
*Bennis, W. G.; Benne, K. D.; and Chin, R. *The Planning of Change*. New York: Holt, Rinehart and Winston, 1967.
Material on AA is available from many sources. One is:
Alcoholics Anonymous. New York: Works Publishing Co., 1939.

Chapter 17

The "hygiene" theory is from:
*Herzberg, F. *Work and the Nature of Man*. Cleveland: World, 1968.
For recent work on satisfaction and its measurement, see:

Smith, P. C., et al. *The Measurement of Satisfaction in Work and Retirement: A Strategy for the Study of Attitudes.* Chicago: Rand McNally, 1969.

For insights into the psychology and sociology of incentives, see:

Lawler, E. E. *Pay and Organization Effectiveness: A Psychological View.* New York: McGraw-Hill, 1971.

*Whyte, W. F. *Money and Motivation.* New York: Harper, 1955.

*Wolf, W. B. *Wage Incentives as a Management Tool.* New York: Columbia University Press, 1957.

For a review of the Scanlon Plan, see:

*Lesieur, F. G., ed. *The Scanlon Plan.* New York: Wiley, 1958.

The overpayment experiments were conducted at General Electric Company. See:

Adams, J. S., and Rosenbaum, W. B. "The Relationship of Worker Productivity to Cognitive Dissonance about Wage Inequities." *Journal of Applied Psychology* 46 (1962): 161–64.

PART 3. PEOPLE IN THREES TO TWENTIES

For general background on group behavior, see:

*Homans, G. C. *The Human Group.* New York: Harcourt, Brace, 1950.

*Shepard, C. *Small Groups.* San Francisco: Chandler, 1964.

For research on the dynamics of groups and other small group problems, two good books are:

Cartwright, D., and Zander, A., eds. *Group Dynamics.* 2d ed. Evanston, Ill.: Peterson, 1960.

Hare, A. P. *Small Group Process.* Chicago: Free Press, 1969.

Chapter 18

The networks research was stimulated and led by Alex Bavelas. For more, see the summary:

Glanzer, M., and Glaser, R. "Techniques for the Study of Team Structure and Behavior." *Psychological Bulletin* 58 (January 1961): 1.

See also:

Collins, B., and Guetzkow, H. *Social Psychology of Group Processes for Decision Making.* New York: Wiley, 1964.

Chapter 19

On T-groups and sensitivity training, try:

Bradford, L., et al. *T-Group Theory and Laboratory Method.* New York: Wiley, 1964.

*Schein, E., and Bennis, W. *Personal and Organizational Change through Group Methods.* New York: Wiley, 1965.

*Likert, R. *The Human Organization.* New York: McGraw-Hill, 1967.

And for an extension of T-group ideas in organizational development, see:

*Beckhard, R. *Organizational Development: Strategies and Models.* Reading, Mass.: Addison-Wesley, 1967.

Chapter 20

For a "contingency" theory of leadership, try:

*Fiedler, F. *A Theory of Leadership Effectiveness.* New York: McGraw-Hill, 1967.

Chapter 21

*Kiesler, C. A., and Kiesler, S. B. *Conformity.* Reading, Mass.: Addison-Wesley, 1969.

Chapter 22

The long example illustrating group conflict is taken from a letter written by John W. May, a Hartford, Connecticut, executive, to the *Saturday Review* and paraphrased in the issue of 1 June 1962.

The innovative work here has been done in large part by:

Sherif, M., ed. *Intergroup Relations and Leadership.* New York: Wiley, 1962.

Much work was also done by R. R. Blake and J. Mouton, one report of which appears in the Sherif book.

Much additional work has been done on conflict in the last few years. Three good sources are:

Pondy, L., ed. "Conflict Within and Between Groups." *Administrative Science Quarterly* 14, no. 4 (December 1969): 499–505.

*Walton, R. E. *Interpersonal Peacemaking.* New York: Addison-Wesley, 1969.

*Walton, R. E., and McKersie, R. B., eds. *A Behavioral Theory of Labor Negotiations.* New York: McGraw-Hill, 1965.

Chapter 23

Most of the interesting work in this area has come out of the human-relations movement, so I refer the reader to the works of Argyris, Blake, Likert, McGregor, and the National

Training Laboratories, all noted elsewhere in these suggested readings.

In addition, some important efforts are being made to develop cognitive training tools, such as business games. See, for example:

*Cohen, K. J.; Dill, W. R.; Kuehn, A. A.; and Winters, D. R. *The Carnegie Tech Management Game.* Homewood, Ill.: Irwin, 1964.

For a novel and impressive approach, see:

*Revans, R. W. *Developing Effective Managers: A New Approach to Management Education.* New York: Praeger, 1970.

PART 4. PEOPLE IN HUNDREDS AND THOUSANDS

Some classic general works in this area (and many new ones are appearing) include:

*Barnard, C. *The Functions of the Executive.* Cambridge, Mass.: Harvard University Press, 1938.

*Drucker, Peter. *The Practice of Management.* New York: Harper, 1954.

*Likert, R. *The Human Organization.* New York: McGraw-Hill, 1967.

*McGregor, D. *The Human Side of Enterprise.* New York: McGraw-Hill, 1960.

March, J. G., and Simon, H. A. *Organizations.* New York: Wiley, 1958.

Simon, H. A. *Administrative Behavior.* New York: Macmillan, 1957.

Chapter 24

The work by March and Simon (see above) is a good place to look for a picture of the organization as a dynamic system. So are:

Cyert, R. M., and March, J. G. *A Behavioral Theory of the Firm.* Englewood Cliffs, N. J.: Prentice-Hall, 1963.

Emery, F. E. *Systems Thinking.* London: Penguin, 1970.

*Lawrence, P., and Lorsch, J. *Organization and Environment.* Homewood, Ill.: Irwin, 1969.

Perrow, C. *Organizational Analysis.* Belmont, Calif.: Wadsworth, 1970.

Chapter 25

For some historical material and concrete pieces of work in these areas, see:

Cooper, W. W., et al, eds. *New Perspectives in Organization Research.* New York: Wiley, 1964.

For good summaries of alternative positions, try:

*Lawrence, P., and Lorsch, J. *Organization and Environment*. Homewood, Ill.: Irwin, 1969.

*Tannenbaum, A. *Social Psychology of the Work Organization*. Belmont, Calif.: Wadsworth, 1966.

And a couple of classics:

*Taylor, F. W. *Scientific Management*. New York: Harper, 1911.

Roethlisberger, F. J., and Dickson, W. J. *Management and the Worker*. Cambridge, Mass.: Harvard University Press, 1939.

Chapter 26

Alexis, M., and Wilson, C. *Organizational Decision Making*. Englewood Cliffs, N. J.: Prentice-Hall, 1967.

For more on the relationship between task and structure, try:

Woodward, J. *Industrial Organizations: Theory and Practice*. Oxford: Oxford University Press, 1965.

*Lawrence, P., and Lorsch, J. *Organization and Environment*. Homewood, Ill.: Irwin, 1969.

Perrow, C. *Organizational Analysis*. Belmont, Calif.: Wadsworth, 1970.

Chapter 27

Addison-Wesley has recently published a set of little paperbacks about organizational development. See especially in that series:

*Beckhard, R. *Organization Development: Strategies and Models*. Reading, Mass.: Addison-Wesley, 1969.

For strong, recent statements of the participative position, see:

*Likert, R. *The Human Organization*. New York: McGraw-Hill, 1967.

*Marrow, A. *Management by Participation*. New York: Harper and Row, 1967.

Chapter 28

A coverage of actual structures of many large companies is provided in:

*Holden, P. E., et al. *Top Management*. New York: McGraw-Hill, 1968.

A fascinating analysis of hierarchical structure in general is:

Simon, H. A. "The Architecture of Complexity." In *The*

Shape of Automation for Men and Management, edited by H. A. Simon. New York: Harper and Row, 1965.

Chapter 29

*Myers, C. A., ed. *The Impact of Computers on Management*. Cambridge, Mass.: M.I.T. Press, 1967.

*Simon, H. A. "The Corporation: Will It Be Managed by Machines?" In *Management and Corporations, 1985*, edited by M. Anshen and G. L. Bach. New York: McGraw-Hill, 1960.

*Whisler, T. L. *Information Technology and Organizational Change*. Belmont, Calif.: Wadsworth, 1970.

Chapter 30

See again:

*Lawrence, P., and Lorsch, J. *Organization and Environment*. Homewood, Ill.: Irwin, 1969.

Thompson, J. D. *Organizations in Action*. New York: McGraw-Hill, 1967.

See also several British works:

Burns, T., and Stalker, G. M. *The Management of Innovation*. London: Tavistock, 1961.

Rice, A. K. *The Enterprise and Its Environment*. London: Tavistock, 1963.

Woodward, J. *Industrial Organizations: Theory and Practice*. Oxford: Oxford University Press, 1965.

Index

a

Achievement need, 12
Action and feelings, 15
Aggression, 32–33
Albrecht, Paul, 353
Alcoholics Anonymous, 158 ff., 211; applicability of methods to management, 159 ff.; and management development, 247
Ambivalence, 16, 109–10, 296
Analytic style: in problem solving, 64–66; in thinking, 75ff.
Anonymity: and coercive power, 150; in large organizations, 301
Apprenticeship, 250–51, 315
Aspiration, level of, 36, 67, 291–92; and problem solving, 62
Assessment centers, 97–98
Assessment of personality, 87 ff.; and atmosphere of organization, 103–4; day-to-day, 88, 98–99; formal methods of, 88 ff.; and information gathering, 100–103; interviewing for, 101–3; scope of, 87–88; "subjective," 102; threat to autonomy, 104. *See also* Tests
Attitudes, 79 ff.; changing, 79–82, 83–85, 328; definition of, 79–82; prediction of, 83
Authority: and coordination, 135; declining place of, 306–7, 331; delegation of, 134ff.; and dependency in organizations, 295–98; formal aspects of, 135–36; and leadership, 218; managerial, 244; and motivation, 143–44; pros and cons of, 139–43; and rank and responsibility, 135, 298–99; and restriction, 137; as tool for

changing behavior, 165 ff.; as viewed by subordinates, 137–38; as viewed by supervisors, 136–37. *See also* Responsibility
Automation, 312 ff.
Autonomy, 44 ff.; effects of automation on, 314; threat to of assessment, 104

b

Barriers to communication, 77–78, 121–22, 203–4
Bavelas, Alex, 356
Behavior: basic assumptions, 5 ff.; effects of organizations on, 291
Behavior change, 125 ff.; and attitudes, 85; and authority model, 134 ff.; changee's power in, 127–28; communication in, 114, 125 ff.; control in, 165–66; diagnosis in, 129, 164–65; and discomfort, 128–29, 166–67; and feelings, 130; and incentives, 179–80; motivation and, 125–27; pattern of in continuing relationships, 167–68; responsibility for, 131–32
Behaviorism, 88
Bethlehem Steel Works, 267
Birth order, effects on needs, 27–28
Blake, R. R., 357
Buddy ratings, 96
Businessmen: decisions of, 5; explosive, 35
Business schools, 67
Business Week, 126

c

Carnegie, Dale, 102
Causality, 7 ff.